*Rattle Conversations*

# *Rattle Conversations*

## Interviews with Contemporary American Poets

Edited by

**Alan Fox**

RED HEN PRESS | Los Angeles, California

Rattle Conversations


Book design by Mark E. Cull

ISBN: 978-1-59709-095-7
Library of Congress Catalog Card Number: 2007940121

The City of Los Angeles Department of Cultural Affairs, Los Angeles County Arts Commission, California Arts Council and the National Endowment for the Arts partially support Red Hen Press.

First Edition

Published by Red Hen Press
www.redhen.org

# Contents

# Introduction

Terrified. That's the word which best describes how I felt more than ten years ago as I knocked on the front door of the home of Charles Webb to conduct my first conversation with a poet. To be sure, I had prepared a list of a few questions to ask, but my only journalism training was in the ninth grade, more than forty years before.

Charles opened the door and led me to a sofa in his living room where I nervously set up my single tape recorder and began to ask my questions. I wanted to listen carefully to his answers, which hopefully would suggest more questions. That was easier to contemplate than to accomplish. The hour or more which we spent together was and is a blur in my mind.

I do remember that the final question I asked was, "Are there any other questions which I should ask you?" Charles looked at me quizzically, then shrugged. "I don't know," he said. At that point I realized that our conversation was over, and even though the role of the poet was more demanding than mine, I still had to initiate the questions. He (or she) only needed to respond. Through more than thirty subsequent conversations, I have never asked that question again.

Now, after more than a decade of conversations with poets, I have become fairly comfortable with the process. In my recent conversation with Jack Kornfield, who is also a friend, I showed up with just my tape recorders. (I now use two, because in earlier days I lost part or all of at least three conversations.) I hoped that Jack would carry the day, and he certainly did. (My editor, Tim Green, told me that this particular conversation was transcribed by his girlfriend. He arrived home to find her sobbing at her desk, and he was sure that tragedy had struck—perhaps Megan's mother had died. But no—she was deeply touched by Jack's stories.)

And that brings me to the purpose of Rattle, which was first published in 1995 as the chapbook for a poetry writing class that was taught by Jack Grapes, a caring and talented writing teacher in Los Angeles. I hasten to say that I love some poetry, and only some—maybe ten percent of the poems I read. I say "some" because many poems bore me silly. In the United States most of us are first exposed to serious poetry at age twelve or older. We quickly learn that only the teacher knows how to interpret a poem, and that we know nothing. Since poetry is something, we learn, that we can't understand without a guide, many of us never read another poem after we graduate from high school.

The primary mission of Rattle, and the conversations with poets which you will find in this book, is to present poems and poets that are accessible, alive, and interesting.

When you read any of the fourteen conversations that follow, you are in for a treat. In the next few hours, or over the next few days or months if you like to extend your pleasures, you will meet fourteen of the finest American poets of our generation. You will meet them, as I did, in their homes, sometimes in their hotel rooms, but always sharing the thoughts of a curious mind, the depth of a fearless soul, and the emotions of an open heart.

My conversation with Alan Shapiro took place in his home in North Carolina while his son was in a hospital room recovering from severe depression. Alan was extremely candid with me and talked about intimate details of his life. My conversation with Sam Hamill was in his office at Copper Canyon Press, which he founded, in the beautiful settlement of Port Townsend near Seattle. I met with Diane Wakoski on the sofa of my office in Sherman Oaks.

The most satisfying ending to a conversation was at the Ritz Carlton Hotel in Marina Del Rey, California, where I enjoyed talking for an hour with Yusef Komunyakaa. At the end of our time together Yusef stood and said to me, "You've asked some very interesting questions. Now I have to meditate on them." He walked into the garden of the hotel where, I presume, he meditated.

The biggest impact on me (and my wife who was with me) was in the New York City apartment where Daniel Berrigan had lived for thirty-five years. He told us that the neighborhood had changed over the years. When he moved in the apartments were not very desirable, and the owner was delighted to rent to almost anyone who could pay the rent. Now the place had become far more upscale, and the owner was trying to replace the old tenants with new, who would pay a much higher rent.

After more than an hour I asked Daniel what he would like to be remembered for.

He immediately said, "The work—that is important. Not the credit." Then he told us the story of a Jesuit teacher who . . . but you will discover that when you read his conversation.

Please note that I am talking about conversations, not interviews. What is the difference? Since I am not a poetry academic, I would be entirely out of my league if I tried to discern where a poem by Sharon Olds, for example, might echo a line from Yeats. I will leave that to more literary types. I am interested in process more than content, in the essence of the poet more than his or her work. I want to know, and share with you, how a poet lives his or her life and how he or she practices the art. I'm convinced that you don't have to know anything at all about poetry in order to understand and learn from these fascinating slices from the lives of fourteen American poets.

On a snowy day in a small village in upstate New York, my wife and I recently spent several hours with Hayden Carruth. Hayden graciously greeted us at noon. His wife was not yet up and about, and Hayden himself was tethered by a long plastic tube to an oxygen tank (emphysema). As you will see, he was most direct and forthcoming. We shared a wonderful conversation.

After an hour or so with Hayden I turned off one of the two tape recorders and thanked him for his time.

"Hmpf," he said. "You came all the way from California just for that!" So Daveen and I stayed, with the second recorder still turning. After awhile he said, "I don't get out much any more, and not too many people come all the way out here to see me. I just wanted you to visit with me for a while longer." We were both touched, and we stayed.

My pleasure, Hayden. My pleasure, Philip. My pleasure, Sharon.

I hope that "listening" to each of these conversations will be your pleasure as well.

Alan Fox
September, 2007

*Rattle Conversations*

Daniel Berrigan's first book of poetry, *Time Without Number*, earned the Lamont Poetry Prize from the American Academy of Arts and Letters, and a nomination for the 1957 National Book Award. Berrigan, a Jesuit priest, has published fourteen volumes of poetry in the last forty years. In spite of this, Berrigan is perhaps better known for his fierce commitment to the cause of peace. He and his brother, Philip, have both served time in prison, and Philip was incarcerated for an antinuclear demonstration in Maine at the time of this interview. The name "Berrigan" evokes images of a pacifist protest. His most recent book of poetry, *And the Risen Bread*, was published in 1998.

Daniel Berrigan (photocredit: John Toolan)

# Daniel Berrigan

January 30, 1999

FOX: Why did you start writing poetry?

BERRIGAN: Well, that's quite a question to start with. I think it had a lot to do with our father who, for years, was turning out awful stuff but who had great ambitions and who was very well read but was stuck, I would say, in the romantics of the 19th century and he never got out of it. He was a big Shelley man, a Keats man, etc., though he knew a lot of Shakespeare, too. Anyway, I was typing a lot of his stuff, under duress [Fox laughs] and much against the grain. We had this old, old manual typewriter, and I was always getting it wrong, because he was meticulous about all this punctuation. I didn't like the stuff to start with, so it was really kind of a bondage. But I guess in a kind of curious way it got me very interested in poetry and eventually, as a very young person in high school, writing poetry. Then, of course, in the order we had a vigorous regime of poetry in Latin and Greek and English, and later in French. So I sort of swam with the tide at that point. I was publishing when I was twenty, twenty-one. And it really never stopped.

FOX: And you've published, what, fourteen books?

BERRIGAN: I think someone said eighteen.

FOX: You seem to command a rich use of language . . .

BERRIGAN: Well, it's the Irish gift of gab. [Fox laughs] And you have to be at least part ham. My father had very little formal education. For a while he was a railroad engineer on the old locomotives where the proud guy sat way up there and the thing chugged away across the plains and he would have Shakespeare in that cockpit and he would be memorizing Shakespeare. And when he came back, he liked to tell the kids stories, he was wonderfully inventive. "Pa, tell us a story." And we'd all gather round. And it was just a feast for a little boy's imagination. And we wanted to hear his stories about the railroad that he could make up on the spot. It was really quite a start.

FOX: How were his stories different from his poetry that you didn't like?

BERRIGAN: Well, that's very interesting. He was on a different plane when he was talking to the kids. He wasn't trying to be literary. There wasn't any varnish to it. He was just being a dad, a dad with his kids.

FOX: How has your work changed over the years?

BERRIGAN: Well, I think I was always sort of reflecting where I was and my sense of surroundings and ecology, urban or country, or foreign, living in Europe, very affected by all of that. It's also reflective of a young person's religion or faith in that it's highly charged with sacramental imagery and with country imagery, because I was in the seminary for so many years in the country. I was quite bucolic for a beginning [laughs] until life caught up with me. [Fox laughs] And then everything changed and, let's see, I got into the civil rights movement with my brother and then that became very electrifying, trying to interpret that, trying to set down some emotional response. And then, of course, the war in Vietnam certainly changed radically my view of the world and of the world of literature.

FOX: In your writing do you sometimes try to get out a message, or affect the course of events?

BERRIGAN: I don't think so. I just felt that I wanted to write poetry even if it stayed in a drawer somewhere. Though, of course, no poet wants that, but I was trying to interpret my life and make sense of it. Also, of course, I always had access either to a classroom or to the public through poetry readings so that there was always the other end of this to be considered. That is to say, is it going to make sense to others or is it going to affect people emotionally or am I at a dead end? I did want to test it out in a certain way, and did, all the time.

FOX: How are you affected by the reaction of others to what you write?

BERRIGAN: I always have a sense that it's a modest gain, and that for a lot of complex reasons I would never be a front-runner, and wasn't particularly affected by that. But I did want to deal with young people and with people at large in a way that would offer something.

FOX: Offer something like a path?

BERRIGAN: Maybe a vision, maybe another view of what we were all going through at the time, because all of us were walking the same tormented earth, and let's see if we can make something of it or even enjoy certain aspects of it, like friendship and children and nature, and let us all also attempt to grieve together over losses.

FOX: What relationship do you find between poetry and life?

BERRIGAN: Well, it's very close. I would say it's almost a mirror image, convex to concave. And everybody goes through very dry periods, but I would think that if something remains so opaque or so labyrinthine or so impossible of entrance, then I better look at it again. I mean, if I can't write about it, is it really there? And not merely a poem, but I've been doing these biblical studies for years now, and if I can't bring a critical sense to the page and find some kind of congruence there, I'm puzzled and I'm stalemated and I'm not very happy.

FOX: Has your writing helped you to make sense of what you go through, what you learn?

BERRIGAN: Yes, at least in a minimal sense, because a lot of life is certainly beyond me. I think it's beyond all of us these days. I mean the depth of, the depth of the death urge, I think, and the extent of it day after day in the world is just simply, I don't know, appalling, it stops one short. It's very hard to make sense of, let's say, a traditional understanding of the human being when you see this kind of behavior. You wonder if those of us who don't believe in killing others are simply residual or if we're just sort of biological sports.

FOX: How did the civil rights movement affect you or your work?

BERRIGAN: Well, as I look back it seems to me that was pretty much the beginning or the opening of a whole kind of gamut of planetary travel. I was seeing the world from a radical uprooting in my own life by going south and by taking part in Selma and elsewhere, and then later [it] became a direct linkage with my work in South Africa in the late 60s. And I was able to join those points across the world in my own understanding and in the way I was talking to people in South Africa or here. It was like landing among people one knew nothing about, and seeing suddenly we have a common burden, we have a common hope, and let's walk with it. And that was very liberating and very beautiful for me, but it was very painful at the same time.

FOX: Painful in what way?

BERRIGAN: Well, it was painful because I saw their pain.

FOX: Ah, yes.

BERRIGAN: And because I could do so little about it. But at least I could be with them and I could walk with them and worship with them and learn from them, and I tried all that.

FOX: Do you feel you've had the impact that you wanted to have?

BERRIGAN: I don't think I ever wanted any impact. I just didn't know what the word meant. I just wanted to be in certain situations that I felt called to, and that I felt maybe I could even be helpful in and that I could learn from, and see where it went.

FOX: What authors have influenced you?

BERRIGAN: Well, I guess a lot of these great people. I carried an all dog-eared copy of Yeats' complete poems for maybe twenty years, and kept marking them up and noting them. Hopkins, of course, was a great inspiration, and, oh, within the last five years, I kept coming back to him. In fact, I did a whole book of poetry on his life and his poetry, as a tribute to his centenary. Others are staples, like Frost and Eliot and Pound. Then I try to keep a weather eye open for young poets and new poets, new to me. The ancients and the moderns both appeal to me from different ways, very different ways.

FOX: Are you still writing?

BERRIGAN: I kind of eased away from it once that book came out and started doing well and getting some very fine reviews. I'm mainly in scripture studies right now.

FOX: It sounds like you've always kept learning.

BERRIGAN: Yes, and of course, these writings all get tested constantly because I'm before people on these retreats across the country, and so I'm just working mainly through the prophets offering what they have to offer today. And it finally coalesces in a book. Now that also, of course, includes especially in Isaiah and Jeremiah a great effort to be faithful to their poetry. And I'm not interested in another translation from the Hebrew; I'm interested in the resonance of those great human spirits in life today. And I had a very hard time with publishers, especially with Protestant publishers, explaining all that, that I was not translating these, I was not going verse by verse, I was trying to say what they would say today. And that was very puzzling, but it worked. I mean, they eventually reach people.

FOX: What do you think they would have to say today?

BERRIGAN: Oh, my, [laughs] where will we start?

FOX: Two hours or less.

BERRIGAN: Well, let me summarize it this way. It seems to me that I see a clear path from, let's say this fifth to the eighth millennium, of the Common Era Before Christ and Christ. The continuity of ancestry and progeny in a spiritual sense to me is quite evident because they are all talking about the God who stands at the bottom with the victims and with the "widows and orphans" and stands with them, witnesses with them in the world, and from that terrifying vantage point which is like the bottom of the dry well that Jeremiah was thrown in, from that vantage point, well, first of all, defines the crime and sin, and from the point of view of the victim indicts the unjust, the oppressor, the killer, the war-maker. And the message is very clear, and it's a very clear indictment of every superpower from Babylon to Washington.

FOX: How do you reconcile what seems to be the fact that human beings can be both so evil and so good? Do you find that to be true?

BERRIGAN: Well, I find it true beginning with myself [laughs]. So that's, it seems to me, a good point, of learning to start with, where are you in all this, where am I in all this, and so on. And then look on the world with a certain kind of compassion. So, drawing from the prophets again, with a very strong bias in favor of the victim and a very strong sense of judgment of evil structures and those who run them.

FOX: That seems to have been true throughout all of human history. What do you have to say to people who don't like poetry?

BERRIGAN: Well, there's not much to be done about Disneyland of the mind, and if people want to go to Disneyland, that's their option. And, of course, Disneyland is right in our living room through the tube, so that kind of moves matters up a little closer. But I like to talk to people. I'm teaching at Fordham this semester and dealing in poetry with a lot of young people who are very new to it. I wouldn't say they dislike it, but it's terra incognita. And I try to give them a sense without being insulting that they're missing something. And I think it takes. I think generally they end the semester very differently.

FOX: What change do you see in them?

BERRIGAN: Well, they've gotten onto the moon and they find they can breathe there, against all odds. And they find that their dislike or their second thoughts or their kind of prejudice has kind of melted in the sun. And I would say the vast majority of them write thoughtfully about this or that poem that struck home.

FOX: How do you teach? What's your style, your approach?

BERRIGAN: Well, let me tell you what we're doing this term. It's called poets in torment and we're starting with poets of this millennium, just finishing this century, who have suffered atrociously for their writing around the world, who have been in gulags, who have been tortured, who have been exiled, who have been disappeared, and it's a very, very tough course. I tread lightly with it because these young people are not emotionally prepared for something this rough. But I think it's very important that they be shown it. It's their world, and the world that they're being shoved into, the world that we're leaving them. And these are the noblest spirits of this century, and this is what happened to them and what are we going to make of it? And what are we to make of their legacy and what kind of resources do young people think are available to be able to celebrate such suffering, and leave those notes in the bottles for us to read? So it's, it's challenging. I say to them, try to remind them again and again that you can best cope with material like this, about human degradation and human glory, you can best cope, with that kind of, electricity, if you are serving others yourselves, but if the campus is your world, this is very dangerous ground for you, and it gives a little ictus, and maybe even an impetus, to grow up to middle-class kids who are very privileged and who are very slow to arrive.

FOX: Do you find your students think mostly of themselves?

BERRIGAN: Well, there's everyone in there. And I think they self-select. Most of them, maybe through their parents, or through other teachers, will know who I am, and some of them will be urged to take that course. I can go to other classes and have a very difficult time just as a visitor because attitudes are so entrenched and so racist or so this or so that, but with the students that are with me week after week it's a very different game. I can start with a kind of sense of common understanding about what a human being is.

FOX: What is that?

BERRIGAN: Well, we have examples of them in these great poets. And it's a very tough definition that emerges by way of, let's say, ricocheting off one's own life and one's own privilege and one's relative unconsciousness of the fate of the majority of people.

FOX: Can you describe the satisfaction that you derive from teaching?

BERRIGAN: Well, I'm very privileged. I'll begin with that admission. I'm amazingly blessed from many angles to have those students. Let me just say, practically speaking, I try to keep a very open classroom. Anybody is welcome. After a while they want to bring their parents if they're visiting town. They want to bring their friends. Last year I was in touch again, while I was teaching, with an ex-prisoner who had been in prison with me, a guy who had been a kind of classical Times Square trickster. He hit bottom and was in jail for endless years. He was an addict, an alcoholic, was just at the bottom of life. He eventually joined a group that Philip and I had formed to do some studying and discussion, and he got his life together when he came out. And he heard about this class. He was now in his middle fifties, a little black guy with a gimp leg and on a cane. And he says, "I come to that class?" I said, "Sure, come along." Very alive intellectually, always, even in prison. So he came to the class. Well, this was really quite a thing because eventually he told his story and told our story and all these kids are going, you know, it's up here, [laughs] and then he died. He died. He was diagnosed in his last weeks as latent AIDS that had really eaten him alive and he died. And a whole group of us went to the funeral. Anyway, it was really quite a saga in the middle of that class, that kind of life and death, and that kind of impact on these students, like, boy, that was another slice of life. Why'd I bring that up? Well, it was all about the variety that can occur because one is open to what might happen.

FOX: You were in Danbury Prison for over a year?

BERRIGAN: Two years.

FOX: How did that affect you?

BERRIGAN: Well, I wrote a book of poems [both laugh], to indulge in a stereotype. It was interesting, too, because there was a little tinge of this atmosphere around us and the officials standing about, "watch their writings, watch their writings." It was almost a little bit of Russia in a sense, a poet taken seriously? We're watching his writings? Anyway, they were, and even later they were preparing for a conspiracy trial, another trial. So we had great difficulty, I had great difficulty getting poems out and I had to use a lot of enterprise because they wanted those poems. And I would put them in my shoe. A kind of Quaker prayer group came in and we were allowed to embrace the women visitors once on leaving, and I could pass these poems to her, she was willing to take them. Now why do I bring that up? Well, it was kind of a backhanded compliment, that they were very interested in my poems [laughs] and that they were considered rather dangerous.

FOX: Why do you think the authorities considered your work to be dangerous?

BERRIGAN: Well, they were on a fishing expedition at that point. They wanted some evidence of criminal intent. But in a larger sense in the world, let's say, from Black Africa to the Soviet Union, poets have acted as the lost conscience of the regime and in very powerful ways have indicted what was going on. Well! And then when you have enormous audiences for poetry as in Russia, you know, this gets to be quite a movement.

FOX: Why do you think there is so much more interest in poetry in Russia than in the United States?

BERRIGAN: I've traveled in Russia but I haven't lived there, so I can't contrast these kinds of psyches very well. I don't know. Poetry has never taken on a major kind of stature here. I guess we have other interests. Disneyland, maybe.

FOX: [laughs] Well, Disneyland is very popular. What is your view on the prisoners that you met while you were at Danbury?

BERRIGAN: Well, in a sense I think Philip and I were, we were demythologizing prison. We were peeling the onion and saying, in a very prosaic way, we certainly have a lot of work to do here just as we have had a lot of work to do on the street. The war was still on and now it took the form of these prisoners. And they needed a lot of attention and counseling and at times, if they were being brutalized, we could get outside attention. They needed worthwhile diversion or to watch something above slimy movies that were being shoved at them so we got literally thousands of books in. And the federal law doesn't allow any convicted felon to practice his or her profession while in prison.

FOX: Really?

BERRIGAN: Yeah, but they didn't know what priests do [both laugh], so the only thing they could think of, because the warden was a Catholic, he said, "Well, they're priests, they can't celebrate Mass." Well, that was fine with us, we went to Mass with the prisoners . . . as a prisoner, and that was just fine. But they didn't know that we were both very experienced teachers, and so before they could frame a new rule, we were holding classes [laughs] and we had all these books; they brought in carloads of paperbacks, a lot of them very good. The prisoners chose what they wanted to discuss and read.

FOX: Did you find the prisoners different than other groups you've come into contact with?

BERRIGAN: Well, you know the sociology that governs life outside, let's say in the class system, was working up close there. That was a lot to learn. They had rich crooks that had the neat front- office jobs and had creased pants and had the best clothing and had access to food and probably drugs, and then you had the minority people that were working the prison factory for slave wages. And as we discovered at one point, they were making parts of fuses of bombs that were being dropped on Vietnam. This is part of the big prison industry.

FOX: Really.

BERRIGAN: So, we had a strike that we engineered in the prison industries, and that was very interesting. One of the prisoners made me this cross on a string. It was made by soldering two screws that were used in the prison factory to make those bombs and he made me that lovely cross.

FOX: That's very meaningful.

BERRIGAN: That's kind of turning things around, isn't it.

FOX: Yes. Have you maintained contact with people you met there?

BERRIGAN: Well, it was very funny. For a number of years I would be walking on Broadway or I would be walking on 125th Street from the subway in Harlem, and someone would dash out of a pub or a betting joint or a numbers joint and yell, "Dan, remember me?" And it was one of the guys from Danbury. I think they're pretty well scattered by now.

FOX: How has being famous impacted your life?

BERRIGAN: Oh, I don't know, it never really got to me.

FOX: Has it made much difference?

BERRIGAN: No, I don't even know what it means.

FOX: People who want to be famous probably become movie actors.

BERRIGAN: Yeah. I've been there, too.

FOX: Tell me about that.

BERRIGAN: Well, I've been in several films including documentaries, but the big blockbuster, I was hired as advisor to the actors, I was trying to make Jesuits out of them. That was called *The Mission* with De Niro and Jeremy Irons and others. So, I was on the set, the jungle set, for about five months, trying to, and it was quite a job because these people were not particular Christians and they, anyway, it was fun. [both laugh]

FOX: Did you feel you succeeded?

BERRIGAN: I think so. I liked the film as it turned out, and I was very interested ever since to note that it became kind a cult film among young people. I go to colleges where they're showing it and ask them, have you seen this before, and they say four and five times. It's very affecting to them, a very tough film. It's in video. It's very interesting, and the music is magnificent. So then they thought maybe I was getting bored down there in the jungle so they said, "Well, why don't you take a few scenes?" so I ended up in the film. As someone said, "If you can't be a Jesuit, go off and play one." Oh, my. That was great.

FOX: Can you describe your relationship between your beliefs and your poetry?

BERRIGAN: Well, it's so much a part of me. I guess it's right in the blood stream, and the family and ancestry that it would be unthinkable that it wouldn't get into the poetry. I think in the beginning it was kind of sacramental, and transparently so. But then it got to be more indirect and I was concentrating more upon the human suffering because it was beginning with myself, and therefore the poetry took on a darker hue.

FOX: For many poets, their poetry has a darker hue. Why do you think that is?

BERRIGAN: It seems to me it's inevitable given the world, unless one can create some kind of nirvana, which wouldn't be very interesting.

FOX: What would you like your work to be remembered for?

BERRIGAN: I'm not sure I even want it remembered.

FOX: Say more about that.

BERRIGAN: Well, I like the little story they told about Gandhi who said that he wanted his ashes to flow down the Ganges and that was quite a symbol for him. Let it go, let it go, let it go. And I feel very much like that.

FOX: Do you feel that people can lead a more meaningful life if they are not concerned with their own ego?

BERRIGAN: I don't know, I don't know. I don't want to generalize. I live with some very marvelous Jesuits here and I think there would be a very diverse response to a question like that. And you would find a number of these very admirable priests who are doing great work, longing to be remembered. The Jesuits I know who have died and all their lives were great teachers; they're the least remembered people. The students go on and they scatter and then you see this great priest after fifty, fifty-five years of teaching, and there might be twenty-five people at his funeral. They're all gone. You just let it go. And I take that as a very powerful kind of instruction from on high. Let it go, and don't, I'm talking about myself, don't ever seek that stuff about celebrity or anything like it.

FOX: Would that interfere?

BERRIGAN: I'm sort of a very interesting outsider / insider in the order. I never met a Jesuit before I applied for the order. I read a great deal about the order and with my best friend came in. Then I was surrounded by these Jesuit hotshots who'd all been through classic schools in New York here. They were way ahead of me on background and languages and everything, and it gave a particular coloration to my love of the order because I always felt I had the right to be a loving critic of what was going on. I was not an inside player. Now, why did I get on all that?

FOX: It was ego, and—

BERRIGAN: See, at least in principle, Jesuits are supposed to be people who do good work without any thought of the outcome. They do good work and they let the outcome go. And it gives a great integrity and substance as far as I'm concerned. Because success is such a weasel word anyway, it's such a horribly American word, and it's such a vamp and, I think it's a death trap. It defines the war industry or something like that. You have to know the outcome before you do the good. You have to know that this thing is going to work before you work on it.

FOX: Your focus is on the work itself.

BERRIGAN: When I studied Buddhism I was living in a Buddhist community in Paris and I was going to the lectures of my dear friend, the venerable Thich Nhat Hanh, at the Sorbonne, and I was finding over those months as we studied together and prayed together and lived together, that there was this terrific congruence between that understanding and Christianity and in Buddhism. Their way of putting it was something like "the good is to be done because it is good, not because it goes somewhere." And their conviction is that if it is done with that kind of purity it will go somewhere. I believe that with all my heart, but I'm not responsible for its going somewhere. Gandhi would say, I think, pretty much the same thing in another way, that the means are the end, the means are in the end, the end is in the means. One day I remember, he wrote something about, "If the British yoke were still on the neck of my people and I died tonight, I would die content, because the whole day has been congruous with means and end." And in true sense, he says, "The end is already achieved."

FOX: Say more about that.

BERRIGAN: Maybe I'm talking out of school, but it seems to me that his spirituality was so profound that he was relatively unaffected by this kind of mesmerizing outcome of things. And yet at the same time he's endlessly fascinating because he was such a brilliant tactician. He wasn't putting tactics to the four winds. He was just, I think, insisting that soul, soul force is what he called it, was the main issue. Spirituality was the main issue. Connection with God was the main issue. And if that were the main issue, the issue of tactics would fall in place. I don't know what more to say. I mean, we're all going to die in a world that is worse than when we entered it. That's true of my great friends who have died. I don't know if you know about Dorothy Day, but she founded a Catholic Worker here and now these houses among the poor are in every city, but when she died at age eighty-four, after fifty-five years on the Lower East Side, the city was filled with much more misery than when she started, and yet that was never the point. The outcome didn't catch her and trouble her, because she kept at work that she knew was pro human and was in accord with her beliefs and the outcome wasn't in her hands.

FOX: You do what's right because it's right, that's the purpose in and of itself.

BERRIGAN: Yes, and then that letting go I think is so, so beautiful, so freeing.

FOX: It's so difficult sometimes.

BERRIGAN: Oh, indeed, not easy, not easy. We'd all like to see the fruit of our labors, but biblically speaking I'd almost say that there's some kind of a mysterious law operating in this way that the more serious the work to be done the less one will see of the outcome.

FOX: Yes.

BERRIGAN: I really believe that. And so you have a very interesting measuring stick about serious work. And that's very hard. I mean this business about peacemaking, it's tough, unfinished, blood-ridden, everything is worse now than when I started, and I'm at peace. I don't have to prove my life. I just have to live.

FOX: If you don't need that outside validation, then it is freeing, by definition.

BERRIGAN: Absolutely, true.

FOX: And then much more can be accomplished.

BERRIGAN: I think of the example of all this that I have in my own family. I think of my brother just out of prison again. He will have spent ten years of the last thirty in prison. The arms race is worse than it ever was, the dumping of creation down a military rat hole is worse than it ever was, the wars across the earth are worse than they ever were. He's completely at peace. And he radiates that in his family, the children are just so admirable and the joy of my life. One of them, the boy is just back from Iraq with medical supplies and is off joining the Catholic Worker in Minnesota to work among the poor. And it goes on like that with the two girls. And they have a very close bond and it's worked. And he has nothing to show for his years in prison except that, except that.

FOX: It's the difference between the superficiality of Disneyland and integrity.

BERRIGAN: Yes, a great help. We have one of our priests in prison right now, Steve Kelly, for his antiwar actions, and three of us in the community are forbidden to visit him because we're all convicted felons. And so they have us on their computers. Well, this is a little bit tough. We all love him very much and just can't see him. But he's very much like my brother. He has a sense of his vocation as being in and out of prison for nonviolent activity against war. And his health is standing up to it and he's going to be back in when he gets out. Now his effect upon our community is just very deep. It just sends us all off to our work more thoughtfully, because of what he has chosen.

HAYDEN CARRUTH was born on August 3, 1921, in Waterbury, Connecticut, and was educated at the University of North Carolina at Chapel Hill and the University of Chicago. For many years, Carruth lived in northern Vermont. From 1979 to 1991 he taught in the graduate writing program at Syracuse University. He and his wife, the poet Joe-Anne McLaughlin, live in upstate New York. Noted for the breadth of his linguistic and formal resources, influenced by jazz and the blues, Carruth has published twenty-nine books, chiefly of poetry but also a novel, four books of criticism, and two anthologies. His most recent books are *Collected Shorter Poems 1946-1991* (Copper Canyon Press, 2001); *Doctor Jazz: Poems 1996-2000* (2001); *Reluctantly: Autobiographical Essays* (1998); *Selected Essays & Reviews*; *Collected Longer Poems*; *Collected Shorter Poems, 1946-1991* (awarded the National Book Critics' Circle Award); and *Scrambled Eggs and Whiskey* (1996), which won the National Book Award for Poetry. Informed by his political radicalism and sense of cultural responsibility, many of Carruth's best known poems are about the people and places of northern Vermont, as well as rural poverty and hardship. He has been editor of *Poetry*, poetry editor of *Harper's*, and, for twenty years, an advisory editor of *The Hudson Review*. Carruth has received fellowships from the Bollingen Foundation, the Guggenheim Foundation, and the National Endowment for the Arts, and a 1995 Lannan Literary Fellowship. He has been presented with the Lenore Marshall Award, the Paterson Poetry Prize, the Vermont Governor's Medal, the Carl Sandburg Award, the Whiting Award, and the Ruth Lilly Prize, among many others.

# Hayden Carruth

December 11, 2005

FOX: You write that everything has the same value.

CARRUTH: I believe so.

FOX: Then why write poetry?

CARRUTH: Why not? [both laugh]

FOX: Okay.

CARRUTH: You do what comes naturally. I started writing poetry when I was a child, and I've been doing it ever since.

FOX: Do you remember when you started, what triggered it?

CARRUTH: Well, my father was a poet, and my grandfather was a poet. My mother was an author of children's books. So, I came from a family that was kind of wrapped up with the wordsmithing business. And, I don't know, I had read to me Mother Goose rhymes and all that kind of thing when I was a child, and I liked them. And I started writing poetry when my father told me what iambic pentameter was, which was when I was about four years old, I think.

FOX: Whoa! [Carruth laughs] Obviously you learned to read before you went to school.

CARRUTH: Yes, I did. He taught me how to read, about that same time. Four, I think, three or four, something like that.

FOX: Your father also had a great vocabulary and was a pretty avid reader.

CARRUTH: He was, he was an autodidact. He did go to high school, he never went to college. And he was a newspaper editor, which was possible in those days. The newspaper business was not so formalized and regularized as it is today, and he didn't have to have a degree or anything to be a newspaperman. So, when I was child he was the editor of a daily newspaper in Waterbury, Connecticut. And we lived in a little town outside Waterbury, about ten miles away, called Woodbury. And that was a nice, very pleasant arrangement for me. I was out in the country, and we lived next to a dairy farm, and I used to hang out in the barn and watch them milk the cows and separate the cream, do all that kind of thing, shovel the shit. And I did it myself in time and I loved that life, that country life, and I still do. That's why I'm here. Munnsville is not exactly the sophisticated capital of the world, as you've noticed I imagine. [both laugh]

FOX: How did you choose this?

CARRUTH: I didn't choose . . . I chose this place, this house. At the time I was still living in Syracuse, and I was still teaching at Syracuse University.

FOX: Mm-hm.

CARRUTH: And I had a girlfriend who lived over here in Clinton. So I was going back and forth from Syracuse to Clinton, Syracuse to Clinton all the time. And it got kind of tiresome. And one time I was driving by this road that you just came on, and I saw a sign out in front that said "For Sale." I took down the number, and called up the guy, and bought the house.

FOX: Ha! And how long ago was that?

CARRUTH: 1988, maybe '87.

FOX: Tell me about teaching in Syracuse. I know that wasn't something you especially chose, but you did it and got into it.

CARRUTH: Yes, that's a good way to say it. I did it because I had to. I needed money, and I couldn't earn any in Vermont because nobody would give me a job.

FOX: Mm-hm.

CARRUTH: They offered me a job there. There were some people on the faculty over there who liked me and my work, so they hired me. And I was scared because I'd never taught in my life and I'd been—well, you know from reading my work . . .

FOX: Mm-hm.

CARRUTH: I'd been a psychiatric case, a basket case practically, most of my life. And so I was very unhappy about having to do this, but I did it. I got over it, and I did it. I became a pretty good teacher, I think, although I didn't know anything about it and I just used my own instinct about how to do it and a lot of the regular faculty members over there thought that I was being very irregular and strange. I gave all my students A's.

FOX: Mm-hm.

CARRUTH: And I never assigned any term papers [laughs]. I had the feeling that term papers were a waste of time because nobody can write a good essay for one other person to read. You've got to have an audience [laughs].

FOX: What do you think were the best things you did as a teacher to help your students?

CARRUTH: Talking to them. The ones who were really interested in writing poetry—and that's what I was teaching—were the ones who responded to anecdote, for one thing. If I told them I'd had a nice chat with Stanley Kunitz last week, they responded to that. So, I did that kind of thing, and maybe I did too much of it. Maybe I was, what do they call it when you flash names around?

FOX: Oh, yeah. Name-dropper.

CARRUTH: Yeah, name-dropper. Yeah, yeah. But anyway, I did a certain amount of that. I also relied on my editorial experience a good deal, because I had been, well, I started out as editor of *Poetry* magazine in Chicago way back in the 1940s, going on from there to various other editorial positions. I'd had a lot of experience reading manuscripts and criticizing manuscripts and helping people along, and I found that I could do that. I'd also been in psychotherapy for years, and a teacher is really nothing but a psychoanalyst, that's all he does [laughs].

FOX: Mm-hm, mm-hm.

CARRUTH: You get your students to sit down and tell you their troubles, and next thing you know, you're teaching them [laughs].

FOX: Well, do you think writing poetry can be taught?

CARRUTH: Essentially not, no. It's a fraud, it's a fake, the whole thing. And I used to tell the students that all the academicization of poetry and literature was a mistake. It was bad for poetry, it was bad for people. And I still think that, and I'd advise my students to get out of a university and go get a job on a farm or something like that—honest work. And that their poetry would improve, and I think I was right. And the ones who took that advice, they've become quite successful. Some of them, they're publishing books all the time, doing things like that.

FOX: You've written that hard physical work is the best aid to composition.

CARRUTH: I think so. For me it was. And I've known a lot of other poets who've said the same thing, poets like me who lived in the country and worked the land.

FOX: Well, today, more and more, we get away from that. We drive cars, we use elevators, there's much less physical stuff.

CARRUTH: That's true. And I was forced into it because I didn't have any other way to make a living. I lived off the land, and when my wife and I went up to Vermont in 1960, we didn't have any money. We had a one-year-old son, a little boy. I had to work hard, I did. I raised all our own food, I cut all our own fuel, and split it and stacked it and transported it. It seems like I was always working with the woodpile. And I had a huge garden, and I raised all of the vegetables and produce that we used, and I raised some animals and slaughtered them—chickens and ducks and God knows what.

FOX: Hm.

CARRUTH: I was never a hunter or a fisherman, however. I don't like to kill things.

FOX: How did you like being an editor?

CARRUTH: I loved it. That's a good job, that's the best job for me.

FOX: What did you like about it?

CARRUTH: I liked the sense of making a product, a magazine, where everything is consistent and goes together nicely, and you have the best work you can get from the people you're working with. And I like to deal with poetry. I write it myself, I like other people who write it, and I like to talk about it, and I like to work with it. I like to say, Look, here, that's not good, you have to change that [laughs].

FOX: What did you find that—when a poem came in and you read it—what did you like or not like?

CARRUTH: Oh, well, it's hard to say. You look for something that's different. You look for something that isn't just the same as all the manuscripts you've read. You look for something that's fresh and original and novel and stands out against the masses of stuff. Sometimes you find it—not very often—and when you do, then you feel good.

FOX: I agree. Our next issue—we've done twenty-four issues of *Rattle*—the next one, which will have your conversation in it, we're doing the "Best of *Rattle*," a little section with all the best poems we've had over the past ten or twelve years, and I agree. Something fresh is very important. It seems to me that we share something in common. I'm pretty shy, used to be terribly shy, and when you say children are not cruel but barbaric, I think I'd go along with that.

CARRUTH: [laughs]

FOX: But it seems that you've chosen to communicate on paper rather than in person, at least as a younger man.

CARRUTH Oh, yes, that's right. That's partly it, that's partly the case. Yes.

FOX: So, people in person are more scary than people that you send something out to?

CARRUTH: It used to be, yeah. No, I've overcome a lot of my problems. I wouldn't be sitting here talking to you if I hadn't.

FOX: Right.

CARRUTH: If you've been through it, you know what I'm saying.

FOX: Mm-hm.

CARRUTH: I had a psychotic anxiety problem, and it was very severe. It crippled me. For long periods of time, I just couldn't do anything—couldn't take a job, couldn't walk down the street, I couldn't do anything. So, I was in bad shape.

FOX: Did writing help you get out of that in any way?

CARRUTH: No, no. It didn't help me, but it didn't hinder me, either. Most people think that there has to be some kind of a big connection between psychiatric problems and art. But there doesn't. A crazy man is just like anybody else when it comes to writing. [laughs] You've got to just sit down and do it, if you can.

FOX: That's true! And do you write every day, or when the mood strikes you?

CARRUTH: No, I don't write anymore at all now. I'm eight-four years old, I can't. I've lost it. I don't have what people often call "inspiration." It doesn't come to me anymore. I don't have ideas, I don't have . . . it used to be when I was working in the woods, I would think of poems, and I'd get strings of imagery running in my mind, and strings of language along with them, and then I could just go home and write them down and I'd have a poem. That doesn't happen anymore. I've gotten too old and too feeble in the head, and in my body, too. It's hard to come to, and I don't like it, but on the other hand, it's silly to try to disguise it or deny it.

FOX: I find that physically getting older is no fun. It's a dirty trick.

CARRUTH: It is, no doubt.

FOX: Would you say that when you were writing, you wrote pretty quickly and edited quickly?

CARRUTH: Oh, yes, I did. I used to . . . often I did do exactly what I just said, I would think of a poem when I was out walking or working in the woods or doing something like that. I'd come home, I'd write it down in longhand on a piece of yellow paper as quickly as I could. And I'd type it up and look at it and change a few words, and that was it.

FOX: Uh-huh.

CARRUTH: I never did a lot of revision. There were other poems, I had projects like writing long poems like "Contra Mortem" and "The Sleeping Beauty," and I worked on them for a long time. And I know what it means to sit down every day and try to continue a piece of writing that you were doing the day before. It's pretty difficult sometimes.

FOX: Hm. I've never read *Walden Pond*, and you've written that it's . . . [laughs]. Why should I not read it?

CARRUTH: Because it's a fraud and a fake, and it's been hoisted on the American people for a hundred-odd years and it's done more harm than good, by a long shot. It's a terrible book.

FOX: Can you elaborate on that? What don't you like about it?

CARRUTH: Well, I don't like the classism. It's all directed to . . . it's against the farmers. It doesn't say so, but he often does make disparaging remarks about the working people and the farmers and other people like that in Walden, around Walden, around Concord, is I guess is where he lived. I don't like that. I don't like the transcendentalism, as it was called at that time. I don't believe that there's any reason to become mystical when you see something pretty, and so on.

FOX: You've always written that loving and being loved were necessities. Can you say something about that?

CARRUTH: Oh, yeah, well, I don't think there's any other way that a human being can live with any kind of confidence or any kind of serenity. You have to have love in your life, you have to have good sex in your life, you have to have all those things. And sometimes it's a struggle to find them and learn how to do it properly, but after a long period, I was greatly helped by that.

FOX: I saw a movie years ago, *Carnal Knowledge*, and it started with an off-screen conversation where someone was asking, "Is it better to love or to be loved?" How would you answer that?

CARRUTH: I don't think there's a way to answer it. They go together in my mind. You can't separate them. If you love someone and you're not loved in return, I think you just stop. It doesn't work. You go on and do something else [laughs]. But I think, in most cases, in my experience, if you love someone and you're really attracted to her, she will respond. And most of the women that I knew did, in one way or another. I think questions like that are fake questions. They don't really signify very much, do they?

FOX: Well, some poets I've talked to said they started writing poetry to attract women.

CARRUTH: No, I didn't do that. [Fox laughs] I can't imagine that very many people have tried to do that. I mean, I've written poems for women and to women, there's no question about that, and so have most other poets. But a good love poem exists by itself, just like any other poem. It doesn't have very much reference to the person who wrote it or the person to whom it's written.

FOX: Say something about Yankee pragmatism.

CARRUTH: It's the only thing that keeps the world sane. William James was my favorite philosopher and author in the old days, and pragmatism was very much of the philosophical and intellectual environment that I grew up in. And I do associate it with New England and Yankees and, kind of, the no-nonsense way that Yankee farmers have about their work and their environment. So, what else can I say? I cannot explain well at this point in my life without making a disquisition about it. I was at one time, but I can't do that anymore. Go read the book *Pragmatism* by James. It's a great book.

FOX: Okay. What authors do you feel influenced you?

CARRUTH: [laughs] Just the other day, I was reading an essay by a former student of mine on Wallace Stevens, and he quoted "Sunday Morning." And I recognized myself in those lines. I guess they influenced me tremendously—that tone, that swing, that rhythm, the kind of diction that he used, and so on. Yeah. I was influenced by him. He was my favorite poet when I was in graduate school at the University of Chicago, back in 1945, whenever it was. And, I don't know what else. Nobody else in particular comes to my mind. I think I was influenced by the age. I was influenced by Ezra Pound and T.S. Eliot and other people who were participating in the so-called revolution of 1910 or whatever it was, and I was excited by that. I was excited by the new poetry, and read a lot of it, as much as I could. I appreciated what those guys did. When I became editor of *Poetry*, I got contributions out of them, to the extent that I could. I got some very nice stuff out of E.E. Cummings and people like that. William Carlos Williams gave me stuff. So, I read all those guys, I was very excited by all that. And I read the magazines at the time. I read Ransom's magazine, *The Kenyon Review*, and *The Sewanee Review* was run by my friend Allen Tate for a while, and other things like that.

FOX: One of my favorite poets is E.E. Cummings, who is certainly not ranked as high as many others.

CARRUTH: Well, I don't know about rankings. I don't pay much attention to them myself, but I don't suppose he is, no. He, uh, he was an irascible kind of a guy. He offended a lot of people [laughs]. But that's all right. He was a good poet. He was a very talented guy, there's no question about it. You can't read his poems without understanding that and realizing that. He had a very good ear and a very deep affection for the past, for the poetry of the English language in the past.

FOX: Mm-hm.

CARRUTH: And there were others like him who nobody pays attention to anymore, but when I was a kid, they were important. People like Conrad Aiken and, who else . . . God, I can't even remember them myself anymore, my mind has gotten so feeble. But there were. It was all around. There were people who were participating in the new poetry and in ideas as new poets, and the new critics, as I recall. It was kind of an exciting time in literature, I think. For me it was, and for other young people like me at that time.

FOX: How did you first get published?

CARRUTH: My first publication was in a little magazine. It was published out in Indiana or Ohio or someplace like that, and I can't even remember the name. It was called something like *Contemporary Poetry*. And I just sent it. It was a little poem, and they took it.

FOX: Yeah, okay.

CARRUTH: That's all. There's no other way to do it, as far as I know [laughs]. And, after that I began publishing in *Poetry* and I got the job there by default, to a certain extent, and got into correspondence with some other people like Ransom and Tate and other people like that, and began publishing in their magazines. I published in *Partisan Review*, I knew Delmore Schwartz, and I knew—what was his name, the guy who ran—there was a guy named Philips and there was another guy named something else, and now I can't think of it. Anyway, it was an important magazine at that time.

FOX: You said we have a "mock humility" of Eliot or Tate. Does that . . .

CARRUTH: Oh, yeah, that was part of the facade that they erected around themselves, this extreme humility, this self-deprecating attitude that they put into their essays. It was bullshit; they didn't feel that way at all. And it was a manner, it was a way of writing, it was a way of getting into language the ideas that they wanted to write about. So they did it, and it worked to a certain extent.

FOX: Well, there's a difference from a facade as being real and genuine, which is something I value. Is that what you're saying also?

CARRUTH: Well, with some of them it may have been. I think with people like Tate and Ransom it wasn't. It was a fake, and they knew it. And they were just trying to be Southern gentlemen, and pretended it was a feasible attitude to have in the 1940s and '50s. All in all, it was a fake.

FOX: Mm.

CARRUTH: But it was a creative fake, and it was, it did have something to do with what they were saying. So, I don't blame them particularly, or I don't find it offensive. Everybody does things like that. I don't know what I've done, but I have done things, I guess.

FOX: You wrote your poem about the age seventy-four knocking the barometer. Can you say something about that?

CARRUTH: [laughs] I've always been affected by the weather, and deeply concerned about the weather, and I do check the barometer all the time. And listen to the weather report, and watch the skies, and that's what the Yankee farmers do, too.

FOX: Mm-hm.

CARRUTH: I used to keep a log, a diary, a weather diary of the weather in conjunction with my spirits and the way I felt. And it was perfectly clear that when the barometer was high, I was high, too, and when the barometer was low, I went down. And I used to have terrible depressions and I still do, but I think they're not as bad as they used to be.

FOX: You've also written that you write in winter because of its cleanness and clarity.

CARRUTH: I do, I love the snow, especially after this last year. It's been so disgusting and so frightening to me. I mean, the temperature, what has it been? Seven or eight degrees higher than normal all year long? And that, to me, is nothing but an indication of impending doom. Like we're all going to be gone in another couple of years. So, a little break like this is nice. It got down to minus five here the other night, and that felt really good to me. I love it when it gets down below zero.

FOX: That's interesting. You've also written about a sadness, a pervasive sadness . . .

CARRUTH: Oh yeah. Well, I think that's the depression that started when I was about three years old and has been going ever since [laughs].

FOX: Mm-hm, mm-hm.

CARRUTH: I don't see how anybody can avoid it, really.

FOX: Well, sadness is actually my favorite emotion. It's real, it's deep, it's important.

CARRUTH: Yeah, yeah. Yeah. And, you know, when you're a little kid, suddenly you wake up someday when you're two or three years old, or four years old, and you're sitting outside looking around at all the trees and flowers and the animals and so on, and then suddenly it strikes you: All of this is going to die, it's all going to be dead in not a very long time from now. And that's what hit me, and that's what caused me to feel sad and sorrowful and melancholy and depressed and everything else. My writing reflects that, I believe. Although I try not to be excessively depressive in my poems, how can you avoid it?

FOX: Mm-hm. You said also that you played dumb in school because you knew how to read. Say something about that.

CARRUTH: Oh, it was a kind of a problem. I lived in Connecticut, and about the eighth . . . no, the sixth grade, I think it was . . . in elementary school, the state of Connecticut administered the Stanford-Benet IQ examination to every public school student in the state. And that year I did it, and everybody else did it. And I came out a genius. And my teachers and the other people connected to the school were terribly impressed, and they told my father, Yes, I need to go to Choate or Tufts or someplace like that right away, and the poor guy didn't have a nickel [laughs]. One of the things they did was . . . my father had already taught me how to read, and I guess that's one of the reasons why I did well on the test. The teachers knew that I could read and that I was happy to read. So, we had a small school—it wasn't a one-room school, but it was one school for the whole town, and one room for each grade—and my teachers would get me a seat in the back of the room, off in the corner, and give me a book to read. Then they would teach the rest of the kids. And when they ran into a problem, they would say, Hayden, what's ten times ten? And I would answer, like a fool, and the other students would all hate me [laughs], and it was very difficult. And that's the way it went. I survived.

FOX: Yes [laughs]. Do you think that we're very different as adults, in that respect, being jealous of those who are . . .

CARRUTH: Oh, no. No, no, no. There's a lot of that kind of feeling in literature among writers, and everywhere, I'm sure. Carpenters have the same problems, I expect. But, well, I don't know. That's why people write fiction, write novels, because they want to explore problems like that.

FOX: Yes.

CARRUTH: I wrote a novel once.

FOX: Did you publish it?

CARRUTH: Yeah. It was called *Appendix A*. It was published by Macmillan in New York, and they actually gave me a contract for another novel, which I started to write. In fact, I wrote it, and I didn't like it, and I threw it away. So, I made a stab at being a fiction writer and getting rich, but it didn't work.

FOX: Well, writing a novel must be very different than writing poetry.

CARRUTH: Well, it is long, and it is a continuous thing. It's like you said before, it has to be something you leave on your desk one day and go back to the next day, and you do that over and over again for 500 days, and then you have a novel. And it's harrowing, it's backbreaking.

FOX: Mm-hm.

CARRUTH: I'm not a novelist by nature, and I'm glad I didn't take it up professionally. Although, many of my friends are novelists. I just had a nice visit a few days ago with Russell Banks. He and his wife, Chase Twichell, live over in Saratoga during the wintertime, and up in the mountains in the Adirondacks during the summertime, and they run that publishing company, Ausable Press, which published my last book. I like them a lot, they're very nice people. I hope I see more of them. And Russell is a good novelist, I think. I like some of his books quite a lot.

FOX: Hm. I haven't got a long attention span, so something that takes more than three or four hours, I'm impatient.

CARRUTH: Well, that's part of the problem for me, too, the length of time it took to do things. And the detail that had to go into it. In order to get somebody from one room to another, you have to go through this whole business of describing the rooms, and describing the people, and everything else. [Fox laughs] It gets to be very tedious [laughs]. I didn't like it.

FOX: Yep. Well, it seems to me one of the advantages of being a grownup, as opposed to being in elementary school, is that you have a broader pool of people, and you can find people who are more attuned to you, because elementary school is just whoever lives there.

CARRUTH: Well, I think that's probably true if you're able to get out and around, which I wasn't for a long time. When I was in Chicago at the graduate school and then at *Poetry*, and then after that at the University of Chicago Press, I did know a pretty good number of people in the arts. I had good friends, and they were poets and writers and architects and musicians and everybody else. And that was good. That was a good period of my life. And then I came to write my novel that I had to write in order to get my book of poetry published. Basically, Macmillan said to me, we'll publish your poetry if you give us a novel.

FOX: Mm.

CARRUTH: And so, that's what I did. And the novel was based on people I knew in Chicago and on experiences I'd had there.

FOX: Did you enjoy your time at the University of Chicago?

CARRUTH: Yes.

FOX: What stands out that was particularly . . .

CARRUTH: It was very lively. There were a lot of good people, both scholars and writers, and critics. Norman Maclean, do you know who he is? The guy who lives out in Montana and writes about rivers and fishing and all that kind of . . . He's a hell of a good writer. I wish I could remember the names of his books, but I can't. He was one of my teachers. And J.V. Cunningham, do you know him?

FOX: No, I don't.

CARRUTH: Jim Cunningham, he was a good poet. He died very young. He was a student of Yvor Winters in California. And I knew him in Chicago, and we were good friends. Henry Rago was a good friend of mine. Do you know him?

FOX: I don't.

CARRUTH: He was editor of *Poetry* magazine after me. He was closely associated with the magazine when I first went out there. And who else was out there? There were people that you probably happen to know about. People like Elder Olson and Ruthven Todd, all dead now probably.

FOX: Mm.

CARRUTH: But it was a lively scene, and I liked it.

FOX: Well, why did you leave editing *Poetry* magazine?

CARRUTH: I got fired.

FOX: Oh! [Carruth laughs] Do you want to say something about that?

CARRUTH: Oh, well, a lot has been said about it. It basically comes down to the controversy over the awarding of the Bollingen Prize to Ezra Pound in . . . 1948, I think. The prize was awarded by a committee of poets chosen by the Library of Congress, and it was given to Pound, and then everybody blew up. The Congress blew up, the House Un-American Activities Committee blew up. And I defended—in *Poetry*—I decided it was *Poetry*'s job to defend the prize and to counterattack the guy who was leading the attack. It was a fellow named . . . he was a pretty well-known poet, he was attached to the *Saturday Review of Literature* . . . Hillyer, Robert Hillyer. He wrote a terrible editorial in the *Saturday Review* blaming T.S. Eliot for *everything*. And the whole modern poetry movement. And he said that Pound was the Antichrist, and so on and so on. He was very belligerent and very snippy. So, I took out after him, and I published a book called *The Case Against the Saturday Review*, and I got a lot of people to contribute to that and to other things. And there were members of the board, members of the Modern Poetry Association, which was mostly made up of Harriet Monroe's friends whom she had enlisted back in 1912, when she founded the magazine, to be the board and to support it. And they were basically rich people, mostly from the North Side of Chicago. And they didn't like what I was doing at all. They thought that Pound was a traitor, and that I was a traitor for supporting him. And so, we came to a parting of the ways. I didn't actually get fired, I don't think. But it was an agreement that I would leave, and I did. But, in effect, I was fired, yeah.

FOX: So, a lot of people are in favor of free speech as long as it's speech which agrees with them.

CARRUTH: Well, that's always the case, I guess. Yeah, Yeah.

FOX: It seems to be. And you've been published by Copper Canyon Press?

CARRUTH: Yes. Unfortunately, that's gone now, too. As you may have heard, Sam got fired.

FOX: Yes, he did.

CARRUTH: And I think that's an awful thing that they did out there. I think it's just absolutely horrible.

FOX: I was shocked. I talked to Sam, I don't know, a year and a half, two years ago. And all of a sudden he's fired, from *his* press.

CARRUTH: Yeah. He founded it, and ran it for years, and trained all the people who worked for it, and did everything. He and Tree Swenson, who was his first wife. And to fire him is just absolutely absurd. It's the most awful thing I ever heard of. It's corporate American politics invading the arts.

FOX: Mm-hm.

CARRUTH: And it's happened here in Rochester. My friend Steve Huff, who is now my biographer and is writing my biography, was an editor at BOA and did good work there. My wife's first book was published by BOA. And he got fired. It's a very similar deal. Somebody got onto the board of directors and started throwing his weight around and enlisted other people, and they conspired against Steve and threw him out. The same thing happened to

Sam. And I've been in touch with Sam a lot, well, ever since he took me on at Copper Canyon, and I know he's terribly upset and depressed by all this. He's busy, he's working now, but for a while he wasn't. I think he's okay. But it was a bad deal, a very bad deal. And I would be ready to get out of Copper Canyon if it were possible. I don't know if it is. You know, I'm under contract to them for all of the books they have published, which is all my books, basically, because that's what Sam did. He took me over and published everything. So, I don't think I can take those titles away and give them to Ausable Press or anybody else, legally. But, I don't know. Maybe something will be worked out. We'll see.

FOX: Yeah, yeah. You once wrote that time is our mortal enemy.

CARRUTH: Well, what's the matter with that? Isn't that true? [Fox laughs] We all die from time.

FOX: That is true! Absolutely. Tell me about death. Is that something horrible, or perhaps a relief, or part of a natural . . .

CARRUTH: It's awful. I don't like the idea of dying at all.

FOX: Uh-huh.

CARRUTH: I, uh, I don't like the idea of being extinguished. I'm a lively guy and always have been, and full of ideas, and to have all that be blown away in a second is dismaying, to say the least. And, so, I don't look forward to it. But it's going to happen, there's nothing anybody can do to stop it.

FOX: Well, that's for sure. Okay, I think that's good.

CARRUTH: That's all you want?

[female voice]: Is there anything else you'd like us to know?

CARRUTH: I have a terrible case of arthritis in my fingers and my big toe.

FOX: Yep. [Carruth laughs] I have gout in my big toe.

CARRUTH: Wow. That's a very hard thing. And, I don't know, I'd like you to meet my wife, but she's not coming. She's not getting up, and she probably won't get up until you leave. [Fox laughs] Can I give you something, anything? Tea? Coffee? What would you like?

[female voice]: I'd like to know more about your love life. You had a couple of wives and girlfriends?

CARRUTH: Yes, I had a number. My present wife is my fourth, and between the four wives there have been probably eight or ten women I lived with at one time or another. It's not a very. . . . um, what's the word I'm trying to think of . . . it's not an entertaining and it's not a very enlightening story. I found that one of the best ways to overcome the extreme anxiety that I had, which psychoanalysis and psychotherapy never really did much for, was to—speaking in the current polite language—to have sex with women who I didn't know.

FOX: Hm.

CARRUTH : And to do it successfully, and do it well.

[female voice]: What does that mean?

CARRUTH: That gave me confidence. I got confidence from my sexual life. That spilled over into my literary life and social life and professional life, and made it possible for me to give public readings. I gave my first public reading when I was fifty-eight years old. And since then, I've given quite a few, and I've become rather good at it. And all of that goes back to overcoming the very acute and chronic anxiety psychoneurosis. I was in the hospital for a long time, a year and a half, and went through doctors, and took all the pills, and so on, and sex was a really wonderful procedure or method for me [laughs] in that respect.

FOX: Mm-hm, mm-hm.

CARRUTH: And also, I've always been terribly fond of women. Probably I was influenced by my mother or something. I'd much rather talk to women than to men, on the whole. I like the company of women. But, I don't have very much of it anymore, except for my wife. Thank you for coming.

[female voice]: [laughs] What about love?

CARRUTH: Love, as I said before, love is essential. You have to learn how to accept it and give it and do it well, intelligently, sincerely, and constructively. A loving relationship is a relationship on which you build your life—your professional life, your home life, your life as a parent, and so on and so on. Everything. If you don't have a loving relationship, and a very loving relationship, then you don't have anything to go on.

FOX: Yep. I agree with that. Definitely.

CARRUTH: And, uh, my life is very screwed, and there's no question about that. And I did things that I regret doing. But, nevertheless, my relationship to women was very important, and got me through to a large extent from the age of, say, about forty-five on.

FOX: Hm. When I was ten, I wanted to invite only girls to my birthday party, but my mother said, You can't do that, you have to have at least one boy. So I invited one boy and ten girls. [Carruth laughs] It was a very nice birthday party.

CARRUTH: I never had a birthday party when I was young, and I don't know any other kids that did at that time, either. [laughs] That came along later, apparently.

FOX: That could be. Well, now it's a big deal, and you have to go to places . . .

CARRUTH: You have to hire a clown and do all kinds of things [everyone laughs]. It's ridiculous, too much.

FOX: That's true.

[female voice]: Can you say something about your children?

CARRUTH: Well, I had two—one by my first wife, a young girl who was named Martha and who became a painter, I think a quite good painter, and then died of cancer when she was still in her forties, which was a terrible blow to me, and I've written about that. And my other child is my son,

David, from my third wife. And he lives up the hill in a trailer with his girlfriend. And we're having lots of problems right now because his girlfriend, who is in effect a member of our family, was diagnosed with MS, multiple sclerosis, a few months ago, maybe two months ago. And then, a couple of weeks ago, she was in a terrible automobile accident, and now she's incapacitated, she can't walk, she can't do anything. So, it's a difficult time for those two, my son and his girlfriend. My son is a guy who is very sweet, a very nice guy, very generous and thoughtful. An intelligent guy who reads a lot, but basically he works with his hands. He wanted to be a sculptor, and I never had money enough to set him up properly in a studio or anything like that, so he didn't get very far with it, although he did make a few pieces. Now he's just gotten a new job as a mail carrier for the Munnsville post office, which I think will be a good job for him.

FOX: Mm-hm.

CARRUTH: I'm very close to him, as I was to my daughter, too, and I spend as much time as I can with him.

FOX: That's good.

CARRUTH: I don't think you've gotten your money's worth, since you came all the way from California.

FOX: Hayden, that's perfectly good. This is good. We talked more about you than about poetry per se, but that's fine. You'll see.

CARRUTH: Okay. No, I'm not complaining. I think it would be nice if you'd stay around a little longer.

FOX: Yes?

CARRUTH: You see, one of my problems, my greatest problem right now, is loneliness. And it helps me a lot when people come to visit.

FOX: Oh, okay.

CARRUTH: So, I like that. I don't have any friends around here. That's one thing that was a mistake about moving to Munnsville. There simply isn't any way to make friends around here, and there isn't anybody to make friends with. So, it's a pretty isolated situation I'm in here.

FOX: We'll what I've found—and maybe you'll echo this—the last two or three months, I wake up in the morning and I'm just really unhappy. And when I'm out with people, I gradually warm up, and it helps a lot.

CARRUTH: Oh, it does, yes, there's no question about that. I like to have people come to talk to me. I'm basically an invalid, I can't go out, can't walk any distance, I can't go up the stairs. And I had a very bad heart attack about three, four years ago, and I've never recovered from that.

FOX: Mm-hm.

CARRUTH: So, uh, I depend on other people to come around and visit me and talk and just be friends.

[female voice]: How often does David come?

CARRUTH: He's pretty busy. He lives right up there on the hill, just behind the house. You can see his trailer from the driveway out there. So he drops in from time to time when he's going to get something or do something, and I call him on the phone every now and then and talk to him, see how he's doing at his new job, and things like that. Yeah. But I don't see a lot of him. He's a very busy guy.

[female voice]: Busy. *Busier* now.

FOX: Well, my father's ninety-one, and he lives near us, and he said—six months or a year ago—he said, I want you to come and see me at least once a week. So, I come and see him once a week and we talk on the phone probably every other day.

CARRUTH: Where does he live?

FOX: Los Angeles, also. Not too far from us.

CARRUTH: Does he have his own place, or does he . . .

FOX: Yeah, he has his own house.

CARRUTH: He's doing very well then.

FOX: He travels everywhere, he drives his car.

CARRUTH: That's great. I wish I would be able to do that, but I don't think I will. Joe-Anne has an aunt, Mary, who lives down in Philadelphia, or near Philadelphia, and she comes to see us. She's ninety-one, too, and she's blind [laughs]. She gets around pretty good for her age. She's never depressed, she's always bright and likable and laughable—a very nice person. I admire her a great deal.

FOX: I saw something on the news a few days ago. They said people who live the longest, over a hundred even, have a positive attitude, they're generally thin—which I, of course, am not. Have you given up smoking? You wrote about that.

CARRUTH: Oh, I had to give it up after the heart attack, yeah. I was a terrific smoker, and I really loved tobacco. I did write about it. It's the greatest vegetable in the world. [Fox laughs] You don't smoke?

FOX: No, no.

CARRUTH: Very good.

FOX: When I was about twelve, two friends of mine took me under their parents' house to smoke cigarettes, and I didn't want to, but socially I couldn't say no. So, I blew into it instead of inhaling [laughs].

CARRUTH: It's a wonder you didn't burn down the house. [both laugh]

FOX: True. Was giving it up traumatic?

CARRUTH: It was difficult, yeah, but the best time to do it is when you've been laid up in the hospital for a long time. I was in the hospital for two months after my heart attack, and there was no smoking there, so I didn't try to. And when I got out finally and came home, I just continued without them. And that was the easiest way for me to break it. I think it would have been very difficult just to stop.

FOX: We have a daughter who just started as a freshman at Cornell, so we're going to go visit her this afternoon.

CARRUTH: That's great. Nice town. Have you been there before?

FOX: We've been a few times since she started, yeah.

CARRUTH: So, what's she going to study?

FOX: Psychology, that's what she started in.

CARRUTH: Well, I guess it's a good school. I had a brother who went to Cornell and graduated who was a landscape architect and did quite well for himself, for a while, until he died. I've been down there. I never gave a reading at Cornell because they never invited me, and that always pissed me off. [Fox laughs] There was guy there . . . that guy who writes those insipid little poems, what's his name? [Fox laughs] Ammons. You know Ammons?

FOX: No . . .

CARRUTH: His first name is Archie, Archie Ammons.

[female voice]: I think he died.

CARRUTH: Did he die? Good. [Everyone laughs] Oh well.

FOX: That's the nice thing about being older, you don't have to curry favor with people.

[Joe-Anne]: Well, I don't think Hayden ever did. [Everyone laughs]

FOX: Yeah, yeah.

[Joe-Anne]: That's why we live in poverty. With our books, lots of books.

[female voice]: You said something about writing a novel. There was the one, and then that was your shot at getting rich, or words to that effect.

CARRUTH: Well, everybody knew in the old days, and I presume they still do, that you can't make any money from writing poetry. You *can* make money from writing fiction, if you hit it right. And in that time, in the '40 and '50s, some of the publishers held out the prospect of getting your poems published if you would sign an option contract with them for a novel. And that's what I did with Macmillan. And I had to write the novel in order to fulfill that contract. At the time, I was told that it was a good novel, and that it would be a good seller, and I would make some money. And we were quite excited at that time—my wife at that time and I—but it didn't happen that way at all. The book got panned in the *New York Times* Book Review, which is death for any book. And it was purely malicious and awful. And so, the book never sold, and I didn't make any money to speak of from it. But I had a contract for another book, which I did write, most of it, I think. I can't remember for sure whether I actually finished it or not, but I gave it up, I threw it away. I didn't like it.

[female voice]: So, did that whole process piss you off?

CARRUTH: Well, yes. Yes, it did. And I still think it's a kind of lousy way to run the publishing business, to run the literary business. But I'm sure it's still going on out there. Fiction is still . . . if you look at the *New York Times* bestsellers every week, you'll see that novels are at the top. Occasionally there's a nonfiction book that gets up there, but mostly they are novels. And people are making money on those things. And they are professional novelists. They write one, then they write another . . .

[tape ends]

Photocredit: © St. Mary's College of Maryland

LUCILLE CLIFTON is one of the most beloved and respected figures in American poetry today, widely acclaimed for her powerful explorations of race, womanhood, spirituality, and mortality. A major voice since her debut collection *Good Times*, in 1969, she has continued to portray the experiences of being an African-American, a woman, and a human with clarity and elegance. Her language, often described as "deceptively simple," strikes a nuanced balance between complexity of thought and economy of words. She has published 12 collections of her poetry, one autobiographical prose work and 19 children's books, with more on the way. She received the National Book Award for Poetry for her book, *Blessing the Boats* (BOA 2000). Her most recent book of poems is *Mercy* (BOA 2005); other titles include *Ordinary Woman, Quilting,* and *The Book of Light*. Her work has been anthologized in close to 200 anthologies of poetry.

Ms. Clifton has received many fellowships and awards for her poetry collections and children's books, including the Shelley Memorial Prize, a Charity Randall Citation, an Emmy Award from the American Academy of Television Arts and Sciences, selection as a Literary Lion by the New York Public Library, a Lannan Achievement Award in Poetry and a Lila Wallace/Reader's Digest Writer's Award. Ms. Clifton served as distinguished Professor of Humanities and holder of the Hilda C. Landers Endowed chair in the Liberal Arts at St. Mary's College of Maryland until her retirement in the fall of 2005. She continues to serve St. Mary's as Professor emeritus and Friend to the College. She served as Poet Laureate of the State of Maryland from 1975–1985. She has appeared on the "Today Show," "Sunday Morning" with Charles Kuralt, "The Power of the Word" with Bill Moyers and "Nightline" with Ted Koppel. Ms. Clifton serves on the board of Chancellors of the Academy of American Poets, and is a Fellow of the American Academy of Arts and Sciences. She is the only poet to have had two books nominated for the Pulitzer Prize in the same year.

At turns sad, exuberant and angry, her voice has always been one of great empathy and wisdom, believing in the redemptive gifts of faith and art. She asserts that the reason to write poetry is to assert the importance of being human. Alternately consoling, stimulating, and emotionally devastating, Clifton's poems are unforgettable. Her readings draw large and enthusiastic audiences.

# Lucille Clifton

December 19, 2001

FOX: When did you start writing poetry?

CLIFTON: I started when I was a little girl. I have been writing since I was about eight or nine, and I wrote very differently from the way I do now, because I was a great reader. My mother wrote poetry, I should tell you, and my mother didn't graduate from elementary school. But she wrote very traditional, iambic pentameter verse. I was telling someone last evening that when I would write a poem and I didn't rhyme all the time, she would say, "Oh, baby, that ain't no poem. Let me teach you how to write a poem." [Fox laughs loudly] And she would write one. But I started; it was a natural thing for me to do. I never questioned it. I never thought about being a poet, because I never saw anybody like me that was, or that could be. I never thought about being published. That wasn't among the things that were possible for me at that time. And still my way of expressing myself, I discovered, was through poems. I wrote answers to Emily Dickinson. I wrote sonnets. But I've never been good at titles so they were Sonnets the First, Sonnets the Second, [both laugh] and so forth. I learned how to write poems. I wrote my way toward figuring out, and read my way as well. I loved reading; I always have been a great reader.

FOX: What did you read that inspired you or helped you?

CLIFTON: Well, I wasn't inspired particularly by what I read, any more than anything else. I've always been inspired by the world, by what happens in the day. I have a great curiosity. Some could say I'm nosy, [laughing] that would probably be true. And I've always wanted to know about things and wondered about things. I read a lot of Thomas Wolfe, not Tom Wolf, Thomas Wolfe, *Look Homeward Angel* and all of that, which is funny because he writes nothing like the way I write. I mean, he's full of things. I am probably not full of things, but I love the language, I love the flow of language. I learned how to speak in my own voice.

FOX: How did you come to your own voice? What was the process of evolution there?

CLIFTON: I think because I wasn't educated into the traditional academic kind of standard written English voice. I can remember the first poem that I wrote in my own voice, and it was called, I don't think it had a title. It was after looking at the Olympics, I think they were in Mexico City. I don't remember when that was, but the announcer was talking about Mexico, this was on the radio, and the natives of the place were talking about "Mehico" and the announcer was acting as if he was right and they were wrong.

*The poem is*
*in the inner city*
*or*
*like we call it*
*home*
*we think a lot about uptown*
*and the silent nights*
*and the houses straight as*
*dead men*
*and the pastel lights*
*and we hang on to our no place*
*happy to be alive*
*and in the inner city*
*or*
*like we call it*
*home*

I have always been aware of the music in our language and I'm a lyric poet so the music matters to me. It's a very musical tongue. And so I didn't see why one couldn't write like that.

FOX: Yes. How did you come to be published?

CLIFTON: I wasn't published until I was thirty-something. By that time, of course, I'd been writing almost twenty years. And I'd say with major intent, which for me is trying to do this well, trying to serve this poem well, trying to serve poetry. My kids were seven, five, four, three, two, and one, and I saw the name of Robert Hayden in a magazine. The magazine at that time was called *Nouveau Digest* which became *Black World* which is now *Jet*, I think, no, it's in the same family of magazines as *Jet*. Anyway, I saw his name and I thought, that's a black guy. He had been part of the literature program of the National Endowment for the Arts, and so I thought, I'm going to send him a poem. I still wanted to know, was it any good? I'm going to send him a poem and see what he says. That was so bold for me, absolutely bold, because I'd never had creative writing classes. I've never studied in that way, though I study everything all the time. I know how to learn. Anyway, I sent two or three poems to him. He was no longer with the Endowment but he passed them along to Carolyn Kizer. Carolyn is now a very dear friend. She took them to the 92nd Street YMHA and I won the Discovery Award, about which I had heard nothing. The prize was a reading at the 92nd Street "Y." I went there and read. There was an editor from Random House in the audience. She wanted to know if I had a manuscript. Well, I didn't know. But I did have poems put in an order. I've always been very careful about the order, not only of word after word but of line after line, of how this poem works together, to help the poem become what it seems to want to be. And Random House read the manuscript and they published the book called *Good Times*. I was so embarrassed [both laugh loudly]. I was really embarrassed, because I had no idea if I could do this again in life, I had no clue. I was going to write poems, but were they going to be a book? I didn't know.

FOX: So you really were writing for the experience itself.

CLIFTON: I was writing for the art.

FOX: Yes, yes.

CLIFTON: I was not writing, when people hear that, they say, "You write for yourself." No, I write, this is what I do.

FOX: What gives you the greatest satisfaction from your writing?

CLIFTON: Oh, dear. If others seem to have a feel for what the poem means, a feeling, I'm interested in feelings. Maybe that, maybe just the act of writing.

It is so exciting to be writing, to have written is less so, [Fox laughs] but to be writing, everything seems okay when you're writing.

FOX: How do you know when a poem is finished?

CLIFTON: You don't. [Fox laughs] You just hope to death. [more laughter] You can murder poems, I mean, I've done it, when you start thinking too hard in your own way and you start intellectualizing, because I think a poem has to come from intellect and intuition. If you get too much intuition you have sentimentality, which is not good, and with too much intellect, it has a whole lot of stuff that nobody knows nor cares. But a poem, it's about a whole human and speaks to the whole human and it has to come from a whole human, so you involve all of yourself. I always tell students to start at the beginning and then when you're finished stop. You have to feel it out, you have to feel it out. I tell students all the time also, they put things in and they say, "Well, I like it." And my reply is often, "The poem doesn't like it." Can you feel the poem being really annoyed with you [laughing]?

FOX: Do you think that writing poetry can be taught?

CLIFTON: It can be learned; I don't know.

FOX: Can you say more about that?

CLIFTON: It's not the same thing. Just that teaching and learning are both activities. You can't teach the inside of a person. Stafford said at some point in order to change poetry you have to change poets. Because the poem has to come from more than the head. You can teach people the craft but I don't know if you can teach them the art. You can illustrate it and give examples and model it for them, but I think that they have to learn it, plus they have to understand that it's possible to learn. Do you know what I mean?

FOX: I think so.

CLIFTON: It seems to me that they have to understand, and we're so accustomed in our culture to think information or knowledge that is valid is completely intellectual information, but a poem is not an intellectual exercise. It is about, Stanley Kunitz says, being human. And I think babies learn to be human. You teach them the niceties but they learn from what they see and understand and hear, etc., to be human.

FOX: Yes. Many people find a distinction between so-called academic poetry and poetry of the streets or more visceral—do you share that view? Is there a difference in your mind?

CLIFTON: Well, I said this last night, or the other day, that people in our culture believe in an either/or culture. I don't believe in an either/or culture. I think it's been a mistake. I believe in a both/and culture. And what does academic mean as opposed to—I don't even believe in those distinctions. People in the Academy seem to feel that in order to be smart, as they think of it, you have to know a lot of facts. I often tell students that a poem has to be true, it does not have to be fact. They are two different things. I want to write poetry that can be understood by the most obscure of humans and also the cab driver. They are not lesser folk, and we forget that poetry is about people, all of them. Now the Academy, since it values intellect above all things, and believes that the only way of knowing is an intellectual way of knowing, it tends to error on that side, I think. I tell students often that if you just had to be smart to write good poetry, Harvard would be full of poets; it is not. And we know it's not. [Fox laughs] And so does Harvard. It seems to me that it's important to understand that there are other ways of knowing. The reason we value the ways of knowing that we do in the academy is because they are the easiest ones to teach. And so they value teaching greatly. They do not value as much learning. And I dare say we go about our lives learning. We know what we know even if oftentimes people don't validate it, you know, because of what we have learned and it's about more than our head.

FOX: It seems that you have a great curiosity . . .

CLIFTON: About everything, why not? I like to know different things. I know lots of things superficially [laughing]. I know a little bit of a whole lot of stuff, because I'm interested in a lot of stuff.

FOX: What do you feel you know in depth?

CLIFTON: In depth? Human-ness. I think I have a pretty good understanding of that. And it is not a perfect thing, nor am I.

FOX: Ah—could you say more about what humanness is to you?

CLIFTON: To me? Humanness is the possibilities in us all, basically, basically human. Basically life is connected, is much the same, but we superimpose on it all our fears and junk and all of that. Every day you get up trying to struggle through that, to touch where you are human. We think that there's supposed to be perfection, as if we understood even what perfection was. I mean, I'm one of the silliest people, I've been told, and I go for it. I am moody, all of that, but I'm probably the perfect Lucille Clifton at any rate. And she's like that.

FOX: Well, it seems that so often in the world we find and emphasize the differences in humans, Muslims and Christians and whatever, and yet you seem to be talking about the underlying . . .

CLIFTON: The samenesses, but, may I say this? What's wrong with having differences? Why has that become a negative? I mean, a world of me would be very boring. I don't think I'd like it. When did being different become such a pejorative kind of thing, a negative? It's wonderful, the differences in people, different belief systems, different ways of seeing things. The world is pretty big. The planet is pretty big. I use an example about language, because poetry students need to think about language, big time, and I talk about the cow and how do I know that is its name. We call it cow. It's kind enough to allow it. I don't know what it calls itself, plus I don't know what it calls me, and I probably don't want to [both laugh]. I'm like the hamburger queen of America. I'm sure that I'm a legend in barns all across the country. There's nothing wrong with having differences. The idea that we must all be like something or other is such a negative on the planet. We accept variety in nature and in animals and we are also animals, but we do not accept the natural variety of humans. So it's like white is the norm, in our culture at any rate, and everybody else is sort of different from that, so therefore lesser, when in fact, first of all the planet is a planet of color. And we are different. I was saying at the reading about teachers, I write children's books, and teachers always tell me, "When I look at my class, I don't see color." Well, that's silly, though I do understand what they're saying and appreciate it, I understand that. But the next step is to see color and have it not matter. Of course, you see color, there it is, but it doesn't matter. And our lives have been different and our circumstances have been different across all kinds of lines, but that does not make us natural enemies. It makes us learn from each other, if nothing else.

FOX: Well, I suppose there's a difference between trying to be politically correct under whatever's going on in the times versus fundamental humanness.

CLIFTON: I don't like the way people use "politically correct," because it's become a touch-phrase for doing tricky things. I think it was Vartan Gregorian who said one time, somebody was saying something when he was at Brown, and he said, "Well, I don't know what people mean about that, about it being politically correct, but it is morally correct and I will continue to do it." You know, it is not a fad or anything that minority people should be admitted to universities on the same basis as others, and that they have not been and so there has to be a little catch-up, that's not opinion. Students now often don't know the difference between opinion and fact, and then there's truth always. People use that as a divisive term, "politically correct."

FOX: Where does moral correctness come from?

CLIFTON: Faulkner has a line, "if the truth is one thing to me and another thing to you, how will we will know which is truly true." Your heart already knows. We know it is wrong to beat old women and to have dogs on them. We know that. The fact that it has happened doesn't mean we don't know it, I mean, people do stuff that they know better than all the time.

FOX: Do you ever think about your writing at all in terms of the effect it will have, and inspiring people to be in touch with their moral center?

CLIFTON: I don't think about that at all. [laughs] Sometimes I know it happens, sometimes it happens, but I'm not thinking about that. Something comes to my attention or maybe that's a way to say what happens, and then I try to serve it. Each poem, for me at any rate, each poem has its own rules. It's not the rules of poetry, it's the rules of this poem trying to be in front of me. I try to obey them, I try to feel them out, feel them out, and then I try to obey them. So I'm a servant for this art.

FOX: So how does the process work for you in creating a poem from inspiration to finished poem?

CLIFTON: How does it work? Something catches my attention. Okay. I live with it for a while, I don't start writing, because when I was writing as a young woman I had six kids and my kids are six and a half years apart in age so I had four in diapers at any time, so I couldn't say, "Oh, excuse me, children, I'm now about to write a poem," [Fox laughs], but they've seen me write all their lives. The way their mother is, is somebody who will write poems and stories, and since, I always say they did not read the parenting manual, they figured that was right. And I would start working in my head a lot, which was what I had to do. I compose on a typewriter or a videowriter, it's an old Magnavox videowriter, it's about thirty years old, I don't think they make them anymore, but it's my thing. I sit down, by that time I have gone a ways along the process of creation, then I print it out and think it's wonderful, and the next day I look it again and think, Oh, my! [both laugh] What was I thinking? I keep trying to help it become what it seems to want to be and if it feels, if it rings true to me, then I'm finished, but I still try to have patience, I still live with it for a while. Like, for instance, I carry around that thing of new poems, poems that are not published, I carry it with me, because I'm living with it, and some of them are okay and some are not quite yet, haven't graduated into the okay ones and [words lost in laughter].

FOX: So do you do a lot of rewriting or. . . ?

CLIFTON: I do a lot of rewriting, yes, I do a lot of rewriting.

FOX: How long did it take you to gain the kind of confidence in your work that you have?

CLIFTON: People ask me that a lot, you know, and I don't feel a confident person at all. What I do feel is, I mean I'm not confident about it yet, but what I know is I do the best I can in this, and I know I'm very fortunate, I've been saying this lately, but what I'm doing, I know, in this area at any rate, is exactly what I'm supposed to be doing. And that's interesting that I know that. I know that these words are what I'm supposed to be doing.

FOX: So you've found your niche in life . . .

CLIFTON: It found me. Stanley Kunitz says, "I did not choose the path, the path chose me." I never even said I'm going to be a poet or anything. Writing poems was as natural to me as breathing. This was just naturally the way that I, this is what I do.

FOX: Is it as much fun for you now as it was when you started?

CLIFTON: Mm-mm. I started hoping to do it well. As a young person, I was clever, and that's not good, you know. Cleverness is a mistake or gets in the way of being creative, but I learned how to fight my cleverness, mostly. [Fox laughs]

FOX: What tips do you have for other writers in terms of fighting their cleverness?

CLIFTON: Well, seeing yourself clearly, moving your ego out of it for one thing. A lot of poets in writing are concerned about the "poet is not the poem." Not that I'm not concerned. I want people to think I'm a good poet. I mean, I give a lot of my life to this and I care about it, but ultimately that's not the main thing. I want the respect of my peers and all of that, my cousins, just everybody. But the main thing is to realize, to have this poem proud of me, to have this poem feel as if she did the best she could. None of us have written the poem we think we're going to write. "She almost did it" will probably be my epitaph, or something. Because, of course, that's what keeps us writing; that was almost it, maybe this one will be it.

FOX: So do you feel your best work lies ahead of you?

CLIFTON: Yes, I do, I really do. It's amazing because I think that's kept me going. I've had some bouts with health. I've had cancer three times, and I have a kidney transplant and all kinds of stuff. All during those times, I thought I'm probably not going to die because I still have good work to do. I know I haven't written my best work yet. And my mother wrote poetry, she wrote very iambic pentameter verse, and she once got a letter about putting her poems in a book. I have a poem about this. The poem is called "Fury." My father wouldn't let her do it. And so she burned all her poems. I watched. I stood on top of the steps and watched her burn her poems. And I said, "My mother's not going to let me stop in the middle; she's not going to let it happen." So I felt pretty sure, and I knew that I was not, I don't think, repeating myself, so I think I have good work left to do. I hope so, I really do.

FOX: Do you ever not write something or not publish something out of fear of offending somebody?

CLIFTON: Oh, no, I don't think about that. If somebody is offended by what is true, they've got a major problem [laughing]. It's a problem that I can deal with.

FOX: It sounds to me like one of your major loyalties is to truth.

CLIFTON: Yes, and to the human condition, really, to life, life in all its interesting forms.

FOX: How do you discover truths in your life, how does that work for you?

CLIFTON: Well, you know, backward. I think you look and say, oh, that was something. I don't, this is the way of discovering it, really, don't you think? I mean, we don't write poems out of what we know, we write poems out of the questions, trying to understand, out of wondering. I always quote Gauguin's "what are we, where do we come from, where are we going." I think that's what art is questioning always, and these poems are a way for me to try to figure that out. I don't think the answers are that important. I think the questions are tremendously important. And there aren't answers that are definitive, you know, that this is the answer.

FOX: How do you think poetry has changed over your lifetime?

CLIFTON: Well, I'm allowed in. [Fox murmurs agreement] That's different. American poetry has become American poetry instead of British poetry. I think that's something.

FOX: Do you do a lot of poetry readings?

CLIFTON: I read, more than enough, I do. [both laugh] I've read in every state in the union. I've read in Alaska and Hawaii. I've read in Jerusalem and London, lots of places. My first translation was in, now I would think my first translation would be into Spanish or Swahili or something like that, but my first translation was Norwegian. And I just got a letter that a children's book is being translated into Japanese. It's really quite amazing how far these words can go. I mean, we don't send them there, they just go.

FOX: Yes, yes. And what do you get out of a reading, in terms of. . . ?

CLIFTON: Oh, the energy. I mean, the energy going back and forth. I like people, so I like to see people. I'm generally exhausted, though, these days. I'm having some health things so I'm more exhausted than usual, but I like the energy and the vibes of people around. Sometimes people seem comforted, sometimes they're annoyed, that's okay. A woman in the autograph line the other day was saying, "Well, you spanked me real good." I said, "Really?" [both laugh loudly] She was an elderly woman. She said, "But I needed it, didn't I?" "I suppose, if that's what you got, it must be what you needed." [words lost in laughter]

FOX: Are you ever surprised by an audience's reaction to something you read?

CLIFTON: Mm-mm, sure. You never know. There's a tendency sometimes, because I read poems that are fun, I get annoyed if an audience laughs then at everything. That doesn't happen that much but it does happen on occasion.

FOX: I was interested that you did a little question and answer session. Is that something you do. . . ?

CLIFTON: I like that; I like to talk to people. I'm not afraid of people so I answer as truly as I can. I don't think the questions are foolish. I'll answer anything.

FOX: It seems to me that in addition to your curiosity you also care a lot about the human condition.

CLIFTON: I do, I do. I get very annoyed with humans quite often, because we know better quite often and I think that in the present, for instance, political situation, someone has to stand up and say some things. Someone has to not just blindly wave a flag, and it might as well be me because I have time, but I think it's important. Stafford has a poem, "it's important that awake people be awake," and I think it is. And I don't mind saying it. I'm not a threatening type of person so oftentimes I've found, I think this is true, that people take things from me that they might not take from, I mean, I'm smiling.

FOX: Yes. What was I going to ask? [laughing] Who are some of your favorite writers?

CLIFTON: Oh, I hate to say that because I'm friends with so many. You know, I always say plumbers are friends with plumbers; I'm friends with poets. Stanley Kunitz is, I think, one of the great poets of our time. I'd be glad to just go around and like wave, fan him, periodically; that'd be fine with me. Oh, after that it's just a lot of people, a lot of people. If I mentioned somebody, I'd offend somebody else.

FOX: Do you have any particular poets that young writers might benefit by reading?

CLIFTON: Just read, read poetry. How do you know you don't like it if you haven't read it? There are wonderful poets in the past and now. I like, I mean I don't like one sort of poetry. There's room for all kinds of poems, all kinds of ways of being good. There's a performance poet, Sekou Sundiata, I love his poetry. Matthew Arnold, I like Matthew Arnold, two different worlds almost. There are all kinds of wonderful poets that people need to take a chance on. You need to read poetry if you're going to write it. I've known people who've said that they don't read poetry much but they write it. That's crazy. You have to write out of your strength, not your weaknesses. Black poets are not a subset of poets, they are poets, after ways of being good. I love poetry, I don't just like it, I really love it, and the magic of the music of words, I just love it.

FOX: Is there a difference to you, as loving poetry, between reading it or being at a reading, someone else's reading?

CLIFTON: I hadn't thought about that. I don't really know. I suppose when I'm reading poems in a book, I know the poet quite often so I'm hearing them even as I read. I think maybe we all do that, sort of. We tend to sometimes hear it in our own voice, if it's not a poet whose work we know, but I think that at a poetry reading I might try to imagine it on the page. They're both enjoyable things. It's not either/or, it's both/and. Many things, I think culturally, we have said they are either/or when in fact it would better if we realized they were both/and.

FOX: Mm-mm, yes. You talk about the order of things being important, word, lines, and I assume you're also talking about the order of poems and function, for example.

CLIFTON: Mm-mm, absolutely.

FOX: How do you sense what order your work should be in?

CLIFTON: I feel it out. I mean, you don't write a book. You write poem after poem. You write a lot of poems, and if you're lucky sometimes they show up, it occurs to you that this could be a book, and for me I have to find the thread that ties the book together. It's not just random poems and then some more random poems. There is a thread, you can feel it if you try, and it doesn't take, it might take a bit, but you can feel it. I have poems that are not in books. Their thread hasn't happened yet. And then once I have the thread, I can go through and feel. I actually put a lot of copies of poems on a big table or the floor even and just feel through one and then what's next and, you know what I mean, feel it through, and then after that I go back and look at it and see what happens and change something. Very intuitive, but I am an intuitive person, and so that can work for me. I understand that it doesn't work for everybody that way, but generally, there is a thread. The most tricky way that I, when I couldn't exactly find the thread, was a book called *Quilting* because quilting can be all kinds of things put together. So I just named the sections traditional quilt pattern sections, and that way I could put some poems that didn't seem to be like each other together as a quilt is, and then I generally have a little introductory poem as that book does.

FOX: What are your biggest rewards from your writing?

CLIFTON: Oh, I've met so many people. I've met lots of interesting people I would never have, I mean, a little girl from Buffalo would never have met the people that I can think of as friends. I never in my life thought that I would know Gwendolyn Brooks. I mean, she was my friend. James Baldwin was my friend. Stanley Kunitz is my friend. You know, Sharon Olds, Sonia Sanchez, my buddies.

FOX: Yeah, I spoke with Sharon about a month ago.

CLIFTON: Oh did you? That's my girl.

FOX: Oh, she was wonderful; she's an original, herself.

CLIFTON: She is. My two best girlfriend poets are Sonia and Sharon, I think. But that doesn't leave out all of the rest of you guys. [both laugh loudly].

FOX: Do you think there's any essential difference between male poets and female poets?

CLIFTON: Male poets have wives. [both laugh loudly] That's significant, because they have somebody who will watch the kids, who do the work, the grunt work, who will give them time, allow them time. I've had males get mad at me about that but the fact is, generally, I have seen female poets do it all and then still write poems. There was an old Peanuts cartoon once where Lucy was talking to Snoopy about this. I think he said, "What do wives do?" She told him and he said, "I gotta get me one of those." [Fox chuckles] Other than that, subject matter, but superficial things. But I think they tend to have time.

FOX: When you look at your work, is there anything you wrote years ago, something you don't think it's as good as what you would write today?

CLIFTON: Well, I mean, what would be the point of worrying about it? But I do have, I have a couple of older poems that I made a mistake in. In one the mistake was to the whole sense of the poem, and one that the ending of the poem was tricky and just false. This is out of a whole lot of poems. I've been publishing for thirty-one years, but we're not going to say which ones they are. [Fox laughs] I know. One is not in the spirit of the poem.

FOX: Which of your poems speaks most deeply to you?

CLIFTON: The next ones. The poem that I think of as satisfying to me is one that came all in one sitting, it's a poem called "flowers," and it's very short:

*here we are*
*running with the weeds*
*colors exaggerated*
*pistils wild*

*embarrassing the calm family flowers*
*here we are*
*flourishing for the field*
*and the name of the place*
*is Love*

That poem just spewed right out and I didn't change anything. Maybe I should have but I didn't do anything and so I'm fond of it for that reason. It's very much an older poem.

FOX: When you publish a book, do you do much re-editing when you get the proofs back?

CLIFTON: Not a lot, no. I don't think I need a lot of editing. Sometimes I do. Sometimes I need some. But for each poem, I mean I have thought it a heck of a lot and if it pleases the sensibility that it seems to have started in me, some editor's thought about it doesn't make a bit of difference. And I have had very understanding editors who know that's not exactly what I'm about. Now, if somebody reads a poem before it's published and has a suggestion that helps the poem, I'm perfectly willing to do it. I mean, I'm about the poem, but a lot of editing attempts to be intellectual exercise stuff. On the other hand, I have no sense of punctuation at all, and sometimes I begin to understand something is needed, but not a lot.

FOX: What would you say is the essential difference between writing poetry and writing prose?

CLIFTON: I teach workshops. I teach some workshops on writing children's books and my children's books tend to be stories. And I think that in prose, one writes the flesh and asks the reader to imagine the bones. In poetry, one writes the bones and asks the reader to imagine the flesh. Somerset Maugham said that the writer of prose can only stand aside when the poet passes. I think he had a point. [laughing loudly] I think poetry is harder than prose, to write. In prose you have room to explain, in poetry you do not.

FOX: What advice do you have for young poets?

CLIFTON: Be true to yourself, listen to the poet inside, the poet inside knows how to write poems, probably better than you do. Read, read, and then write. If somebody can lead to you to writing, somebody can lead you away from it. You have to take yourself.

FOX: How have important people in your life responded to your poetry?

CLIFTON: Well, my kids are used to it. My kids, my youngest is in her thirties so they're not children. I don't know. This is what I do. They are quite accustomed to this is what she does. I think it explains things for them; they think their mother's not a regular mother sometimes. Generally, I have had good responses to poetry all around. It's interesting, sometimes people try to figure out if I'm popular, am I also good? How that can be? And I do seem to be. People have a time with that but that really is not, I mean, I've got enough to think about. My kids think it's all right. They think poets are kind of nuts, though. [both laugh] That's all right.

FOX: Do you have a favorite environment for writing or a place?

CLIFTON: I can't have. I write in my head so much that wherever I can do it, I do it there.

FOX: Is that unusual? My impression is that most poets put it on paper, rather, that's the first draft and you're saying. . .

CLIFTON: I've never written longhand. I've never done that. Often the first draft for me happens in my head. But most poets didn't have six kids under seven when they were writing. When I was very young, I was very formulaic.

FOX: What life experiences have affected you most as a writer?

CLIFTON: Being an African American woman in America and all that that involves, entails, and all the rest, and then being a mother and a woman. I said to Adrienne once, Adrienne Rich, that my strength, if there is one, is that I have lived an ordinary person's life, pretty much, an ordinary poor person's life, not as poor as I used to be, but that has stood me in good stead.

FOX: I was reading an editorial a few days ago saying that with Condoleezza Rice being an advisor and a very close confidante of the president, no one even comments that she is a Black woman which. . .

CLIFTON: Mm-mm. She probably, don't say this, she probably likes that.

FOX: Uh-uh [both laugh loudly].

CLIFTON: But we won't put that in our edited, I'm not a great fan of Condoleezza Rice.

FOX: Do you think, though, that the attitude of America has changed significantly?

CLIFTON: In some places, in some places, but it's easy for America to say I'm different. It's harder to recognize that I'm not. A lot of my circumstances have been, you know, but say that. I mean, mention that I'm Black, I am, so what. If you mention that and automatically negative things come to your mind, check yourself out, 'cause you have a problem. I mention, you know, that you're white, I know that you're white. I know what that generally means. Let's see about you, you could be different from what the norm is. I'm willing to, Black people are the most forgiving people on the planet in a lot of ways. We've got crooks and thugs and stuff and so have you. We've got remarkable people and so have you. We are amazing and we don't even know it. We don't realize how truly amazing we are, and if we were not here how sterile this country would be, because we would take our stuff with us, 'cause we don't keep our stuff anyway, and together with the new populations that are coming, it's quite a wonderful mix.

FOX: It seems to me the essential mistake we seem to make over and over, many people do, is to identify a person Black, white, Japanese, whatever, as all of what you are rather than a part of who you are. It could be an important part, but it's only a part.

CLIFTON: Excepting that, if I may say, white people identify, they don't even have to mention it anymore, you know what I mean, because it is for them quite often the norm, and what I am is also the norm, do you know what I mean? It's interesting to me, this may be not even relevant, but I do a thing in classes sometimes, I teach a course among other things, called "unpopular American history." And we talk about stuff that they don't get in other classes, and I do it simply because I don't like people to say, "nobody ever told me." And they know that. I don't want anybody to say, "I never heard that," so we talk about all kinds of things. And one of the things that we talk about a lot is stereotypes. I have a little game where we go around in the classroom and everybody tells a stereotype about their own sort and then a stereotype about "the other." And everyone knows about a stereotype about them as Black or Asian or something but white people never know of a stereotype about them as white. They have them according to culture, French are so and so, Italians are so and so, and it occurred to me that white people don't think of themselves as a race in that way, they think of themselves as people and others are a race but "we are the people." In those classes, actually, it's great fun that the other people volunteer them stereotypes, which is fun, we laugh and we become a community quite easily. I remember at Santa Cruz once, I taught at Santa Cruz for quite long time, one of the arguments was that the African American students said that white people's hair when it was wet smelled like dogs. And the Latino students said, No, it smells like chickens. And so there was this cultural clash going on between these two groups. I always said that the white people were sitting there keeping their hair dry, "Lord, I don't want [lost in laughter]." It was hysterical, and we laughed and learning to laugh is a good thing.

FOX: What's the place of humor in poetry?

CLIFTON: Oh, very important. Humor can keep us alive. I'm alive because of a sense of humor, I think. A lot of things are funny. They're awful sometimes, but they're funny. I think poetry with humor in it is great. It sort of breaks down a lot of stuff.

FOX: What sort of things do you learn as a teacher?

CLIFTON: Oh, from students, all kinds of things. I love my students. I had a student there the other day from when I was in Santa Cruz which has been twelve years. Something about what's going on. I learn to validate their world and hope that they try to validate some of mine. They know that I care about them.

FOX: It seems to me that's a very good area to have a connection on a deep level with other people, some of your students.

CLIFTON: I'm not particularly, I am perhaps in some areas, but not particularly judgmental and I try to tell them straight what I think, you know. I announce nobody can come into my room high. You just can't do it and can I tell? Yeah. And so they don't do it. I trust them. I talk about doing your best. At the end of every class we hold hands. I've been doing this thirty-one years, every class I've ever taught. We hold hands and say something to get us through the day. Other teachers often say, "Well, I can't possibly do that." I do not understand why, but fine, I can so I do. In our "I, Too, Sing America" class at St. Mary's College of Maryland, we were in a circle, and I start the first time but then other people start, and we go around the circle saying something. Next to me on the left was a young man, white, from New Mexico and he had not been around African American people. Next to him was a young Black guy, a street guy from D.C. He'd been around everything. And this was the first meeting of the class and they had heard about it, people know what I do at St. Mary's, I've been there 11 years. So the white guy said, "Well, I think you ought to know and I feel like I can say this, that this is the first time I've ever touched a Black person." And when he said that the class was kind of surprised and the Black guy from D.C. next to him looked at him and just held open his arms and they just embraced each other. And I felt, oh, okay, that's why I teach, that's what it is, because that broke down a barrier that was, I mean, I was so proud of them both. It took courage to do both things, more courage for the white kid, and so they hugged each other and it was almost born a community. Somebody said, "I went to work and told them about so-and-so and so-and-so" and she said that a Black person at her work was offended and walked out of the room. Some people, but you know what you saw was good, so if somebody's offended, they got a problem.

FOX: Well, I suppose one could view poetry as a process of breaking down barriers between people, whatever those barriers might be, gender, race. . .

CLIFTON: Mm-mm, defenses quite often, defenses.

FOX: Ah, say more about that.

CLIFTON: Well, because people, poetry can be healing. After 9/11, people turned to poetry so much as a healing kind of thing, healing our insides, and they turned to others and to poetry despite any kind of defenses against "the other." But the problem, of course, is that they then united against people who looked as if they were Arab and that's a great, great, horrible mistake. I've talked with my students in the "I, Too, Sing America" class because we had just talked about Japanese internment, and I have always told them that these things are connected and they began to see a connection here and you really can't have that. A lot of things disguise themselves as arrogance and they're really fear, disguise themselves as belligerence and it's really fear, and it's good to study and know the difference.

FOX: Yes, I think fear has many faces.

CLIFTON: It masks itself.

FOX: Yes, yeah. Could you talk a bit more about how poetry is healing.

CLIFTON: I don't know how it works. I don't know it does that. I just know that it does. And I've had enough people talk about it. Somebody asked me once if I wrote to heal others—I write to heal me, if anything. Because I am not different from others, others can be healed as well. Some of it is mystery, how poetry works. Some of it is mystery, how it comes to you is mysterious, what happens after it does is mysterious as well.

FOX: What effect would you like your poetry writing to have on the world, on people?

CLIFTON: Well, it hasn't done badly. I've had letters from people in Serbia on both sides of the war. Now why in the world I have no idea. But people feel that maybe I understand something about what they are going through, because I do try to talk about those basic things. I don't know, I would just like to be doing the best I can.

FOX: I agree with you about diversity and I think the biggest mistake, but I don't like to see groups not like other groups because they aren't the same.

CLIFTON: Sure. I like to say that it's possible and it is an American culture that we all share, of course. It seems to me that so often when people say that, what they mean is the more you're like me the more I like you. I tell my students all the time that I love all my students and they know that, I don't have a lot of minority students. St. Mary's College does not have a lot of minority students, but I say I love you all, I love the minorities, the African American students first because they have been last so long but that doesn't have anything to do with if I love you and they know that, my students know it perfectly well. I have never had a problem with students about this.

And I don't agree with the African American ones all the time; they often don't know what they're talking about, just like all the other kids.

FOX: Well, it seems to me that the problem among other things centers around fear, we fear the unknown. Someone who looks different or is a different culture to that extent is unknown and therefore is to be feared.

CLIFTON: Yes, let me, can I take this off, what's interesting—[loud laughter] because we know you all really well, we have been there, in the kitchen, or in somewhere for a long time, so it isn't an unknown. You would not be an unknown but oftentimes our fear is because there is the possibility of rejection so often and you never know when it's going to happen. So, especially our young people, their defense gets up and so they do, now it's gotten to be a thing where if you're articulate, you tryin' to be white, which is really not, and I talk about to them all the time. The poets who don't know, I was very pleased, I went to this poetry thing last night. This was a young Black woman, and we read some poems, poems that we didn't write but that, but I loved that in this group, somebody read Intasake, somebody read Mary Oliver, that was wonderful, wonderful. There is a fear, a lot of times I think the fear for white people might be the fear that somebody is going to "get back atcha," you know what I mean? Because I think there's a knowing that these people have not been treated that well. Well, I didn't do it but my grandmother did. And there becomes a thing where I wonder if they're reacting to that. Some will, some will. There aren't any guiltless people. It's kind of a big drag, you might say, but there aren't any guiltless people, but one has to do the right thing anyway. I know that I certainly in the earlier years, not now, you win the National Book Award and a lot of good stuff happens, but I was not reviewed very much, etc., because I was always reviewed as primitive [Fox laughs uproariously] sort of like the Grandma Moses, and without craft. I have craft, okay. I think about this stuff, too. As if I could have stumbled on poems, spewed them out, whatever words come, I don't care. That was in the early years and I was always compared with Langston. I do not write like Langston Hughes. I don't write like him at all, but I understand what the mind set that says that is. I'm not mad about it. I mean, you're a product, I saw the same movies you did. I always say, you're a product of what your life has been.

SAM HAMILL is the author of fourteen volumes of original poetry, including *Destination Zero: Poems 1970-1995, Gratitude*, and *Dumb Luck*; three collections of essays, and two dozen volumes translated from ancient Greek, Latin, Estonian, Japanese, and Chinese, most recently, *The Essential Chuang Tzu, Narrow Road to the Interior & Other Writings of Basho*, and *Crossing the Yellow River: Three Hundred Poems from the Chinese*. He is editor of *The Gift of Tongues: Twenty-five Years of Poetry from Copper Canyon Press*; *The Erotic Spirit*; *Selected Poems of Thomas McGrath* and (with Bradford Morrow) *The Complete Poems of Kenneth Rexroth*.

He taught in prisons for fourteen years, in artist-in-residency programs for twenty years, and has worked extensively with battered women and children. He has been the recipient of fellowships from the National Endowment for the Arts, the Guggenheim Foundation, the Woodrow Wilson Foundation, the U.S.-Japan Friendship Commission, two Washington Governor's Arts Awards, a PEN Anti-censorship Award, and other honors. He is Founding Editor of Copper Canyon Press. In 2003, he founded Poets Against the War. His new and selected poems and translations, *Almost Paradise*, was published by Shambhala Publications in March, 2005. A collection of essays on poets and poetry, *Avocations*, is available from Red Hen Press, 2007.

# Sam Hamill

September 3, 2004

FOX: First, I have to ask, how did you come by this unusual, wonderful location?

HAMILL: Well, I was looking for a place for Copper Canyon Press in the Northwest. I was even actually thinking about moving to Canada in 1974, when the folks at Centrum started the Port Townsend Writers' Conference, and they thought it might be a good idea to have an editor and a press in residence. So, through Centrum, Copper Canyon was able to rent this building and become artist in residence under the umbrella corporation of Centrum. We've been here now for thirty years.

FOX: Wow, that's neat! Some writers feel that they write well in one place and not in another. Does this affect you at all?

HAMILL: Well, no. [Fox laughs] Although the poetry *of place*, as it is often called, or what John Haines calls the "Place of Sense," I think is a very important ingredient in who and what I am and who and what Copper Canyon is. We are Northwest Coast, we are Pacific Rim. That's a direct connection to Asia. I translate, as you know, classical Japanese and Chinese poetry. The landscape, the geography, the flora here, is very reminiscent of northern Japan. We have volcanic mountains. The land-bridge, anthropological idea that the people we often refer to as Native Americans may in fact be Mongolian, Chinese, Inuit, who knows?

FOX: Yes.

HAMILL: So all of that, I think, comes into play, both in my poetry and in, sort of, my general sensibility. Certainly in my Buddhist practice.

FOX: And how does your Buddhist practice impact your poetry?

HAMILL: Well, Zen mind is Zen mind. [Fox laughs loudly] I can't really answer that question. People sometimes will come up to me and say, "You know, I really like your Zen poems." I don't know what that means. Which of my poems are not Zen poems? [Fox laughs] But, Zen is an attitude and a conduct, and that attitude and conduct infuses one's poetry, theoretically, with the spirit of Zen. I don't often write about Zen as a subject. But, certainly, Zen, Mind-Zen attitude, um, ever present in . . . I mean, I hope it's ever present in whatever I do. But I'm the last one to know.

FOX: [laughing] Yes. Over the course of your career, has your writing changed in any significant way?

HAMILL: Well, it's certainly evolved. For the last ten years, I've been writing a lot of poems in classical Japanese measure, so that requires 5-7-5-7-7. A block of short poems. Except I link them together and turn them into long poems of thirty-one-syllable stanzas. That happened because I translated so much of that poetry, and began performing with a shakuhachi player named Christopher Blasdel, who uses a lot of classical Japanese bamboo flute music in our performances. Those rhythms became just sort of part of my body knowledge. And I found that I could write a certain kind of discursive poem in those measures and be very comfortable with it. So, that would have never happened had I not been translating a lot of classical Japanese. Twenty-five years ago, before I was translating that stuff, it never would have occurred to me, probably, to try a measure like that. But, generally, I've always written in I guess what we would call a projective line, or Denise Levertov's line, if you will. Certainly, I think she was the largest influence on me in terms of lineation or how I construct the poem on the page. So one's poetry, I suppose, evolves. And I'm restless by disposition anyway, so I'm always trying to find a new poem or a new kind of poetry. And yet there are certain kinds of poems that I seem to return to, like the longer forms . . . the ten, fifteen, twenty-page poems. Those sorts of poems don't get readily published in magazines, and they don't often invite a lot of new readers; but I think it's very important work for me, and I enjoy working in those longer forms. So I do what I do.

FOX: So, the reward to you from writing, the writing itself?

HAMILL: I don't know that reward has a lot to do with it. [Fox laughs] I think the practice of poetry is like the practice of medicine or the practice of law. One engages in it as a way of life, not as "this incident" and then "that incident."

Although, in one's memory there are certain incidences that become sort of profound in retrospect. But really, it's the long view. It's the practice of poetry that engages me. And whether I'm writing a lot or whether I'm not writing much at all, has never really concerned me a lot. I haven't gone through long periods of not writing, and I'm almost always translating something. So I'm always engaged, and I'm an active poetry editor. So I'm living in poetry basically twenty-four hours a day.

FOX: How does the editing impact your own work?

HAMILL: Well, it helps me be more clear about what I care about.

FOX: Yes.

HAMILL: It helps me sometimes see my own poems from a slightly disengaged point of view. But who can say for sure? Certainly, I'm a sponge when it comes to influences, I mean, every poet that we publish is an influence on my work. And when you line-edit someone else's poetry, you read those poems very, very closely. And to me, that's the real reward. It's all of the poetry that I get to see, and the poetry that I get to discover, and the poetry that I get to present. And *presenting* poetry is very important to me. I really enjoy doing that.

FOX: Presenting in . . .

HAMILL: Well, giving poetry readings . . .

FOX: Ah.

HAMILL: . . . writing criticism, publishing books. Whatever is engaged in the process of presenting poetry excites me.

FOX: And during a poetry reading, how do you find audiences react?

HAMILL: Well, different audiences react in different ways. Let me give you, for instance, two examples. A couple of years ago in California, I guess it was just a year ago in California, I gave a reading for the Buddhist Peace Fellowship in Beyond Baroque. And that's not a very large venue, so the place was really packed, which sort of makes you feel good. Although it also makes you feel bad, because a lot of people don't come, because it's a very small venue. But, I talked a little bit about Poets Against the War, and I read a few poems, and people were really very appreciative, and seemed really deeply engaged with the poetry reading. Now, that's one way to do a poetry reading. Shortly after I started Poets Against the War, I went to New York City for what is now a legendary reading at Lincoln Center during "the storm of the century." Snow was literally hip-deep walking up 5th Avenue. Couldn't get a cab. I mean, nothing was running. The entire city was shut down. And there were about twenty poets reading that evening. There were 3,000 people there, stomping, screaming, applauding every poem.

FOX: Wow.

HAMILL: Yup. That's a whole different kind of experience. Frankly, I prefer smaller venues. I like reading to an audience that I can feel personally engaged with. And when I'm on a stage in front of two or three thousand people, I can't really be engaged with those people.

FOX: Yes. Talking about Poets Against the War, what motivated you to start that?

HAMILL: Well, I was invited to the White House for an evening discussion, I guess, of Walt Whitman, Emily Dickinson, and Langston Hughes. And the night before my invitation arrived, I'd been on the Internet reading about Bush's proposed "Shock and Awe" attack on Iraq. And I've been an anti-war activist from the day I was discharged from the U.S. Marine Corps., more than forty years ago. Not only that, but I grew up on Walt Whitman. At one point he referred to the White House as our national "cesspool," and that's exactly how I think he would refer to this White House. And to have these people try to co-opt Walt Whitman, Emily Dickinson, and Langston Hughes, three of the most individualistic American poets to ever live, three of the most decent poets who ever lived, after reading about "Shock and Awe" attacks, just infuriated me. And it put me in the untenable position: if I decline and keep my mouth shut, nobody is aware of this, nobody cares. And the White House had done this before with writers, and some writers objected—my dear friend Hayden Carruth, who wrote an eloquent letter declining an invitation to the Bill Clinton White House. Adrienne Rich declined an invitation to the White House. So various of my friends had . . . and when Denise Levertov was queried about becoming Poet Laureate, she simply said, I'm not an American. I'm mid-Atlantic, she said, neither British nor American. [Fox laughs] So, I made the decision to e-mail thirty or forty friends and invite them to give me a poem, and I planned to present—just send it—an anthology to the White House. Well, it hit the Internet and, twelve hours after my first e-mail went out, the entire Port Townsend server was about to collapse from the response. My invitation I went out at six o'clock Sunday morning. Monday morning the poetry symposium was canceled.

FOX: Yes.

HAMILL: So, I wasn't even given an opportunity to decline the invitation. [Fox laughs] And, of course the shit hit the fan with the media. We ended up on March 5th—I mean, there were readings around the world, readings nationally, the C-SPAN broadcast an entire reading from Massachusetts with Bill O'Daly and Galway Kinnell, and some really great people. On March 5th of '03, I delivered to Congress 12,000 poems by American poets—12,000 poets expressing their "shock and awe" at this administration and its polices. And the role of poetry in our culture was debated on the op-ed pages of every major newspaper in American.

FOX: Yes.

HAMILL: The good old liberal *New York Times* hired one of Tricky Dick's old speechwriters to do a hatchet job on me. *The Wall Street Journal* hired another Nixon speechwriter to attack me not once, but twice. And the interesting thing in all of this was how little any of these people know about poetry. I mean, they don't know *anything* about poetry. And then they would say, "Well, why can't you just keep the politics out of it?" And I would say, you know, "Why didn't Homer? Why didn't Sappho? What great poet can you name who is apolitical?" And, of course, they all named exactly the same one, Robert Frost, who wrote one kind of poem, rather well, [Fox laughs] and who was really a very unhappy, miserable human being. Not a very good model for any poet that I know of. [both laugh] And even Frost was political, you can't say that he wasn't. Simply by being a rural poet instead of an urban poet, he made a political decision that affected his entire career. So, it was fun being interviewed on the radio and on CNN, with all of these functional illiterates who worked for the nine corporations that control 90 percent of the American mass media. [laughs]. And discovered just how empty those minds really are. [laughs again]

FOX: Do you think people with political sensibilities become poets, or poetry pushes you that way?

HAMILL: I think you cannot be a poet without being politically engaged in some way. You think of how reclusive Dickinson was, and yet she's one of the most political poets in the American tradition. She's every bit as political in her own way as Whitman is in his. And, of course, the FBI had followed Langston Hughes around for twenty-five years, trying to nail him as a Commie or Socialist or *something*. Get this guy on *something*. And, of course, they couldn't get him on anything because all he wrote about was being black. [both laugh]

FOX: In what way do you find Emily Dickinson political?

HAMILL: In every way possible. I mean, if I pulled Dickinson off the shelf and started looking at poems, I could show you poems that are in-your-face political. But even famous poems like "Wild Nights! Wild Nights!"—it's political. I also think that Langston Hughes, Emily Dickinson and Walt Whitman were *three gay poets*. Isn't it interesting that this White House would think of *three gay poets* [Fox laughs] to have a symposium about.

FOX: Was it, George W. or Laura . . .

HAMILL: Laura.

FOX: Yes.

HAMILL: But I don't think she had read those poets deeply enough to even realize that they were gay, or what it might mean to say to American poets, "Let's celebrate Whitman at the White House." And a lot of we poets have actually *read* Whitman. [both laugh] You know, "Resist much, obey little." [both laugh]

FOX: You think those words are . . .

HAMILL: The Whitman who inspired Ed Abbey, I might add. [both laugh]

FOX: Are you pleased, then, with the impact that Poets Against the War has had?

HAMILL: Well, there are now Poets Against the War organizations in forty or fifty countries.

FOX: Whoa!

HAMILL: And on September 11th, all around the world, we will remember September 11th. We will remember, the world remembers, the Attica Prison riots. The *world* remembers the fall of the Allende government. And the *world* remembers Manhattan Island. Those three events are all September 11th events and we will memorialize them, and we will, we will think about them and what actions we can take to make the world a better place to live through engaged poetry, beginning in Tokyo on September 11th and closing on the West Coast of California and Hawaii that night.

FOX: What is it about the human condition that seems to call human beings towards war over and over and over?

HAMILL: Cynicism, pessimism, and greed.

FOX: Hm.

HAMILL: I mean, if you really think about it there's really only two reasons to go to war: "I hate you," or "You have something I want." There really isn't anything else. You can't say, well, we're going to war over a philosophy, because philosophy is a discussion. By definition. So, it's just, . . . the reason Sappho expelled man from her community wasn't because she was a lesbian, it was because she thought that men were childish, and they made war. And she was so vehemently anti-war; she simply didn't want war-makers, childish war-makers, in her community. I agree with Sappho. War-making is childish behavior. Bush is infantile in his language, in his conduct, and in his thinking.

FOX: Well, we may get in trouble for publishing that, but . . .

HAMILL: I mean, this guy, this guy is so fucked up, [Fox laughs] that when bin Laden bombs Manhattan, he goes after Saddam Hussein.

FOX: Yes.

HAMILL: And he said, when he switched from bin Laden to Hussein, he said bin Laden doesn't matter now, we got to get Hussein. Who never attacked us! It's irrational. This is Oedipal. This is, uh, Oedipus on acid. [both laugh]. Right now, my Iraqi friends can't translate my poetry into Iraqi. But my Iranian friends are translating my poetry in Farsi.

FOX: Why can't your Iraqi friends translate . . .

HAMILL: Well, it's because all of the, all of the communications are getting interrupted.

FOX: Okay.

HAMILL: We can't have Iraqi poets talking to American poets [laughs].

FOX: Iraqis are our friends. We're going to give them American style democracy, aren't we?

HAMILL: I raised a lot of eyebrows with a poem called "Amerika, Mon Amour" by referring to the Bushes as fascists. But, Mussolini defines the perfection of fascism as the marriage of corporation and the state. And if you look at the American political system, it is the epitome of fascism. It is a political system completely controlled by corporate money. The Democrats, the Republicans . . . as George Wallace used to say, there ain't a nickel's worth of difference between 'em. They have their big convention and they all go have a big party on Enron money, or on Halliburton money, or on Conoco money. And all of these corporations supply all of the money for all of this nasty-ass, stupid, beside-the-point political advertising to keep us distracted from looking at the real issues.

FOX: Do you vote?

HAMILL: You bet.

FOX: Okay, so . . .

HAMILL: I hold my nose and vote. [Fox laughs]

FOX: Well, this election . . .

HAMILL: There have been a couple of elections that I simply couldn't do that in. But that was in the late 70s, early 80s, when it was just so awful, I was utterly disgusted. But we weren't under the kind of threat to our Constitution that we're under with this administration. I mean, the Patriot Act is the most evil document, perhaps, since the incarceration of the Japanese. I mean, it's just a flat evil document. It's either you're on my side or you're a terrorist, and if you're a terrorist, then I can arrest you and not charge you and hold you forever.

FOX: To change it a little bit, do you remember the first poem you ever wrote?

HAMILL: No, I was four or five years old.

FOX: Ha!

HAMILL: I grew up on a ranch in Utah, a farm in Utah, and my old man, my adopted father, loved poetry. And he would sometimes recite poetry while he worked. And he would explain to me, the rhythm of the work would help you decide what poem to sort of say. The way you sometimes hum or sing when you work—well, he recited poetry that way, and I think that was what first turned me on to poetry. And I would go out and do my chores, and I would make up a quatrain, and that evening we would all sort of work on it and write it down. But I don't have any of that stuff.

FOX: So you started writing poetry at a very young age.

HAMILL: Yeah.

FOX: What relationship do you find between music and poetry? You mentioned rhythm . . .

HAMILL: Well, I believe that all poetry aspires to the conditions of music, which is to say that my muse is Calliope, the muse of lyric poetry. Its rhythms in speech have always fascinated human beings, rhythms in sound. I suspect that before we learn to actually make words, we first learn to imitate animal sounds. If you could, you know, moo like a cow, the cow would come closer, and then you could kill it and eat it. So, I think at a very practical level, listening to our own sounds and mimicking the sounds around us, and organizing those sounds, I think is fundamental to human nature. And I grew up in what I think is the greatest era of jazz, and that's the era of Miles Davis, and John Coltrane, and Dexter Gordon, and all of those folks. Monk. And when I was young I was a piano player and a trumpet player.

FOX: Hm.

HAMILL: So, the idea of music was sort of everywhere in my world. I discovered Elvis when he was still recording for Sun Records.

FOX: Whoa.

HAMILL: So I grew up with folk music, rock music, Delta blues, Chicago blues and that sort of 1945 to 1965 period of jazz. Music was an amazing world in those days. It's still amazing, but in those days so much was opening up. Black guys could play in white clubs. [laughs] A lot of things were happening. And the music was part of the social revolution that the Beats were a part of. I mean, it was all a big social revolution, breaking down the hard barriers of racism, the soft barriers are still there.

FOX: Mm-hm, mm-hm.

HAMILL: So it was natural for me to sort of get to some point in my life where either I had to think seriously about being a musician or think seriously about being a poet.

FOX: What turned you toward poetry?

HAMILL: Well, I was an orphaned kid, and a battered child, and had a pretty unhappy childhood. I think I was really looking for a family. I was looking for some human being who gave a damn about me. And I found that world, eventually, in poetry. I really felt when I was reading D.H. Lawrence's animal poems that he was somebody that I shared something with. Or when I was reading Robinson Jeffers' narrative poems like "Roan Stallion," his love of mountains and Western America and the desolation of America, I really felt that in my bones, having grown up basically atheist in Mormon Utah, with those gorgeous mountains and deserts. I mean, Jeffers' feeling of isolation was my feeling of isolation, his despair was my despair. His cynical view of civilization was my cynical view. I was a kid. [laughs] And, you know, discovering Roethke and the Meditations, not the, not the anthology Roethke, but the "Meditations of an Old Woman" and the "North American Sequence." To me, that opened vistas in the same way that "Sketches of Spain" opened vistas. It was like there had never been anything like that before.

FOX: So you found kindred spirits.

HAMILL: Yeah, yeah. And, you know, Rexroth, who was really sort of, *I* adopted *him.* [both laugh] Yeah, he used to write that review, those columns for *The Saturday Review*, "The Classics Revisited." And I couldn't wait for the next *Saturday Review*, and then I'd run out and I'd buy *Tale of Genji* or I'd buy Tolstoy, or I'd buy Whitman. And I'd read Rexroth's essay, and read whatever it was he was telling me to read. So he was really sort of my first professor. [laughs]

FOX: Many people feel that poetry is a very intimate way of communicating. Would you?

HAMILL: Well, it can be, but it doesn't have to be. A lot of Whitman's poetry, some of his most famous poems are public rhetorical poems. Certainly, there's nothing private about "When Lilacs Last in the Dooryard Bloom'd." That's a speech. It's an elegant, beautiful, moving speech, but it's not intimate. It's a public speech. Poetry is a large house. And I think people have a tendency to forget that. We get concentrated in our little chamber in the house, and we forget that all those other rooms are still there, and they're all occupied. [laughs]

FOX: I guess the house of poetry contains multitudes.

HAMILL: Yeah, exactly.

FOX: When you edit, do you change much, or ask the poet to change much?

HAMILL: Some people get more editing than others. Some books get more editing than others. Not too long ago there was a poet who we had published previously, who sent me a book that I really didn't like. And I just sort of said, you've got to completely rewrite this book, and you're gonna have to cut it in half, or I'm not gonna do it. And we sort of had a little war over it, for months! Finally the book got rewritten and cut in half. The poet's delighted with the book. And so is the editor. [laughs] So, sometimes you have to draw those real hard lines.

FOX: Yes.

HAMILL: But for the most part, line-editing here is not heavy handed. If we're not really, deeply engaged with the poetry to begin with, . . . You know, being a good editor is telling the poet that really terrific line in that four-line is so beautiful, it's gotta go. [both laugh] But most of it's little stuff.

FOX: Do some poets just refuse the editing?

HAMILL: Not if you want to get published here. We don't have those kinds of conversations. [both laugh] When you have devoted as much of your life to your poem as I have devoted to Copper Canyon Press, then we'll have that conversation. Until then, I'm the editor. [laughs]

FOX: When did you learn Japanese?

HAMILL: Well, I began learning Japanese when I was an eighteen-year-old Marine in Okinawa, which is where I began *serious* Zen studies. I'd read a lot of Zen before then. I grew up with Whalen and Snyder and Rexroth and Alan Watts and all of those people. But I was two years in Okinawa, and I began learning some Japanese and learning some Zen, and that's where my deeper engagement with Asian cultures, that was the . . . I've always wanted to go back to Okinawa. I love the Okinawan people. And, I've forgotten the Okinawan term for it, but the local language, called Uchi-something, it's "family language," I've forgotten what the language, *Uchi* is "family," I've forgotten what the "language" part is. I don't remember any of that, but I would love to go back to Okinawa one day, and deliver my diatribe against the U.S. occupation of that poor, beleaguered little nation, because it's not a Japanese nation. The Okinawan people are Okinawan, not Japanese.

FOX: How does the process of writing work for you?

HAMILL: I write mostly by ear. So, on a shorter poem, nothing goes on the page until the poem's done. So, when I send my manuscripts to my archivist at WSU, she opens my manuscripts, what she gets is basically finished poems. There may be a word or two that get changed between there and the actual book, but I don't revise the way most people do that go through MFA programs, where they do a lot of fool with this and fool with that, and . . . I look at pages of poets, and the only one of those things that ever interested me much was the Ezra Pound facsimile edition of "The Waste Land," where you can see Ezra Pound's editorial mind really at work on a great poem. Well, on a mediocre poem that he made great. [laughs]

FOX: Yes.

HAMILL: I do a little of that on my longer poems, but not, not heavily. I'm not a big reviser, I try to get things right the first time.

FOX: Has technology had an impact . . .

HAMILL: No. It's very helpful in writing *prose,* which one does have to fool with constantly.

FOX: Mm-hm.

HAMILL: But, for poetry, in the longer poems, sometimes I'll shift passages or something. But in a poem of two or three or four pages, there are very basically no drafts, because I do it all by ear. And then I write it down, and then I try to get it out of my mind to make room for whatever's going to happen next.

FOX: What would you say has happened with poets of the United States over the past thirty, forty years?

HAMILL: Well, the first, most obvious thing is that when I was a teenager in the mid-50s, early 50s, there were no Black poets. There was Langston Hughes and Jimmy Baldwin, they were the Black writers. [laughs] And there were, like, three women poets. And there were no Hispanic poets. There were no Asian-American poets, and no Greek-American poets. There were no *hyphenated* poets. And poetry lived entirely within the university community. And there were no public poetry readings. Dylan Thomas was the only poet who ever gave public poetry readings.

FOX: Mm.

HAMILL: And then along came the Beats. And all of a sudden, there was poetry in cafes and poetry in bars and poetry in the streets and poetry in bookstores, and there was underground publishing. And there was, became a great vitality in the American language though that. And it was revolutionary in prose because of people like Kerouac, revolutionary in poetry because it brought poetry out of academia and right back where Whitman always said it belonged—in the streets, in the hearts and mouths and ears of everyday Americans. So that's the first huge thing. The second revolution came with the invention of non-profit publishing. There were hundreds of tiny, little presses around the country, some of them making exquisite handmade books, some of them, like George Hitchcock, cranking things out on a mimeograph machine. That work was really important. And with the creation of the NEA and the advent of non-profit publishing, things like Graywolf Press, Copper Canyon Press, Allan Kornblum—the Coffee House, BOA . . . All of a sudden, there were places we could go and ask people to donate, and help us do what we want to do, and become more professional about it, those of us who needed to become more professional. And that created an explosion in publishing. Unlike anything ever before in all of history. I mean, just a *huge* explosion. And now it's perfectly normal to have 2,000, 2,500 books of poetry published in the United States, *every year*!

FOX: Yes.

HAMILL: Some of the editions are large, some are small. But you think about that, 2,500 poetry . . . 3,000, *a year*! And, whether it's four or five hundred copies, or three or four thousand copies, or eight or ten thousand copies, that gives you some idea of the *extraordinary* spread of poetry over the last forty years.

FOX: Yes.

HAMILL: When I have to listen to people pissing and whining about American poetry, I just wanna slap 'em.

FOX: okay.

HAMILL: This is the greatest time for poetry since T'ang Dynasty China. At whatever time in our history have we had the magnitude of poets that we've had in the last seventy-five years? Beginning with William Carlos

Williams and H.D. and Ezra Pound and that whole generation, Rexroth and Carruth and that generation, and this *incredible* generation of the 20s that included everybody like Jim Wright and Dick Hugo, to Gary Snyder and Merwin and Rich and Levertov and Creeley and Duncan, and on and on . . . it's just an endless fucking list.

FOX: Mm-hm.

HAMILL: And it's an incredible list. I mean, this may be a greater time for poetry than T'ang Dynasty China. Nothing like it in history.

FOX: And the audience, perforce, has increased enormously.

HAMILL: Absolutely! To have great audiences, you gotta have great poets. [laughs]

FOX: Many people see a great gap between academic poetry and poetry of the streets. What's your . . .

HAMILL: Pointless arguments, you know. [Fox laughs] It is, it's pointless. You know, I can't listen to rap, 'cause I can't understand what they're saying. And often, when I do understand what they're saying, it offends me. That doesn't mean that rap isn't important. It doesn't mean that there aren't people making rap poetry, or performance poetry of any kind, that doesn't help people become more human and more humane. These are matters of taste, not matters of philosophical argument.

FOX: Yes.

HAMILL: There are poets who have been influenced by the language poets, whom I don't read. But I love the poets that I read who've been influenced by the language poets. So, there's really no point in trying to make an argument, a logical argument, out of what are really matters of taste. You simply have to come back and look at the entire "household" of poetry one more time. And, you know, you may not like that branch, it may be misshapen, you may like this perfect branch over here, well, okay, write metrical poetry. Over here, we've got the free-versifiers, things are a little disheveled. [laughs]

FOX: What happened to rhyming poetry? It seems to be way out of favor now.

HAMILL: Well, I use a lot of rhyme, I just don't use a lot of metered end-rhyme. I think any poet worth his or her salt would be a fool not to make use of rhyme. I suspect there's a lot more rhyme out there than you may realize. It's just that we don't put it where it's expected any longer, because that got boring. [laughs] "a-b-a-b" just doesn't stay interesting for a long time, most often.

FOX: Yes, yes. Do you think the writing of poetry can be taught?

HAMILL: To a degree, sure, yeah, sure. I think every, everybody who's able to learn how to read and write can learn how to write a decent little poem. I think learning to do so will make any life a better life. Do I think that anybody has great poetry in them? Of course not! I've been wholly devoted to the study and practice of poetry for forty years, fifty years, and I don't have a clue whether I'm any good. And I never will. I mean, I will die not knowing whether any of this mattered, except that I'm convinced that my work as an editor / publisher *has* mattered. But I'll never know whether any of my poetry is worth reading.

FOX: In what way do you feel your work as an editor and publisher has mattered the most?

HAMILL: Well, I think I've made a gift to American poetry. There's a little poem by Antonio Porchia that Merwin translated long ago, that I've always loved—"I know what I have given; I cannot know what you received." [laughs]

FOX: Yes, of course. What advice do you have for people who are just starting to write poetry?

HAMILL: Well, I think there are two fundamental attitudes. First of all, I think if you want to, you can do it. But in order to do it, you've got to practice. You can't ride a bicycle without a scraped knee, nobody ever did. The second is, if you're going to be real serious about it, then you have to write every day, for twenty years. Doesn't matter whether you feel like writing, it doesn't matter whether you have anything to say, it doesn't matter whether anybody thinks your writing is any good or not. And, in fact, the worse thing that can happen to you is to get too much praise too soon. If you don't invest ten years in bad writing and becoming a mediocre writer, you haven't done your homework. And the second thing is, what you read is what you feed your *anima*. What you feed your soul, what you feed your spirit, determines what kind of poet you're going to become. One of my great heroes is the T'ang poet Tu Fu, who said, "Poetry is about character." And I like to pair that up with an observation of Ezra Pound's that more poets fail from lack of character than from lack of talent.

FOX: Could you say more about that?

HAMILL: Yeah. [long pause]

FOX: Would you say more about that? [both laugh]

HAMILL: I'm sort of gathering my thoughts here. Well, if we go back to the idea that what you read is what you feed your *anima*, all over America there are MFA programs where you can go to school for a couple of years, and study three or four poets, and read them pretty closely and become certified Master of Poetry with a *terminal* degree. And then you go off with your two or three poet knowledge, and you spend the rest of your life teaching those two or three poets to more people who hunger after terminal degrees. I don't think it's a dishonorable thing to do. But, if to do that and declare that poetry really *matters* to you, seems to me a bit hypocritical. Because, if you talk to any *great* poet (and you can decide for yourself who is great), you're gonna find the same universal answer, and that is, you gotta do more homework. You've gotta dig more deeply. You've got to be more self-critical. You've got to put your own bare ass out on the limb. And if you don't take those psychological risks, those philosophical risks, then you're not going to have those risks in your work, and your work is destined to be less than minor. That's a failure of character, not a failure of talent.

FOX: So, a poet shouldn't hold back for fear of offending his parents, or friends . . .

HAMILL: Absolutely not! When I used to teach in the prisons, and one of the reasons I taught there was because I didn't have to put up with the bullshit that you have to put up with in academia, I used to tell my students, "I'm not wasting my time on any 'poor me' poems. If you want to write the blues, you can write the blues, but no 'pity poor me' poems. The only poem I want from you tomorrow is the poem you write tonight if tomorrow's 'your day.'" And then I would give them a little talk, about Sappho, about Hikmet,

Akhmatova. When the Turkish government went after Hikmet (you know he was a socialist and the government was a military government, so he was on the run for several years there), and when they got him, to humiliate him, they threw him into the bilge on a ship. And, of course, all of his accusers stood around on the deck and watched him wallow around down there in the excrement. And he rose up out of the bilge, and he looked up at his oppressors, and he began to sing. And for hours, he stood there and he sang at the top of his lungs. He sang poem after poem. When Akhmatova stood at the prison gates at St. Petersburg, an old woman came up and tugged her sleeve and said, "You're Akhmatova." She said, "I am." The woman nodded toward the prison and the horrors that had happened in there, and she said, "Could you describe it?" And Akhmatova said, "I could." That's what it means to be a poet.

FOX: Yes. Do you show your work to anybody before you send it off?

HAMILL: Oh, I guess that happens. I don't sort of do it intentionally. But there are three or four people that I often send new work to. I don't have time to write Hayden nearly, nearly the number of letters that I would like to write to Hayden. So whenever there's a new poem, I send it to Hayden. And when I'm working on longer poems, I just finished a twenty-eight-page poem, I find Hayden and my old friend Bill O'Daly, who was one of the cofounders of Copper Canyon and a great translator of Neruda, I find Hayden and Bill both very helpful. Cold eyes for my struggling poems.

FOX: A few years ago, we read in the newspapers that a woman gave $100 million to *Poetry* magazine.

HAMILL: Mm-hm.

FOX: What impact do you think that had?

HAMILL: Well, nobody knows yet. I mean, they've completely reorganized the modern *Poetry* organization that runs *Poetry* Chicago, etc. I noticed they've also raised their fees for advertising, which kind of amused me. [Fox laughs] But frankly, I've never paid a whole lot of attention to the *Poetry* Chicago people. Almost every poet that I love has published in there at some time or another, but it's never been, I've never felt very warm towards *Poetry* Chicago. That probably comes from me being a Pound scholar, and thinking back about

Harriet Monroe and where *Poetry* has been. And that is, it's been incredibly uneven. And it's ninety percent college crap, and five percent good poems by more or less famous poets. It's published important work. I hope the new editor enlivens it.

FOX: What would happen if Copper Canyon Press got a $100 million bequest?

HAMILL: Well, we would certainly become stabilized, more or less forever. But it wouldn't change things. I don't want to publish more books than we're publishing. I don't want a bigger staff than we've got. Um, I think we're a good mid-sized, we're not a small press, we publish eighteen books a year. I think we're the best poetry publisher in America. I don't mean that pridefully, I just mean that, I think, practically. So I would love a gift like that for the long-term stability. I would love at my age to have a little financial security. I have nothing for retirement, and one disastrous medical bill, and I'm right down the toilet. And I've lived like that my entire life, and my first twenty-five years here, I lived in really pretty desperate poverty, lived for several years with no running water and no electricity. So that kind of thing would be *nice*. But, you know, we're managing okay. [laughs]

FOX: There doesn't seem to be a whole lot of money in writing poetry . . .

HAMILL: Well, it's not about money. Somebody told Auden once, why do you write poetry, there's no money in it. And he said, well, there's no poetry in money, either. [both laugh]

Jane Hirshfield is the author of six collections of poetry, including *After*; *Given Sugar, Given Salt* (finalist for the 2001 National Book Critics Circle Award, and winner of the Bay Area Book Reviewers Award); *The Lives of the Heart*; and *The October Palace*; as well as a book of essays, *Nine Gates: Entering the Mind of Poetry*. She also edited and co-translated *The Ink Dark Moon: Love Poems by Komachi & Shikibu, Women of the Ancient Court of Japan*; *Women in Praise of the Sacred: 43 Centuries of Spiritual Poetry by Women*; and *Mirabai: Ecstatic Poems*. Hirshfield's other honors include The Poetry Center Book Award; fellowships from the Guggenheim and Rockefeller Foundations, the National Endowment for the Arts, and the Academy of American Poets; Columbia University's Translation Center Award; and the Commonwealth Club of California's Poetry Medal. Her work has appeared in *The New Yorker, The Atlantic, The Nation, The American Poetry Review, Poetry*, five volumes of *The Best American Poetry*, and many other publications, and has been featured numerous times on Garrison Keillor's *Writers Almanac* program, as well as in two Bill Moyers PBS television specials. In fall 2004, Jane Hirshfield was awarded the 70th Academy Fellowship for distinguished poetic achievement by *The Academy of American Poets*, an honor formerly held by such poets as Robert Frost, Ezra Pound, William Carlos Williams, and Elizabeth Bishop.

# Jane Hirshfield

April 20th, 2006

FOX: How did you come to live in this lovely home in Mill Valley?

HIRSHFIELD: I had been living at Green Gulch, in Muir Beach, very near here—[phone rings]

FOX: I will turn this off.

HIRSHFIELD: I should turn mine off too. [laughing, unplugs hard line telephone]

FOX: I was at a dinner—James Ragan had been the head of the Masters of Professional Writing Program at U.S.C. for twenty-five years and they had a dinner last night. They had a number of speakers including Shelley Berman, who's one of the teachers there, and Shelley was speaking when my cell phone went off. I think Shelly got one of the biggest laughs of the evening when he looked at me and said, "Take the call." [both laugh] I put the cell phone under my leg and I turned it off. All right, we were talking about how you were . . .

HIRSHFIELD: Let me start earlier. I arrived in California in 1974, in a red Dodge van with tie-dyed curtains, as one would do at such a time, and soon went into eight years of formal Zen training. The last place that I lived as a full-time practitioner was Green Gulch Farm, in Muir Beach, just a ridge over from here. I made a very gradual transition back into lay practice life, and didn't go far. That's how I ended up here.

FOX: Are you familiar with Spirit Rock, which also isn't far from here?

HIRSHFIELD: Yes, I edited two of Jack Kornfield's books.

FOX: Oh! I'm a very good friend of Jack's.

HIRSHFIELD: Really? Maybe at some other event we'll say hello then.

FOX: Absolutely. What impact did your Zen practice have on your writing?

HIRSHFIELD: Well, those eight intensive training years were from age twenty-one to twenty-nine, so I can't really know who I might have become had I not done that. The most honest answer I can give is to say the influence is both complete and unknowable.

FOX: That's good. When did you start writing?

HIRSHFIELD: As a child. My mother still has one of those big brown sheets of writing paper that they give you in first or second grade, with the wide-spaced blue lines. On it, it says, "I want to be a writer when I grow up."

FOX: Wow.

HIRSHFIELD: I don't remember writing or thinking that, only that I was always a lover of words. I read voraciously. I'd choose books over sleep every time.

FOX: And what types of things did you write when you were a child?

HIRSHFIELD: Always poetry. For school I'd write whatever I was asked to, but it was always poems for myself. I don't have a narrative mind or aptitude. If you're a person who wants to investigate the world through language and you don't tell stories, what's left is either the essay or poems. I think most deeply through image, the mind-leaps of metaphor, sentences carried by music and tone. Poems suited the ways my mind already liked to move.

FOX: And how did you first get published?

HIRSHFIELD: When I was a senior in college, *The Nation* magazine started what the next year became The Discovery Awards program, a prize given to four young writers of promise. It still exists. In 1973, it wasn't yet called that, but I was one of the first four winners, and that meant my first published poem was in *The Nation*. I didn't try to publish again for seven or eight years, and during the three monastic years, at Tassajara, in the wilderness inland from Big Sur, I didn't write at all. We were told to do nothing but practice while there.

FOX: I'm always interested in how people discover whether they're a poet, as opposed to a personal essayist or a textbook writer, or whatever. Do you have any insight into that process for you?

HIRSHFIELD: It's hard to have insight into something that feels inevitable. It's like asking a plum tree why it makes plums. Poetry was what I did. I can, though, say that the desire to write was probably part of the desire, again from earliest childhood, to comprehend my life and the world more deeply. I was a very curious child, but also a child who had to clear a way through a kind of thicket to find my way to myself. My family wasn't very forthcoming, and I hungered for something, without even knowing what it was. But I knew that a path towards it could be found in poems.

I think two kinds of people become poets. Extroverts who go out and entertain the family friends, and introverts who hide in the bedroom and put what they write under the mattress. Allen Ginsberg, I imagine, was the first kind; I was the second. For me, words were not about pleasing or entertaining others but about creating a place of refuge, where I could find something out about what it means to have and be a self. Scholars say that introspection only became truly possible with the development of writing. Writing allows the self to be set down and looked into, questioned, changed. On those unseen late night pages, I could experiment, I could fail, it didn't matter. There is an immense freedom to writing for oneself alone. This is something I still feel. I wrote most often in the middle of the night, after everybody else was asleep. It was a way to investigate and craft a self, a soul, undisturbed, unjudged.

The desire for Zen practice must have come from the same rootstock. It's not so much that poetry and Zen influenced each other in my life. They were both ways to try to do the same thing, to know the world and my own experience, to feel and think more deeply, with greater saturation. You develop a craft and a practice in order to make a vessel of yourself that can take you where you want to go.

FOX: Mhmm . . . would you say then you were born into the wrong family or . . .

HIRSHFIELD: Oh, I could never say that. Every circumstance goes into making a person who he or she is, so how can I question any of it?

FOX: [laughing] So you wouldn't change anything?

HIRSHFIELD: Well, actually, no. If I want to be who I am, I have to accept every part of what has gone into that, what's sometimes called the whole catastrophe.

FOX: Absolutely. Could you describe the thicket that you talked about?

HIRSHFIELD: Well, one reason I'm not writing those personal memoirs we talked about earlier is that I'm not inclined toward autobiographical revelation. The poems don't talk directly about my family. Very few give you any sense of the circumstances of my outer, visible life. The poems come from my life—I think we always speak through and of our own experience—but at the level of the x-ray, perhaps, rather than the nude. I should add that many poets I read with fierce pleasure are autobiographically revealing. It's just not what I myself do.

FOX: Would you say that the truths that you unearth are universal, personal? Both?

HIRSHFIELD: I'd say there's no distinction. Where does the universal live except in the particular? There is only the truth of this moment and its manifestations. What I'm talking about is a matter of perspective, not of residence. A good poem's address is always "here."

FOX: Mhmm.

HIRSHFIELD: In my 2001 book, *Given Sugar, Given Salt*, there's a line that appears in two different poems: "You work with what you are given." And so, as an example of what I'm talking about, in the new book, *After*, there are some good number of poems that speak about looking out the window at the mountain that's there, right now, behind your left shoulder. Now, it's in the poems first as itself, Mt. Tamalpais, which is the first thing I see every morning when I wake up, if it's light out and there's not heavy fog. It's also in the poems as what mountains stand for in the human psyche, and for its instruction to the psyche in what mountains teach. It's a slope and presence by which I can investigate and question. Other things come in—in one poem, Vilnius and St. Petersburg, in another, a line from Gerard Manley Hopkins, in a third, an imaginary herd of bison. All these things are themselves and are also prism-lights of my own psyche, and perhaps of the reader's psyche as well. I also feel that through the shared life of poems, mountains in some way can know us. They enter us, when we bring them into words, just as walking in the mountains enters our bodies and changes the strength of our legs, the capacities of our lungs. We aren't just ourselves, once we have walked those paths—we are also our history of being changed by the mountain. This is interconnected life. Poems are one way we make ourselves more transparent to the fullness of existence.

FOX: It seems to me that you're very sensitive to your environment. Would that be accurate?

HIRSHFIELD: Yes.

FOX: Can you say more about that?

HIRSHFIELD: [silent for a moment] I'm going to be a tough interview for you. [both laugh] Could you try asking that in some different way?

FOX: Oh sure. What do you like to avoid in the environment?

HIRSHFIELD: Oh, what do I like to avoid? That I can answer. Noise, distraction, superficiality—in other words, the entire contemporary world. [both laugh] And yet, and yet . . . I'm creeping up on present-day life, or it on me. A little more of the contemporary world enters my work all the time. My early poems drew almost entirely on the imagery of the natural, but in the past two books especially, there's much more reference to the shared cultural landscape. In *Given Sugar, Given Salt*, for instance, there's a line that says "a shopping mall swirls around the corpse of a beetle." [both laugh] So there you have it. The natural world is still at the center, but a shopping mall has wrapped itself around it. [laughs]

FOX: Would you say this has enhanced your work, or corrupted it?

HIRSHFIELD: Oh, I think expansion is always good. We begin life with a certain set of powers, tools, loves, and one of the tasks of a life is to enlarge that field, until, along with the Roman writer Terence, you can say, "Nothing human is alien to me."

FOX: Well, even the Dalai Lama is involved in scientific research, I saw him speak in Boston, he works with people at MIT . . .

HIRSHFIELD: Oh yes, I know some of the people involved in those meetings, and my beloved is a molecular physicist, so . . . Yes. [laughs]

FOX: Mhmm.

HIRSHFIELD: Knowing scientists has unquestionably changed my poems, has given me new images and landscapes and also allowed me to think about things I might not necessarily have been thinking about otherwise.

FOX: And in what ways has that, I'm not going to say transformed your work, but directed it . . .

HIRSHFIELD: Well again, it's an expansion of possibility. A new bit of knowledge or vocabulary is an expansion of world. So, for example, in the new book there's a series of seventeen very short poems, the ones I've called pebbles, several of which have some biological context. They're all very brief, and somewhat recalcitrant, reserved, as a pebble is. As I also like to say of them, they aren't jokes and they aren't riddles, but they function a little bit like a joke or riddle in that they aren't complete until the person receiving them takes them in and has a response. When you throw a pebble into the pond, the ripples are part of the phenomenon.

FOX: Mhmm.

HIRSHFIELD: So, to get back to science, among these pebbles, there's one about global warming, there's one about tool use in animals, there's one about evolution and glass. Another poem, "Jasper, Feldspar, Quartzite," I fact-checked with a friend who's a geomorphologist, and I suspect that talking with him over the years was what allowed these stones of different nature to come into my work as images.

A poet really needs to know everything. Yet no poet does. So what we find is that Stephen Dunn can write certain poems because he knows gambling and basketball. Pattiann Rogers's poetry is an encyclopedia of the natural world and its phenomena. Philip Levine's work is founded on his growing up in Detroit, doing factory work, and coming into adulthood in a community and time where the Spanish Civil War mattered in a deeply personal way. We are given our charges to some degree by our lives, to some degree by our choices. But however it happens, what poets know, or learn, will become the material by which they think and feel. The deep issues of human life are not that many. But the images and stories through which we can approach them are infinite. And every such exploration throws a subtly different light on what it means to be human on this earth.

FOX: So then, I think you're saying that you can find these truths anywhere, or everywhere, and where you go with it depends upon your own personality?

HIRSHFIELD: That, and a great extent depends also on the circumstances of life you were born to, and on what the world gives you in the course of that life. We were talking before the recorder was turned on about something closely related to this, what for me has been a life-haunting question about how much choice people actually have in what happens to them in their lives.

FOX: Yes.

HIRSHFIELD: Somewhere in each of my books, I've noticed, there's a line or two that considers that question. It haunts me. Anybody reading this, and you and I, sitting in this room—we have some choice. We're lucky, and we have some choice about our fates. There are many people who have next to none. For them, it takes some great force of world and soul to break through the pressures of non-choice they were born into. It can be done, but it's rare, and it's hard.

FOX: Why do you think many or most people have such limited choice, or relatively limited choice?

HIRSHFIELD: Because life is simply too hard. If you're a child born in the Sudan right now, you don't have a lot of choice, besides suffering and starvation. One recent poem about this, the last to go into *After*, too late for any magazine, is "Those Who Cannot Act." That poem came out of thinking about the tsunami two Christmases ago, which led me to think also about the Iraq war. In the one, no one at all had a choice; in the other, the carnage and vanishment are caused by human decision. Yet many of the people who die in war are as without choice as those villagers and beach going tourists who vanished inside the waters. There's a much-repeated sentence from Aeschylus's *Oresteia*, "Those who act must suffer, suffer into truth." But that is the protagonist's prerogative. The tragic hero will die but so will the chorus. Many people, most, suffer without the catharsis of meaning. The poem is for them. It ends mid-sentence, broken off, as lives do, every day, in Iraq, in the Sudan, in New Orleans, in Indonesia, in Kashmir.

FOX: Yes, yes.

HIRSHFIELD: And I think that those of us who do have some choice have a deep responsibility to those who don't.

FOX: Say more about that.

HIRSHFIELD: We have the responsibility of doing whatever we can to alter those circumstances, whether by writing about it directly or indirectly, or donating, or volunteering, or political activism—again there's a full spectrum of possibility, and all parts of that are necessary. But also, I think, there's a responsibility to make, of these lucky lives we've been given, what we can.

FOX: Yes.

HIRSHFIELD: Not to throw them away, because so much opportunity is given to leave the world better. And to know joy. Simply to know joy. You mentioned the Dalai Lama earlier, and one of his central teachings is that happiness matters. Perhaps you have to be the Dalai Lama, a person who has known exile and the dismantling of country, a person who has spent a lifetime in a practice that originated in the recognition of suffering to say that and not be taken as a simpleton. And, of course, one corollary of a joyous heart is that it allows some chance of behaving better, of acting out of richness and generosity rather than selfishness, grasping, and fear.

FOX: And yet there are many people who are not born in the Sudan, who feel themselves victims, and they have no choice, because things happen to them . . .

HIRSHFIELD: Something I wrote in one of my essays may speak to that question. It's in my mind because it was quoted recently, first in something called the *Little Zen Calendar*, and then by the director of an Episcopalian church, whom I was told used it in her Easter Sunday sermon. The sentence was "Habit, fear, and laziness conspire to keep us in the realm of the deeply familiar." There are forces of inertia in the soul, and there are forces of awakening in the soul, and for each of us, that's one of the very few places of choice—which way we turn—towards inertia and the comfortable habitual or towards the unknown, frightening permeability of awakened heart. To make one choice in that realm rather than another, even in the smallest way, will change a life. There's an eight-line, early poem I love by the Greek poet Cavafy. The title is an Italian quote, from Dante, "Che Fece . . . Il Gran Rifiuto." And the poem begins, "For some people the day comes when they have to declare the great Yes, or the great No." That is a life-changing poem, I think.

FOX: Yes.

HIRSHFIELD: I can give you the rest of it if you'd like.

FOX: Yes, please, absolutely.

HIRSHFIELD: [laughs] This is Edmund Keeley and Philip Sherrard's first translation. They revised it, but I like the first one better:

*For some people the day comes*
*when they have to declare the great Yes*
*or the great No. It's clear at once who has the Yes*
*ready within him; and saying it,*

*he goes from honor to honor, strong in his conviction.*
*He who refuses does not repent. Asked again,*
*he'd still say no. Yet that no—the right no—*
*drags him down all his life.*

FOX: Yes.

HIRSHFIELD: I love the poem both for its reminder of the possibility of declaring a great Yes and a great No, and also for the koan held by the phrase "the right no." What does that mean, "the right no drags him down all his life"? Sometimes I think it means one thing and sometimes I think it means the other. For me it's a question you can weigh a life against.

FOX: That's, to me, another central issue which you touched on before, death versus superficiality . . .

HIRSHFIELD: Yes.

FOX: Most people it seems to me are into superficiality . . . cocktail parties. What are you supposed to do?

HIRSHFIELD: A cocktail party is an almost untenable set of circumstances to navigate. [laughs] You find one person and go in a corner with them, or else you circulate and pretend you're someone else. Someone who enjoys cocktail parties. Sometimes you even fool yourself. [laughs]

FOX: Yeah. Why is it though, that death, intimacy, seems to be something which most of us avoid?

HIRSHFIELD: Well, to be truly vulnerable is terrifying, isn't it? It's to put yourself at risk for devastation and abandonment and ridicule, experiences we all had as young children on a regular basis, from our peers, from our family, from our siblings. To live exposed in this world is hard, and to be willing to be permeated by that pain, rather than try to avoid it, takes immense courage, effort, and energy. There's another poem that's been central to my life that talks exactly about this question, written by the Japanese woman poet Izumi Shikibu around 1000 A.D. I first came across it when I was translating *The Ink Dark Moon*. Mariko Aratani, my co-translator, was the language expert on the team, giving me the literal possibilities for the Japanese words. I'd then go off and work on the poems by myself. With this one, it was strange—I had the words, I had the grammar, and I knew the poem meant something, but I simply couldn't figure it out. And so it lay there, inert on the page. Then suddenly, I understood it. And from that time on, it changed my life, in the way of exactly this question you're asking: can we become intimate with devastation, can we face the full spectrum of our own lives and deaths? Here it is:

*Although the wind*
*blows terribly here,*
*the moonlight also leaks*
*between the roof planks*
*of this ruined house.*

Shikibu is saying that if you wall up your house so tightly that no cold wind will get in—nothing difficult, nothing painful, no grief, no loss, no sorrow, no rage—you'll be very safe, but you'll also wall out the moonlight, which in Japanese poetry can mean all beauty, and also the fullness of love, and also the fullness of enlightenment, of deep awakening. Thirty-one syllables in the Japanese, and Shikibu put into words a touchstone for a life.

FOX: Sounds like a much better sound bite than what we see on television today.

HIRSHFIELD: Just so. You know, there's something to ponder about poetry and sound bites. Sound bites interest me not least because, as you can already tell from this interview, I'm not very good at making them in ordinary conversation. Prose sound bites, thought sound bites, come hard for me. And yet what is a poem except a sound bite? A piece of knowledge, infinitely complex, somehow compressed down to a few words that can cast light about them in all directions.

Good poems show what a sound bite could be, as opposed to the slogans we get from our current politicians, which, besides being so often brazenly lies, are also thought-deadening, compassion-deadening, heart-deadening. This administration gives us the sound bite of a blindfold over the eyes and cotton in the ears; their adamance is deafening and blinding. But they're memorable. Try, with all we've seen since, remembering this one—Bush, in his first campaign, saying "I'm a uniter, not a divider." The bitter memorability of that phrase, I'm sorry to say, sits at poetry's door. It's the music that makes it stick.

FOX: Well exactly. Why is it that there seems to be such a large appeal to those kinds of sound bites and, at least in this country, a much lower popularity of the deeper . . .

HIRSHFIELD: Habit, laziness, and fear, it must be. I do think that it is difficult for human beings to wake up. If it were easy we'd all have done it already. It's difficult to attend to the subtle, to look past the immediate, to think and question and go against the ease of self-interest, the ease of turning away and letting others deal with the difficult. And I'm not sure that this country and culture is worse than most. Fifth Century B.C. Greece, it could be, was better, but compared to most times and places in civilization's history, we're probably more awake. Just not enough. Especially given the exponential increase of effect we have, with all our technology. But how do we change? There's the question.

FOX: It seems to me that the best an individual can do is to be true to him or herself, really without proselytizing, per se.

HIRSHFIELD: I agree. The poetry of propaganda is just another blindfold.

FOX: To me, it's kind of like catching a feather—if you go after it you chase it away, and if you wait it might land, and it might not.

HIRSHFIELD: Yes. And certain people demonstrate this as a possibility for others. Czeslaw Milosz. Gandhi. A more mixed case, perhaps, Simone Weil. And it is contagious.

FOX: Well, hopefully . . . You mentioned you travel a lot. Could we talk about that?

HIRSHFIELD: Oh, it's not that interesting. [Fox laughs] I do a lot of poetry readings and they involve many airplanes.

FOX: Yes. [waits]

HIRSHFIELD: Ok, with this new book just out, let me see if I can reconstruct this. . . it's now mid-April, and since January I've been in Florida, New Jersey, all over California, Maryland, upstate New York, Massachusetts, Indiana, Virginia, Oregon, and I'm about to go down to L.A. . . Oh, I'm sorry, I'm just this moment realizing that if you'd known I was coming down to L.A. you wouldn't have had to come up here. I'm going to the LA Times Book Festival.

FOX: Oh!

HIRSHFIELD: I'm so sorry, it was added after this interview was already set up, it must have been, or we'd be doing this there, wouldn't we?

FOX: Well, this is a nicer environment. Do you like to do readings?

HIRSHFIELD: One of the great surprises of my life is that the girl putting her poems under the mattress, who spent three years at a Zen monastery in silence, a person who was introverted, shy, and timid, has somehow, by poetry, turned into a person not only able to speak with strangers, but able to find in that some real pleasure . . . Two nights ago I gave a reading for 400 people, at the Portland Arts and Lectures Series, and it actually felt intimate. It felt like being present with people in some deep and connected way.

FOX: Mhmm.

HIRSHFIELD: I don't think this would have been imaginable to me when I gave my first readings—hands shaking, voice trembling, wishing only to be anywhere else. But, again, we were talking before about how life wants to expand your perimeters. I think it also wants to counter your inborn tendencies. If I'd been born an outward-turned person, perhaps I would have had to get myself thrown in jail for a few years, until I learned to quietly study the self.

Anyhow, it's interesting that the path of going out and being physically present and saying the poems on the voice, into the ear, has become so central a part of poetry's life in American culture. It's almost a return to a bardic, oral tradition. Spoken poetry may be the main way that many people know poetry at all, though I'm also fairly certain more books are being bought now as well. People are hungry for what poetry has to offer. And part of that hunger is for intimacy with depth and with grief and with the serious, what you were speaking of earlier. It's for being in a room where something real is said aloud without cynicism or glitz or commercial purpose, and where something happens between and among living people. It's different from the experience of entering a poem on the page. I wouldn't want to lose either, and not only because if I needed to hear Emily Dickinson read in person before I could appreciate her poems, I might have to wait a long time. For me, poetry on the page has been one of the great friendships of my life. Look at the company available, right on this bookshelf. . . Dickinson. Basho. Dante.

With an attuned inner ear, you can hear the poems as if they were speaking directly to you. But for many people to hear poems outwardly spoken is a necessary point of entry. We all have friends who don't know or care much about poetry. Yet if at the right moment a poem is said to them, they are completely taken inside the experience. Which of course is why poems are still read at weddings and at funerals.

FOX: Mhmm, mhmm.

HIRSHFIELD: This is my answer to the question, "Is poetry still alive?" As long as poems are read at weddings and funerals, and exchanged between lovers, and given to people in times of duress, poetry is doing its work. And all the rest is a kind of scaffold to support the endeavor, so it can be there at the moments it's needed.

FOX: I'm thinking that you can experience so much intimacy at a reading because your audience is able to enter into the experience without being exposed, and so they can really feel as one with you and with the other people there.

HIRSHFIELD: Well, that's right. It's such an ancient human thing, isn't it? Go back to the Greek tragedies, Homer, *Beowulf*, traditional *griots*. People sitting together in a hall or an amphitheater or around a fire, listening to somebody set forth what it is to be human, in interesting and memorable ways. Participating in that ritual and shared vision is how culture is made and preserved, and how certain qualities of being are created and transmitted, one generation to the other. And consider what it means for people to be in a room together, paying attention to something. That in itself has an effect, very different from the passivity of watching television. Though I have to confess, there are moments when there's nothing I want more than to sit watching television, to escape myself and my life. Still, too much television leaves the feeling of overdose. You can take a vacation for awhile, but then it's like being in a room that's too hot—you suddenly need to throw open the windows or go outside and roll in the snow.

FOX: I'm thinking that the fear of being intimate is perhaps the fear of losing one's individual identity.

HIRSHFIELD: [silent a while] I have no doubt that you're right, and yet. . . To lose your individual identity is one of the most profound things a human being can do. And it's something we seek out continually, isn't it, whether by mind-altering substances or going to a concert. I have no question that falling out of the self is one of the deepest pleasures of music, that we enter into music in order to become it and no longer ourselves. And yet you are also right that this is terrifying to people. My maternal grandfather, who was a Rosicrucian for a while, and the only person in my family with an interest in mysticism, told me a story when I was a child. He had been given anesthesia, and as he went under, he said, his mind traveled out into the universe, into the vast blackness of the universe, until all he saw was a single point of light which he understood as the beginning of all time and all space. Now, I thought that sounded extraordinary, absolutely wonderful. For him, it was so frightening that he never consented to full anesthesia again. Every operation after that was done under only a local.

FOX: Wow.

HIRSHFIELD: So, what do we make of this? I can't make anything of it. What to one person is an ecstatic gnosis, to another is a hell-realm.

FOX: You learn in the third or fourth grade to find the lowest common denominator. To simplify. And simplistically, to me, it seems that life will end in disaster, relationships will end in disaster, if nothing more than death, illness, or separation. That is a given.

HIRSHFIELD: Yes.

FOX: So you might as well have the moonlight, because you're going to have the destruction anyway. [laughs]

HIRSHFIELD: So true—everything we love will be taken from us. But you know, in order to enter the attitude you're describing, you need to be willing to lose it all right now, this very moment. That's the only way to stop clinging. And it's the clinging that narrows us.

FOX: Uh-huh . . .

HIRSHFIELD: The same principle, I think, can be seen in many aspects of a life. For instance, in the writing of poems—if you aren't willing to risk making a fool of yourself, you'll never write anything good. To enter what you didn't know before is to risk a kind of death. You have to be willing to make terrible errors in order to do anything new, different, unfamiliar. Every time, every moment. You know, I have a deep compassion for all this fearfulness and hesitancy. There's a great deal of both in me. It makes perfect sense. Evolution gives us two basic modes of being. One mode is self-preservation and the other is seeking, and some balance between the two is going to decide your fate. And I think my whole course as a human being has been a navigation between those two things. Because I really am a terrible coward, yet I have not wanted the narrow life that comes with cowardice.

FOX: Yes.

HIRSHFIELD: From our conversation earlier, I'd say that you are courageous by nature. That you come naturally to what for me has been a struggle.

FOX: Well, I think there are different areas of timidity or fear. And, for myself, where I've been most successful in life is where I just don't have fear. But I'm certainly afraid of relationships or vulnerability. I'm fearful of physical pain, and that, that's big.

HIRSHFIELD: Yes, it is.

FOX: So would you say for yourself that there are certain areas you have a large fear and other areas you have not very much?

HIRSHFIELD: Well, you know how they can take puppies and test them for their nature?

FOX: Mhmm.

HIRSHFIELD: I'm sorry to say that I was probably the timid puppy. [laughs] What's interesting, I suppose, is that something else in my nature caused me to hammer against that condition. This goes once again to the question of how much we can change in our lives. Here, I think, the pivot point is, do you feel your life as malleable clay or do you feel only "That's the hand I was dealt"? My good luck is that, given the hand I was dealt, I also felt my life to be malleable clay.

FOX: There's a movie, *The Last Samurai*, with a Japanese man who played the samurai. He was writing a poem about cherry blossoms, and at the end of the film, as he's dying, he finds the end of the poem, "They are all perfect."

HIRSHFIELD: This is also, of course, one of the central teachings of certain schools of Buddhism: You're already a Buddha, so you might as well act like one. And everything that happens is the perfection of what happens, including the losses, the pain and suffering, the death, and also the joy. It's never too late to awaken—you can recognize the perfection of things even at the moment of death. There's a remarkable haiku by Issa—

*On a branch*
*floating downriver,*
*a cricket singing.*

I think that this is a perfect portrait of life in seventeen syllables [in the Japanese]. You're going to go over the waterfall, but you are here, now, a cricket, and so what do you do? You sing.

FOX: I'm thinking that . . . we all have the ability to be the cricket, in fact we are, and yet I'm thinking of the line from e.e. cummings' "Everyone Lived in a Pretty How Town," which is, "down they forgot as up they grew." It takes a lot of intention and work to delve into that which we knew.

HIRSHFIELD: Yes, yes it does. And I think that is one central role of poetry, especially in this culture and at this time. Historically, poems have done lots of different work—the work of lullaby, of prayer, of love song, of elegy, of work song . . . unfortunately, also of war song. Poetry is a concentration of language that permits transformation. Poems enable you to do or know something you couldn't have done or known in the same way without them. In contemporary American culture, all the arts, and particularly poetry, have as a central task the work of paying attention to whatever the mainstream culture ignores or dismisses. Now a great deal of our current mainstream culture is asking us to deaden ourselves—to close heart, eyes, mouth, to thicken skin, to stay inside a perimeter of consuming and protecting. Art's example reminds us that it is possible to develop an awakened and courageous and indecorous soul, in the face of a world that mostly asks us to be obedient sheep.

FOX: Mhmm.

HIRSHFIELD: Who was it who said. . . a French poet. . . "There is another world and it is in this one." Paul Éluard. Good poetry reminds us that that other world exists, and that we can find our way into it.

FOX: I'm thinking of the Zen joke about the brigands who attack the Zen community and they're looking for the gold, and they finally . . . do you know the joke?

HIRSHFIELD: I'm not sure. Keep going.

FOX: Well they finally accost the Zen leader, and the chief robber puts a sword to his throat and says, "Where's the gold?" And the Buddhist monk just looks at him. Again the robber says, "Where's the gold, don't you realize that I have the ability to kill you?" And the Buddhist says, "Don't you realize that I have the ability to let you kill me?"

HIRSHFIELD: Oh, yes! There's also the wonderful story about a Zen master who comes home and finds that his little meditation hut has been ransacked and everything's been taken, only a single pot is left, and he runs after the thief, "Wait, wait, you forgot something, take this!" [both laugh]

FOX: That's reminiscent of the line from *Les Misérables* where the priest says, "You forgot to take the candle sticks . . ."

HIRSHFIELD: Yes, and then another Japanese poem, "Barn's burnt down, now I can see the moon." That one's on my refrigerator. Masahide.

FOX: I'm thinking again about choice. I sometimes think that there is no choice. If I took a pebble and let go of it with my hand it would drop, and we can predict that, and we could tell you how fast it's going to go, and if it would bounce. So, to the extent that we are creatures of a universe with rules—the rule of gravitation, whatever—then don't we inevitably have to just drop like the pebble, according to our nature and the nature of the universe? No choice at all.

HIRSHFIELD: It's the old problem of free will versus determinism.

FOX: Yes.

HIRSHFIELD: You know, much as I care about this question of choice in people's lives, I myself find the free will/determinism question simply not useful. You know, it's one way or the other and it actually doesn't much matter which is "true," because our experience is that we have to figure it out.

FOX: Mhmm.

HIRSHFIELD: That even if whatever we end up deciding to do is inevitable, even if we could never have done anything else, part of that is still the experience of struggling with it, and our sense is that in any moment we could do one thing or we could do another. If I were a proper Zen master, right now, I'd take my teacup and pour the tea over my head and walk out. And thus exhibit something relevant, perhaps, to this kind of discussion. The thought crosses the mind. The tea is cool enough. Not being that dramatic, or a Zen master, I probably won't do it. But here, have a macaroon. [both laugh] I'll have one too.

FOX: Well this is either—

HIRSHFIELD: An inevitable macaroon?

FOX: Absolutely. Because it is, of course.

HIRSHFIELD: [laughs] Does it still taste sweet?

FOX: Yes.

HIRSHFIELD: I hope you like macaroons.

FOX: Yes, I do. [both laugh] Well, you said this would be a difficult interview, but I like what you say, it's important, it's touching, it's um . . .

HIRSHFIELD: Thank you. No, I'm only difficult when people start asking me personal questions. I just don't answer them for the most part. [laughs]

FOX: When you're writing a poem, don't you have to go where it leads you, rather than where you want to force it to go?

HIRSHFIELD: Absolutely. I've never once written a poem by will power. I can't do it.

FOX: Ah, good. See that comes back to choice also, are you going to impose your will on the universe or are you going to just discover what is there?

HIRSHFIELD: I've always wanted to discover. It is the only thing I've wanted. Everything else in my life stems from that. What is this life, this moment, and how fully can I know it? And the interesting thing is that if you pursue those questions, astonishments step forward, and you find things that you never would have guessed were there to be found. I think this is true for any inch of ground, looked at with the mind of open awareness. There's the famous story about E.O. Wilson, the entomologist, in his office at Harvard. There's a plant in the corner. He looks at the plant and discovers a new species of ant. [both laugh] Anyone else would have thought, "Ants! Get the Raid!" But because it's E.O. Wilson, it's, "Ants. . . What have we here?" and then, "Write a paper!" You just have to open your eyes.

FOX: Do you ever reach the point of wondering, why write anymore?

HIRSHFIELD: In one way, finishing every poem feels that way, for me. It's done, and my life's work is over. At that moment I never know whether I'm going to write another. And I've had in my writing life many periods of extended silence, during which months might go by between poems. Some day those months might extend into years. So far that hasn't happened. And so far the silences, I think, have all been deeply necessary for my psyche and my unfolding. One gift these periods of sequestration seem to give is that when I begin to write again, the poems have usually changed. They know something new, because I haven't been reinforcing old patterns, old subjects.

FOX: So what you're saying is that you can't successfully force yourself to write?

HIRSHFIELD: That's right. I can't. I sometimes feel like I'm the last poet in America who's not writing a poem every day. [laughs] It seems that everybody else has taken up William Stafford's practice of writing a poem every day before breakfast. But, as I say when this question comes up in public, I'm the poet with the bad work ethic. There are times when I do write every day, but there are many more times when I don't. I write so terribly badly when I have nothing to say that, as Emily Dickinson used to say, "It would embarrass my dog." [both laugh] And my dog's been dead eight years [Fox laughs] and she'd still be embarrassed. And that then depresses me, and I really do feel, "Why write anymore?" I don't want my relationship to poetry to be dutiful. Poetry is not obligatory, it's not work. It's an inner request far subtler and deeper than that.

FOX: Well it seems to me that you've become very comfortable with yourself. And perhaps that's one reason you're comfortable with an audience, whereas perhaps you wouldn't have been years ago.

HIRSHFIELD: I think that's a very astute insight. One of the lists in Buddhism—Buddhism is full of lists—is the Five Great Fears: fear of death, fear of madness, fear of pain, fear of loss of livelihood, and fear of public speaking. [both laugh] It's pretty universal that human beings are nervous about standing up and talking in front of others. Forgive me if this is reductionist evolutionary psychology, but the antelope who stands out from the herd is the one who is eaten by lions.

FOX: Mhmm, yes.

HIRSHFIELD: And so there is a real and genuine protectiveness of self in not being seen. The paradox though is that the cost of that self-protection is a diminished life.

FOX: Ah, absolutely. That's a good place to stop.

YUSEF KOMUNYAKAA was born in Bogalusa, Louisiana in 1947. Komunyakaa's books of poems include the following: *Taboo: The Wishbone Trilogy, Part 1* (2004); *Pleasure Dome: New & Collected Poems, 1975-1999* (2001); *Talking Dirty to the Gods* (2000); *Thieves of Paradise* (1998), which was a finalist for the National Book Critics Circle Award; *Neon Vernacular: New & Selected Poems 1977-1989* (1993), which won the Pulitzer Prize and the Kingsley Tufts Poetry Award; *Magic City* (1992); *Dien Cai Dau* (1988), which won The Dark Room Poetry Prize; *I Apologize for the Eyes in My Head* (1986), winner of the San Francisco Poetry Center Award; and *Copacetic* (1984). Komunyakaa is currently professor and Distinguished Senior Poet at New York University.

# Yusef Komunyakaa

November 28, 1997

FOX: Who do you see as the audience for your work?

KOMUNYAKAA: Initially, of course, I write for myself. I think most authors do, but in giving readings throughout the United States it's quite open, so I'm willing to keep surprising myself. I don't specifically write for a single individual in mind. I basically deal with images. The poet deals with images, metaphors and language like it's music. Consequently, it has a possibility of connecting to a variety of people.

FOX: When you give readings is there any generalization as to the type of audience or response or the type of your poetry they respond to?

KOMUNYAKAA: Well, it's quite varied. Young and old, educated, unlettered. There's a whole spectrum, I think, and I'm quite blessed, perhaps, in that sense. It becomes a challenge for me as a writer to connect to those various communities and conjure some emotional intersection.

FOX: Do you find that the poetry audience has changed over the past ten or twenty years in the United States?

KOMUNYAKAA: I think there are more readings and people are aware of the oral tradition and poetry's connection to that tradition. Not as entertainment but as a place of, at least you could say, a place of meditation. There are readings all over the place from bars to University centers and art centers, that's healthy actually, but it's not confined to one location or one intellectual group as such, but essentially it parallels a democratic tableau. And in that sense, one thinks about William Carlos Williams' idea about achieving an American idiom. I think that's important. But one also thinks, of course, of Whitman, Whitman's need for a democratic premise operating in the language, underlying each metaphor.

FOX: Some people find a distinction between what they refer to as academic poetry and the poetry of the street. I see you smiling.

KOMUNYAKAA: Well, I don't really see a distinctive difference. I feel the poet has to be aware of what's around him or her. So I think that involves the academic arena as well as the so-called streets. I think it's all one, part of human experience. I think that it all merges, that it overlaps, that we tend to create at least psychological bridges between those places and that's a voice that we risk in poetry. I think that's the reason Plato questioned the service of the poet in his ideal republic. We trouble the waters, we tend to pose questions, and perhaps poets are really the active philosophers in this time and age. Of course we're, hopefully, but not necessarily, attempting to answer questions as much as posing questions, where the listener or the reader provide the answers through a process of elimination, through deductive logic.

FOX: When did you start writing poetry?

KOMUNYAKAA: I wrote my very first poem in high school. I found myself raising my hand saying that I could write a poem for my graduating class and I agonized about that for weeks before I actually pinned myself down to the chair and produced a hundred lines, twenty-five traditional rhymed quatrains, perhaps influenced by Tennyson or Longfellow. It was quite a surprise for me. Then when I went to Vietnam I took with me two anthologies of poetry, Hayden Carruth's Anthology entitled, *The Voice That Is Great Within Us*, and then Allen's Anthology, *Contemporary American Poetry*. So I'd read poetry for the most part. When I attended the University of Colorado, I found myself in a creative writing class in 1973, and I've been writing ever since.

FOX: What encouraged you? What made you stick with it?

KOMUNYAKAA: Well, I tend to think that one has to have a need in order to do what one does.

FOX: How?

KOMUNYAKAA: I had the need to write but also, I received some positive encouragement early on from Dr. Alex Blackburn, who was my first creative writing teacher at the University of Colorado in Colorado Springs. I really think that poetry has, or art itself, has to have surprises. First it has to surprise the person who's creating it in order to surprise the audience.

FOX: One winner of the Nobel Prize for literature was asked by the media what he thought about winning the Nobel Prize and he said, "I don't know, I haven't written about it yet." Is that what you're talking about?

KOMUNYAKAA: Yes, I think that's the positive energy that comes out of that experience, that meditation on possibility. That's really what the poem is. That's a plus sometimes. I laugh out loud. Damn, where did that come from, but besides the matrix of surprises, engagement, evolution, all of this becomes a composite.

FOX: As a writer, how do you know that you're a poet and not a novelist or a short story writer or all of these?

KOMUNYAKAA: It's the form of the poem, the aesthetic. However some novelists have started off as poets. Faulkner poems are not as interesting, of course, as his novels. But I think it's interesting that he did start off as a poet. Or look at Tennessee Williams' work as poetry. His poetry, of course, isn't as provocative as his plays. Amiri Baraka started off as a poet, long before he wrote *The Dutchman*. Baraka says that every poet should be a playwright. In a way I'm drifting towards plays myself. I read a whole lot of literature, of course, especially short stories, novels. I like reading plays as much as seeing plays produced.

FOX: How do you go about teaching poetry?

KOMUNYAKAA: First, I do believe that the young writer has to have some idea about the tradition in order to become innovative. So I end up teaching literature as well as Creative Writing. I do think that writing is intricately connected to reading, so automatically I help students compile their individual reading lists. And I tell them it's not just reading literature as well as reading a science text, philosophy, history, psychology, anthropology, everything. I do think that one has to have a work habit as well. He or she should write every day, so I talk about that. I talk about my method of composition, not dictate it to them. I tell them they must choose their method of composition. I tell them I write everything down, and then I systematically go back and revise. Revision is so important. Revision basically means to re-see. So I talk about that, the ability to come back to the poem again and again to refine it into, not necessarily an artifact as such, but something that is in motion, something that has action as part of its dynamic. And I tell them, don't be afraid to surprise themselves.

FOX: That's a very good point. Do you have any source of inspiration for young poets?

KOMUNYAKAA: I think everything around them should be a source of inspiration. If we are really engaged with the world, it can be the small things, those things that we think of as insignificant. It can be a meditation on something as basic as a maggot, which I have a short poem about. Usually many poets start out with those grand abstractions—victory, truth. I tell them, yes they can wrestle with those grand abstractions, but don't be afraid to face the world that they can put their hands on.

FOX: Who are some of your favorite authors?

KOMUNYAKAA: Oh, it goes and goes, [laughs] but I usually say Robert Hayden is a very important voice for me. Gwendolyn Brooks is important. Michael Harper, Whitman, Blake is important. I tend to go back to Shakespeare and especially since he had such an intense, monumental imagination. I admire that. And also he was able to put his fingers on some things that were quite contemporary. Elizabeth Bishop is important. I can go on and on. So many voices: C.K. Williams, Charles Wright, Pablo Neruda, Pushkin.

FOX: What was the role of your Vietnam experience in your writing?

KOMUNYAKAA: Well, it took me fourteen years to really come to that experience. I sort of internalized the pathos of the Vietnam conflict. I was there for a year, '69 to '70, and six months in '70 and was renovating a house in New Orleans in 1984 and I found myself writing a poem entitled "Somewhere Near Phu Bai". That poem came as I was moving up and down the ladder. I had a pad of paper on the floor writing down a few lines, and I found myself writing that particular poem. It just opened that experience for me as poetry, as images, because it came back to me in images. It was a sort of excavation and I suppose it happened at the right time. If it had happened earlier, perhaps it would have come out differently.

FOX: So then it incubated inside for a period of time?

KOMUNYAKAA: Yes.

FOX: When you sit down to write, do you have an idea to start with?

KOMUNYAKAA: I usually have an image, sometimes no more than a word, that I meditate on to improvise on. For me, jazz is important. It has taught me a lot about method of composition. I like to have everything set, by an improvisational tone. That's why I write everything down. Initially a poem might start off 120 lines long and it ends up about forty lines or even less.

FOX: So initially you don't want to censor.

KOMUNYAKAA: Right. I just want to go with it. I just want to see just how I can extend a moment of improvisation.

FOX: How do you know when a poem is finished?

KOMUNYAKAA: Often we don't know. [both laugh] But we wrestle with it. Often I've realized that one perhaps goes past the ending of a poem. I like to have a poem open-ended. So I'll put a sheet of paper at the bottom of a poem I've started working on, to see just what the possible endings are. If there are three or four endings, which is the most important for me? Which ending helps the reader or the listener enter and become an active participant in the creation of meaning?

FOX: What effect has winning the Pulitzer Prize had on your writing or your life?

KOMUNYAKAA: Well, I was lucky because I was midway into some ongoing projects, books of poems, collections, I should say. That's the way I write. Usually I'm writing three collections, side by side. So it didn't really stop me in my tracks.

FOX: Do you find it's interfered in terms of more readings and more demands on your time?

KOMUNYAKAA: I'd already begun to read a lot. I've done a lot of readings especially after the Pulitzer. But I think reading is one way of bringing poetry back to oral tradition. So it is sharing more than anything else. I taught poetry in the schools, in New Orleans for a year, that's one of the things that I told third graders and fourth graders at the onset, that poetry has to be a sharing. It's a way of sharing a voice.

FOX: In this issue [of *Rattle*] there is a tribute to the poetry of children. What was your experience teaching poetry in the schools?

KOMUNYAKAA: It was really amazing because of the surprises. These young third and fourth graders, they weren't afraid. They weren't afraid to put their emotions down on the page. They weren't afraid of images that leapt out of their psyche and I was quite surprised by that and also there's a freshness usually. Not necessarily severe innocence, but a kind of surprising, almost accidental maturity.

FOX: Many poets who teach school children notice that the so-called bad students are often the ones who have the most to say, have the freshest voice.

KOMUNYAKAA: Well again, that's taking us back to Plato or Plato's argument with Euripides. They might be seeing something a little differently and perhaps wrestling with those small and big questions side by side. And confused, so the poem becomes a method of getting to a certain understanding and it's not necessarily an understanding about the exterior world as much as an understanding about the interior world, the world that's inside.

FOX: Do you find that at a college level you have to encourage students to reveal their interior world?

KOMUNYAKAA: Well, they have created the mask, the facades, the detachments. They have to relearn to share which is frightening, often that which they do not fully understand so there's a certain risk involved, but not always. What's interesting I think is this idea about poetry. Often they don't realize the everyday things their lives are made of is subject matter for poetry. Usually it's the grand abstraction, the big questions.

FOX: Some poets I've talked to feel that they may censor themselves because they don't want to offend other people and write about their parents or other subjects. Is that a concern of yours?

KOMUNYAKAA: It's not really a concern of mine. I think they may be offended if I protected, shared in their transparent illusions, that would be offending.

FOX: So in your work you don't feel that you hold anything back.

KOMUNYAKAA: I try not to. But as I say that, I realize it's an ongoing process. We're getting to new territory over and over, as long as we live as artists.

FOX: Do you feel you've done your best work or is that yet to come?

KOMUNYAKAA: I feel like my best work is before me. I like to think of it that way.

FOX: What in your work has given you the biggest surprise?

KOMUNYAKAA: Well, actually the book I'm working on, one of the books I'm working on now has been a huge surprise. It's a long book, it's probably a trilogy. And that is a book entitled, *Pleasure Dome*. For years I've read a lot of history, especially African American history, history that touched on the Black experience worldwide. I've never really thought of that as subject matter for poetry until I began to pose questions to many young students during conferences. And they didn't even know what I was talking about, and I'm a stickler on names. I am now finding myself writing about Pushkin, about Alexander Dumas, writing about George Washington Carver, Charles Drew, uh, all these characters that history shares.

FOX: Is there an essential theme, or message from you that you find in your work or that is most important to you?

KOMUNYAKAA: I suppose for me it's the uncovering of things that's important, not necessarily with any kind of design, but as a series of surprises. Presently I walk about three miles to school. And I've been writing sixteen line poems and often I find myself meditating on something that one might see as trivia, but then I come to find myself wrestling with it walking there and back, sometimes when I return home I'll have a complete poem. It could be on the virtues of animals, insects, whatever. Perhaps it takes me back to Bogalusa, Louisiana. I remember as a child I pretty much observed everything around. I remember observing the rituals of insects, and animals, and consequently observing the practiced rituals of human beings as well.

FOX: As an observer, do you feel more a part of the human story or apart from it?

KOMUNYAKAA: I feel a part of it. The way that I feel a part of it is a kind of hopeful celebration, a celebration of those small moments and how they all lead to the larger moments of human history.

FOX: What would you like your work to be remembered for?

KOMUNYAKAA: Persistence. [both laugh]

FOX: I think persistence is very, very important. So walking to and from school you can sometimes actually compose a poem?

KOMUNYAKAA: Well you know, what I wanted to do was write a large book, rather a long book of sixteen line poems. I wanted to impose a structure on the poems. I began writing odes and meditations, all those things that we sort of overlook and take for granted. And then I realized that I wanted to broaden the canvas. I wanted to deal with ontology, I wanted to deal with psychology, philosophy, history, all of those questions. I wanted to deal with universal relationships.

FOX: Do you prefer to write longer or shorter poems?

KOMUNYAKAA: I like the idea of being challenged to write longer poems. I would like to even write a book length poem, if possible, but also I like writing these small sixteen line poems as well because what I've been looking for is a kind of compression. Everything's so compressed, and at the same time, when it's read it expands.

FOX: What about the role of ambiguity as compared to clarity in a poem?

KOMUNYAKAA: That's an interesting one. I don't mind the ambiguous because, especially if it's interesting, it forces me back to the poem again and again. I like to read poems like that. I don't like to have an immense clarity from the onset. I don't know if I actually compose poems that way. I like the idea of coming back to the poem, the same way that I don't think poems should be resolved. The idea of coming back to the poem again and again and consequently you understand more and more and you feel like you're participating in something that's organic or something that is alive and almost breathing at times.

FOX: What gives a poem an enduring quality, something that you want to return to?

KOMUNYAKAA: I think the music is important, the language inside the music, I think the images, the metaphors, the overall style that pulls us into the poem tells us, we can trust it, and it is the music of trust that endures.

FOX: Do you regard yourself as a spokesperson for any particular point of view such as Vietnam?

KOMUNYAKAA: No. I don't really regard myself as a spokesperson. I just feel like I'm a part of the human community. And we were all observers. We're all participants.

FOX: In that context do you find any significant differences between American poetry and poetry from other countries?

KOMUNYAKAA: That's a good question because I do think that poetry from the United States, at this moment, is probably the most engaging, the most important and yet there are those isolated individuals writing in other parts of the world who are important. And it isn't just because of Creative Writing workshops. Although Creative Writing workshops are influencing communities. And I do think the artist needs a community that he or she can embrace or that community can embrace him or her. But, there is something in the air—poetry slams, poets in the schools, all of these things happening.

FOX: So, it's a pretty vibrant world then?

KOMUNYAKAA: Very vibrant. It seems like it's inclined to engage celebration and critique.

FOX: Have you ever been to a poetry slam?

KOMUNYAKAA: Yeah, [laughs] not that I've participated in poetry slams. But I support anything that generates active language and communication.

FOX: One hallmark of the American experience today seems to be participation. So many people attend readings, write poetry and are interested in it.

KOMUNYAKAA: Yes, it's quite an experience in democracy.

FOX: Can you say more about that.

KOMUNYAKAA: Just the fact that a democratic society can engage participants, that poetry engages individuals from various neighborhoods, various economic experiences and so forth. One can be at the top of the heap or at the bottom and still be an active participant.

FOX: What advice do you have for a young poet?

KOMUNYAKAA: Read everything. Write every day.

FOX: [laughs] That's a fairly universal approach.

KOMUNYAKAA: It's true.

FOX: Do you find that your students do that?

KOMUNYAKAA: I think often they realize the importance of that and yet seem afraid of being influenced. I tell them not to be afraid because the artist never really operates in isolation. We all are influenced just by the language we speak.

FOX: But if you have to be influenced any way, why not be influenced by the best? I'm intrigued by your ending lines from *The Thorn Merchant*, "he knows how death waits in us like a light switch." Could you follow that up?

KOMUNYAKAA: Oh God. [laughs] I wrote that, matter of fact, in graduate school at Irvine and I remembered when I wrote that line down, that image down, it was something that made me laugh and at the same time, it was something that caused a great deal of internal fear.

FOX: Can you say more about the fear?

KOMUNYAKAA: Well, it's a realization about death, how it can come out of nowhere, it seems that it isn't something that we can rehearse for. Something we can't control. So, I think that's where the fear comes from. That we're not put here to control everything.

FOX: [laughs] Yes. Very true. Some people see poetry as a search for truth. Do you?

KOMUNYAKAA: It's not necessarily a search for truth as much as a search for confrontation. And I'm talking about confronting that which is real, by finding that which is inside oneself. So I've pretty much defined poetry for myself as a celebration and confrontation.

FOX: Could you say more about the celebration.

KOMUNYAKAA: The celebration is that we care to describe something a hundred different ways. I'm willing to observe an insect, I'm willing to observe someone playing basketball, putting the whole body and mind into that observation and consequently getting even closer to the experience, in a sense.

FOX: And when you talk about confrontation, are you talking about an internal confrontation or . . . ?

KOMUNYAKAA: It's an internal confrontation, I think for the most part although it can be an outward confrontation as well. I don't necessarily rule that out because, let's face it, language is political. We are social beings, but we are political beings as well and we don't have a grasp on that which could be classified as a truth or truth. It seems as if the foundation is often shifting under our feet, and perhaps that's good because as least we can have some kind of grasp on the cosmos. There's no system or guarantees.

FOX: In what way do you see your work as political?

KOMUNYAKAA: I think it would be political to say it wasn't political. I think silence is political. We are using tools such as language. Language is a political construct. A good example would be, if I look in the dictionary, everything that is prefixed with black, 90% percent of it would be negative. And vice versa. So I'm very much aware that language often is political and I think the young writer, I think the young thinker has to be aware of that as well.

FOX: What sort of influence would you like your work to have?

KOMUNYAKAA: I don't want it to influence, I want it to be an instrument of meditation. I want it to be understood. I want people, at least momentarily, to be willing to embrace it. I'm not talking about the work being didactic, but as part of who we are. I would like for literature to be accepted that way. I would like knowledge to be accepted that way. I don't think we should be fearful of knowledge. I don't want everything nailed down; I don't want my feet nailed to the floor. I think that is imprisonment. So about literature, I like to be challenged.

FOX: I find that some poems, which I like very much, I read and I say, wow, I like that. I don't understand it. But I like it. [both laugh]

KOMUNYAKAA: That's the interesting thing about it. It brings you in, in a psychological, emotional way. Sometimes I notice when an individual comes to me, he or she may understand certain things about it that I didn't even have in mind. That's positive for me.

FOX: When I was growing up my high school teachers taught poetry as something arcane which only they could really explain. I think many people have shared that experience.

KOMUNYAKAA: I don't think poetry is that way. I think automatically coming to Dorothy Wordsworth's journals, or coming to someone such as George Moses Horton, or any of these voices. Certain things we are not going to understand immediately and that's fine, but if we reenter the territory of the poem with care, with insistence, with love, then we understand it. We don't necessarily have to understand it a certain way. We understand it in relationships to who we are. What we've brought to it.

FOX: Do you think readers might understand the same word a little differently?

KOMUNYAKAA: I really do.

FOX: And you wouldn't necessarily say that that's wrong.

KOMUNYAKAA: I don't necessarily say that, because I could be wrong. It's what he or she brought to the experience and connotation.

FOX: What do you see happening with poetry in the United States over the next ten or twenty years?

KOMUNYAKAA: I hope poetry won't be shortchanged by technology.

FOX: How?

KOMUNYAKAA: That technology doesn't make us become emotionally, psychologically, and intellectually lazy. That everything is set up and thought out for us and we become slaves to that which is pre-programmed. I want poetry to keep its surprises.

FOX: Do you think that involves individuality, surprise?

KOMUNYAKAA: Yes.

FOX: Well what aspects of technology would concern you in that respect?

KOMUNYAKAA: [laughs] I expect medical technology for the most part. Well, no, I shouldn't say that, but many aspects of technology because what it does is it sets out to make things easier. That is what always underlies, you know. Some things are difficult and that is what distinguishes us as human beings, that we have the kind of dexterity to negotiate those difficulties.

FOX: Do you feel it's the computer, the internet or . . . ?

KOMUNYAKAA: Internet, things that just go boom and wham for us, you know and we realize we are consumers of pre-digested—we are not participating in this as thoughtful and inquisitive human beings.

FOX: Does it surprise you, in an age of Arnold Schwarzenegger and action movies that poetry seems to be undergoing a renaissance?

KOMUNYAKAA: I think one of the reasons that poetry is having somewhat of a renaissance is because there is a need, and the need is even more severe now, because of what it contrasts. It contrasts often that which dehumanizes us.

FOX: Say more about that.

KOMUNYAKAA: Well, I still admire the capacity of the human brain to negotiate so many difficult questions, so many difficult problems. I admire that capacity but for some reason there is an attempt, and maybe not a full design, to bypass certain avenues. I am frightened about the amount of time spent in front of computers. I think people should be talking with each other a lot more. I'm frightened about the amount of time spent in front of televisions. What made me start thinking about this in the early 80's, I think it was 1981, May of 1981, I went back to Louisiana and my grandmother was talking on the phone, her friends would call her, and they were talking about people I didn't know, and it dawned on me they were actually talking about soap opera characters. And it really saddened me.

FOX: Do you find students nowadays different in any meaningful way than ten or twenty years ago?

KOMUNYAKAA: I think it becomes problematic with education, especially with the liberal arts, when individuals are not there for the love of learning. That the university has become essentially a trade school. I have real problems with that and so there's always questions.

FOX: You seem to value life experience itself; the observation, the paying attention to the environment, to yourself, is more important than looking for the outcome?

KOMUNYAKAA: I think we have to go through the emotions of experience, wondering about, how the day is going to lead us towards the future. Appreciate what is.

FOX: I think there's something about the issue of control. Couldn't you say that the history of human evolution is seeking more and more control over the environment?

KOMUNYAKAA: Well, it's even within the context of the Bible if we think about it. Man is given dominion over the animals and I'm frightened by that statement. That, one, because we're born to human skin that automatically we are given dominion over everything that isn't human. It's commodity. The problem with that, I think, is that it's a selfish thing because everything we think of is sacrificed as commodity. We know it's going to run out.

FOX: And yet don't we tend to treat other people as commodities, living I-it instead of I-thou?

KOMUNYAKAA: Right, that's right. So, it's almost as if we're living for the moment. We feel as if we have to use up everything in our lifetime and I see that as immensely selfish.

FOX: What role do you think selflessness should have?

KOMUNYAKAA: I think it has taught us to survive as a species. But we should also be selfish about that which is good.

FOX: With that idea in mind, is working together the means for evolving communications?

KOMUNYAKAA: Yeah, but its not just communication. Because what I've been able to look at, it's not communication for good as much as selling products. It baffles me what people have done through technology to convince others they need this or that. And we make a profit off these illusions.

FOX: It's purely commercial.

KOMUNYAKAA: I think something is extremely wrong about it. We have brainwashed small children to think in a certain way. They begin to measure themselves against their friends; we're talking about two and three-year-olds. Something is awfully wrong and perverted here, because people think wearing a thousand or two thousand dollars worth of clothes creates a better person, but that isn't the case at all. He or she could be the worst person.

FOX: It seems to me that's one way we deal with our insecurity.

KOMUNYAKAA: Yeah, I think so. I couldn't understand for a long time how boys could be killing other boys over brand name sneakers. Those kids must have been brainwashed to believe that those things are going to make them more complete people. Many times brainwashed within their families, or by television. I think we have to share in the responsibility of that. For what makes us human? I think the brain has a lot to do with it. And also compassion, the possibility of compassion.

FOX: That's nice. It has to make a big difference in teachers, parents with their children. We're all influenced, if not by being more human than television, then probably by being more selfish.

KOMUNYAKAA: Thank God. We have this possibility for compassion. It's amazing.

FOX: Do you find compassion reflected in your work?

KOMUNYAKAA: I hope so. I like to be able to see things from the point of view of other humans, and even the animal world.

FOX: Any last thoughts?

KOMUNYAKAA: No. [laughing] We've been going on for awhile now.

JACK KORNFIELD trained as a Buddhist monk in the monasteries of Thailand, India, and Burma. He is one of the key teachers to introduce Buddhist mindfulness practice to the West. He is a founding teacher of the Insight Meditation Society and Spirit Rock Center and has taught meditation internationally since 1974. He holds a PhD in clinical psychology, and is a husband and father. His books include *A Path with Heart*; *Buddha's Little Instruction Book*; *Teachings of the Buddha*; *Seeking the Heart of Wisdom*; *Living Dharma*; *A Still Forest Pool*; *Stories of the Spirit, Stories of the Heart*; *After the Ecstasy, the Laundry*; and *The Art of Forgiveness, Lovingkindness and Peace.*

# Jack Kornfield

June 28, 2006

KORNFIELD: It's somehow been so much better to have a place that's dedicated to writing than trying to write at home in my home kind of office upstairs. It just doesn't work, there's always my daughter coming in or my wife saying "Oh dear would you mind—"

FOX: Yes, yes. Well, we're with Jack Kornfield. This is June 28th. We're in a, how to describe the setting, a treehouse, at Spirit Rock in Marin County. So Jack, you have a lot of manuscript material and books on the floor. What is that?

KORNFIELD: I brought some of my poetry library because it's a pleasure to sit with a poet and there's this ancient Chinese tradition that when a poet comes you bring out your favorite poetry books and a bottle of plum wine and the cherries from the garden trees and read to one another and take enough time to listen so that you can feel into the poem, and have it touch you. And one of the things that I love about these books is that they're all battered and marked and pages turned and so I pick up William Stafford's book and immediately it drops open to one of my favorite poems and I could just go from there, "A Ritual To Read To One Another," or to Etheridge Knight or Naomi Nye or Alison Luterman, so it's—the poems become like, they become companions.

FOX: When did you first discover the world of poetry?

KORNFIELD: About the same time that I became interested in Buddhist practice, in university at Dartmouth. I was starting to do science and pre-med and then Dr. Wing-tsit Chan, an emeritus professor from Harvard, came to start a department at Dartmouth and I took a course in Asian philosophy and he sat cross-legged on the desk on occasion and would hold forth about Lao Tzu and the Buddha and I found it touched me in a way that organic chemistry didn't. [Fox laughs] Although there is a poetry in chemistry as well. And then living as a Buddhist monk for years in the monastery, there is a deep tradition of poetry as an expression of the awakened heart. The very first words that the Buddha uttered after his enlightenment was a poem where he begins, "Oh house-builder, thou art seen at last" and house-builder means "the builder of this house of sorrows, you are seen at last, smashed is the ridgepole, broken the rafters, open to the freedom of the world, no more imprisoned by sorrow am I." So his very first words were a poem and as I began to study in the monastery, I saw that poetry was really the linguistic voice of the inner life that meant a lot to me.

FOX: How does poetry differ in that regard, the inner life, from other types of writing, novels or whatever?

KORNFIELD: It's hard to say. But I know it's spare and tough and tender and gets under your flesh down to someplace deep in the psyche and in the bones. And anyway I'm not so much a poet as kind of a poet groupie; I'm a follower of poets. People would follow their favorite rock star; for me it would be much more thrilling to go and hear my favorite poet. And so I, I'm more of a storyteller and I use poetry, I use the poems of others to help remind people of the possibilities in their spirit and in the world. One of the things I love these days is reading from Middle Eastern poets because we're in this insane war. I think Rumi's now the most popular poet in the USA, due to Coleman Barks and all these wonderful translations—and so here we are at war in Iraq and Afghanistan and this is Rumi and Hafiz's home. Hafiz says—oh, where he explains what a poet is. . . does it matter if there's a little pause—

FOX: No, no, not a bit—

KORNFIELD: Oh, good. Oh, I want to find this and I know it's here—

FOX: That's fine, take awhile—

KORNFIELD: The one I want. I may have to do it from memory, which isn't very good. [Fox laughs] He says a poet is someone who can create a goblet out of words and fill it with the most delicious wine for your parched lips to drink. Something like that. And so to me poetry is a kind of a force that has risen out of out of our cultures worldwide, and now we're in this amazing position because we have the greatest poetry of the ages in front of us. I have Rilke and Rumi and Kabir from India and Li Po from China. Actually, it's kind of intimidating in terms of writing poetry because we have these masters, and they touch me very deeply and then I just want to pass it on to people. But I want to say a couple of other things about poetry and then you may have another question.

FOX: Sure.

KORNFIELD: Well I'm going to stay with the Middle East for a minute because I want to honor all these fantastic books of poems from Rumi who described in the Mathnawi that his poetry was like an ocean. He was like Mozart. I don't think Mozart wrote his symphonies, I think Mozart heard them, there was a divine inspiration. And Rumi would walk around and then someone would walk around "cooking the joy soup" as he said, and someone would walk around next to him with a notepad and Rumi would spew forth language of divine inspiration and vision and someone would write it down. So in the. . . .

FOX: I will say you are more prepared than anyone I've ever talked with.

KORNFIELD: Well this is fun, this is sort of like jazz—I just pick up a poem—

FOX: Yes.

KORNFIELD: And think, oh what would be the right poem or story. So Abdul Kassem Ismael, the Grand Vizier of Persia in the 10th century, couldn't bear to part with his 117,000 volume library of sacred texts and poetry when he traveled, so he had the books carried by a caravan of 400 camels trained in such a way to walk to keep the library in alphabetical order. And I like it for its humor but I also like it because it speaks about how when we become a poet and when we read great poetry, we're really part of a lineage of thousands of years of human beings trying to give voice to something that's inspired or, or heart-breaking and often both. Let me talk a little about poetry and inspiration if I can.

FOX: Sure.

KORNFIELD: Um, first a story. In London, there was a study that was done, a sociological study—and I'm a little dubious about them at times, but—in London some years ago, in which they took two parallel streets in a London ghetto, an economically depressed area that had a high crime rate. One of the streets they left the same and on another parallel street about a mile away, unbeknownst to anyone in the community, they ordered that the street should be cleaned every day, that the trees be watered and replanted if they had died and the graffiti cleaned up and that the street be kept beautiful for a year without anyone knowing that anything different was happening. And after a year, they measured the crime rate on the two streets and found that it had dropped fifty percent on the street that they kept clean and beautiful. There's something like this about poetry. It is an expression of beauty, even the necessary beauty of the words that speak our tears and our sorrow, and this beauty allows us to live in a different way. I believe that it's our human impulse to creativity and art that saves us. One of the posters that I carry when I teach is a photograph of Vedran Smailovic who was known as the "cellist of Sarajevo" and for the three years that Sarajevo was under siege in the Balkan War—mortar fire, snipers, no one could get in or out except some UN helicopters and many, many people died. Every afternoon, Vedran would put on the tux that he wore to the Sarajevo national symphony, and take a folding chair and his cello and go out into the square and play music for the residents of Sarajevo, so they wouldn't give up hope. He played in spite of the fact that he could have been easily killed by a sniper or a mortar fire. Since, he's gone around and given concerts. And in a certain way I see Vedran doing what a poet does, offering art in the face of the beauty of life and the horrors of life. Aung San Suu Kyi, the Nobel Peace Laureate, who's been under house arrest for fifteen years in Burma, wrote about house arrest and what kept her alive. Part of what's keeping her alive, is the poetry of Rabindranath Tagore. Rabindranath Tagore was one of the first poets to win the Noble Prize for literature and there's a passage she quotes in which he writes, "If they answer not your call, walk alone. If they are afraid and cower mutely facing the wall, oh thou of evil luck, open the mind and speak out alone." And Aung San Suu Kyi writes, "When I feel alone and I read his words and I realize that I have to keep the flame of my heart alive in this place for myself and for the people that I love. And it's poetry that keeps this flame alive." Anyway . . .

FOX: When we take the wisdom of poetry in the $10^{th}$ Century, or whatever, and then remember that we're living in an age of cell phones and television and internet, what do you think the interaction of poetry is in this present day?

KORNFIELD: I think poetry is still, remains a voice that can heal and transform. I watched Martin Scorsese's film history of Bob Dylan not so long ago, which I loved, and when it was given to me, a friend put it in my hand and said, "This is the life of a poet." And when I watched it through those eyes, I saw him stand up not as a rock singer or as a cultural icon, but as a man who others tried to capture politically, economically to get him to speak for their cause, but he simply wouldn't be caged. He had a poet's voice that had to speak the truth. I worked together with some poets like Luis Rodriguez, who you know, and Michael Meade, who's a mythologist and poet, and we work with youth, in schools, coming out of youth gangs, juvenile hall, and so forth, and one of the forms that Michael and Luis use quite a lot, is to get young gang members to begin to listen to and write poems. When you first say to these young kids, "We're going to talk about poetry," their eyes roll and they pull their backward hats down further on their heads and they seem to disappear. And then Luis will stand up and read a poem about shooting heroin down the viaduct in L.A., and the agonizing loss of community and dignity for the immigrants, and Luis reads like a Mayan sacrifice, it's like he opens his veins and passion and love and desperation and eloquence pours out, and the eyes of the young men start to open wider and wider as they sit in their chairs and Luis reads another poem and by the time he's read four poems and starts to pass out paper, they realize, this is a voice that's in me that wants to speak, and their own voice starts to come out. And I see it even in popular music; I see it in rap music. There's terrible rap music but there's also a voice that comes out of desperation that has to be heard, so I see poetry coming out like grass, or weeds sticking out of the sidewalk, in unexpected places, because it's really the voice of people that need to say something wildly important to them. And I trust it. William Carlos Williams wrote "You can't get the news from poetry but men and women die every day for lack of what is found there."

FOX: A few years ago we published a number of poems by prisoners and they were very honest and touching and, as you say, trustworthy. Say something about the relationship of poetry and truth.

KORNFIELD: Another story. I recently listened to and had a few moments to speak with Mubarak Awad, who is the Palestinian Gandhi figure. For his whole life he's been dedicated to non-violence. He's now a silvery-haired eloquent professor at an American university. The Israeli government kicked him out years ago because he was being successful and he's unable to go back, although he has created centers for non-violence around the Middle East. And he said, "I wanted to bring the Palestinian and the Israeli people together to hear one another's sorrows because I believe that if that could happen, there is a chance for peace." He said, "I made some mistakes. We brought together politicians—bad mistake. Then we brought together religious figures—even worse. We tried academics; I'm sorry to say, it may have been worse than the first two. [Fox laughs] There were two groups that could hear one another. The mothers: when we brought Palestinian mothers and Israeli mothers to tell their stories, they could really hear one another. And the artists. We brought one hundred Palestinian and one hundred Israeli artists together—poets, writers, painters—for four days, thinking in a few days they would be able to hear one another. Within two hours, they were creating art of the voice of their sorrows together."

FOX: It seems to me that those two groups, mothers and artists, were better able to touch each other through their common interests and outlook and set aside the fact that they were Israeli or Palestinian—that aspect of their being.

KORNFIELD: Yes. Or to say that in some way they were connected to a voice and an imagination that was much bigger than their national identity. To be connected as a mother is to be connected to all mothers and to that which gives birth. And to be connected as a poet and an artist is to be connected somehow to the heart, to the voice that was in you before your parents even told you your name. And then I hear these words of poetry—Hafiz again, he writes, "Fear is the cheapest room in the house, I'd like to see you in better living conditions." And in one sentence—

FOX: Wow.

KORNFIELD:—he says, All right, here you could live as an Israeli or a Palestinian or an American who's frightened and lost in the whole sense of insecurity and terror, but that's an awfully small room to live in. Or there's a much greater possibility as a human being, to live fearlessly with vision and courage and heart and art. He does it in two lines, and that's the art to me of poetry. Here's another short verse I love of Annie Lamott's words, because I teach meditation in groups where we come together to do the contemplative work of the heart and she writes, "My mind is like a bad neighborhood, I try not to go there alone." [Fox laughs] And I think one of the things that makes it hard to write poems—you know in the little poetry I write, but I do write a lot as a writer—is that you do have to go into that neighborhood, you have to go and wrestle with, I have to go and wrestle with my demons and insecurity and somehow look to find the words and voice that will come from a place that's deep enough and vulnerable enough and honest enough, as you were saying, to be worthy of sharing. And I heard an interview with a great writer sometime ago on National Public Radio, I can't even remember who she was, but she was asked the question—might have been by Terry Gross—she was asked the question, how do you know when your book is done, when you've really finished the last draft and your book is done, and she answered, "When you're not disgusted with it anymore." [Fox laughs] And it was both a terrifying and honest answer, that there's some way in which you really have to look into the mirror of your writing. Rilke writes also that it's upon our vulnerability that we depend, that there's a certain way in which we have to be honest about our vulnerability to one another, that we depend on one another, that we can't make some fortress around ourselves or around our country, and that when we are honest in our poetry it also speaks from that place of vulnerability, and that's the real courage and strength. I love the poem in one of the earlier *Rattle*s, about the horses in World War II in the Crimean Peninsula, that were all taken to the edge of the cliff, and then, because the army was losing that battle, the soldiers who loved their horses and used them had to shoot their horses. And I could hardly bear to breathe, bear the poem as I read it, and what I saw is that it made me feel the vulnerability and the terror of war in a new way because the channel of my love for animals wasn't yet sullied by so many bad television war images and movies and that the poet had found a way in to say, all right, here is an image that will tear you, tear you, and let you feel this human planetary vulnerability that we share.

FOX: You mentioned sorrow several times, and many people if not most regard sorrow and sadness as something to be avoided and locked up. You seem to feel differently.

KORNFIELD: Poetry is both erotic and passionate and deadly in some way. What is the word that Carlos Castaneda put in the mouth of Don Juan—that death is always just over your left shoulder and if you catch a sense of him waiting there, just even a glimpse, all of a sudden your life becomes more real to you. We live in times—and maybe it's always been these times because the Buddha spoke of the sorrow of Dukkha as one of the things that we need to come to terms with as humans. We live in times where we see the images of the sorrows of the world and one of the great tragedies in our culture is that we don't know how to grieve and weep very well. When the heart opens, it can't just open to joy. If you open the door, you get everything, you get the ten thousand joys and the ten thousand sorrows—those are the words of Chuang Tzu. And so, we need our tears. If I see a politician on television saying we're going to go to war and they're not weeping, I can't fathom what's going on. My good friend Malidoma Some, who is a West African medicine man, who also has two PhDs in world literature, one from La Sorbonne and one from Brandeis—he's also a poet and professor—when he came back from his initiations in African shamanic tradition and his inner vision was opened, he said, "I could barely stand to walk on the streets of your cities in America because I saw with these new eyes that your streets were full of the ungrieved dead." And so we asked what did that mean and he said, "The ones who died in wars that you don't want to pay attention to, the ones who died in your prisons, the ones who died in gang violence, the ones who died in your old age homes—it's as if their spirits are still among you because they haven't been wept and grieved, and until we can grieve honorably, we can't tend the earth. The tears make it possible for some new vision, some new imagination to come." So I hold up Carolyn Forche's book *Against Forgetting: the 20th Century Poetry of Witness*, where it says, "One person will always be left alive and tell the story. Humanly speaking, no more is required. These poems are like those that keep Ang Sang Suu Kyi alive. They're the poems that speak that voice that has to be heard for us to, to be willing to fight for justice. We have to see the injustice, we have to feel the suffering, and then we have to say, "I am a part of this and I will do something," and that way, that's a part of the voice of poetry. There is an account that I got, I think out of *Harper's* magazine—and this is jazz for me, this is just doing jazz—not long after 9/11 there was a professor at Columbia University who was walking down the hall in the school of the arts and ran into someone who said to him, "It all feels so absurd making art, what's the point?" And obviously this person was in a great deal of trauma from the collapse of the World Trade building and the thousands of people who had died. And this professor answered, "To which I couldn't answer anymore than I could have answered if he'd been arguing about the redundancy of breathing or beauty. What could I say? That in June of 1945 workers reclaiming the Reich's prisons in Buchenwald found poems folded into thick squares, stuffed up into the electrical wiring, so that a person locked in a cell awaiting interrogation or death would choose to write a poem on a piece of toilet paper so that their spirit facing death would never die." And so there's a kind of responsibility in poetry, if we take it, not just a political responsibility, a responsibility to love, a responsibility to our children, a responsibility to the fading iris in the vase on my poet's desk that shows me the declining cycle of my own sixty-one years.

FOX: Well what would be the first steps, for—you mentioned grieving—for grieving?

KORNFIELD: For grieving. . . .

FOX: How does someone who's never grieved start to do that?

KORNFIELD: [laughing] I'm laughing because I'm thinking, "Should I tell this story?"—which I will, of course. It took me a while to learn to grieve. In my family my father was a brilliant scientist and a paranoid and angry, often violent man who would beat my mother to the point where she had to wear long sleeves in summer sometimes to cover the black and blue marks or hide bottles behind the curtains in the house so she could grab a weapon to defend herself. So, emotion was not an easy thing in our house; we were frightened by it, whether it was anger or fear or grief. And I fit very well into the monasteries where we would meditate and be contemplative and quiet, but somehow I knew that to be more alive I had to learn how to grieve and with that then how to feel joy; they're the same gate. I learned through meditation how to feel my feelings that had been unfelt before. When I was angry one day I went to my teacher Ajahn Chan, and I said, I'm really angry I was mistreated by this senior monk and he said, "Great, good!" That was his first response, different from my family. He said, "If you're going to be angry, do it right. You have a little hut in the woods, close the one window and door, go in there—it's the hot season, right—put on all your monks robes and sit in the middle of the hut all day and be angry and really study it, learn about it." So I sat there and I was raging in anger and very hot and it wasn't the anger at that monk, it was the anger of a lifetime.

FOX: Yes.

KORNFIELD: And what does it feel like in my body? Burning, throbbing, emergency, dynamite, desperation, strangling. What does it feel like in the heart? Molten iron, poured down my throat, fireworks. What are the stories it tells? And it had all these stories, all of them saying, "I'm right," somehow, underneath it, or "they did me wrong." I mean this huge enormous world creation of myself—

FOX: Yes. [laughing]

KORNFIELD:—you know, in relation to how it should be. And so I really studied it and I got very good at knowing anger and with it my sadness would come; when I could let out my anger, then I could also feel the hurt that I carried, which we all have. We've all been betrayed and we all carry this great measure of sorrows. But I wasn't very good yet at expressing it. I—at least I could feel it, that was a step, but I think, whether as a teacher as I am, or as poet, one needs to then give it voice. So I decided when I came back home from the monastery—I got myself in therapy and that was partly to figure out what happened to me and how to integrate it more. And I saw Dr. Myron Sharaf, this old Reichian who was on the faculty of Harvard Medical School, but had also lived with Wilhelm Reich up in Maine in his community. And Myron started to work with me and he said, "You know, you're an interesting case, because you have a lot of access to your inner life from meditation. You can tell what kind of thoughts you're having and if there's fear or anxiety or anger or joy and you describe how they feel in your heart and your body. But you don't know how to express it." He called it the monks' defense. "I want to see your tears; I want to hear your rage and your voice." So he would have me breathe and do these Reichian exercises and not much came of it. Then he looked at me and he said, "Okay, I want to know what time of day is the hardest for you." I said, "Morning. I hate getting up in the morning. At the monastery they ring the bell at 3:30 and I get up, always disliking it." He said, "Good. Our therapy sessions are now going to be at 6:30 AM. That's when your ego defenses will be down." So I would come and see him at 6:30 AM and lie on this bed and do these Reichian breath practices to charge up my body. And then he would put on arias from operas, wonderful music, and after my body was charged up, he would say, All right, tell me the story of your childhood, or the story of this, have me tell the story, and then push on my body and try to get me to let the feelings come out. He actually cracked two of my ribs once—

FOX: Whoa.

KORNFIELD:—so it was a kind of—which was fine, it was worth it. It worked! And by the end of my time working with Myron, I could weep and I could be angry. It was as if he helped me unblock something that I'd been frightened about. And now when I sit with someone as I teach and they come in and they say "I'm afraid" or "my sister just died" and they're grieving, I feel my own grief come and we weep together and I know, and I understand it. Or I teach and I know how important it is somehow to have a voice, a word, or the poem that can touch the heart of someone so that they can feel again, because a lot of what contemplative life is about is to feel that, feel deeply in yourself that wisdom and that love that's been locked up for so long. So I might read a passage like this—and I see this as a poem—it was left at the Vietnam Veteran's Memorial Wall, and I took it from a book called—I believed it's called *The Wall*, or *Offerings of the Wall*, where people have left prayers and poems and letters. "Dear Sir, for twenty-two years I have carried your picture in my wallet. I was only eighteen years old that day that we faced one another on the trail in Chu Lai, Vietnam. Why you didn't take my life, I'll never know. You stared at me for so long, armed with your AK-47, and yet you did not fire. Forgive me for taking your life. I was reacting the way I was trained. So many times over the years I've stared at your picture and your daughter. Each time my heart and guts would burn with the pain of guilt, for I have two daughters myself now, and I perceive you as a brave soldier defending his homeland. Above all else, I can now respect the importance that life held for you. I suppose that is why I'm able to be here today. It is time for me to continue my life and release my pain and guilt. Forgive me, Sir. Please forgive me." And I feel as I teach, when I read a poem like that, that I open in myself, and in those who listen, a gateway to feel all the things that we would like to ask forgiveness for. And I believe that if we, that if we cannot forgive we really can't live wisely. And to forgive isn't a matter of the mind, but it's somehow a matter of the spirit in a very deep way, and that when we can learn to do it, then maybe we can also live in a different way with one another, individually and collectively.

FOX: I think that you touched on a central issue which all of us face—that is, how to live our lives, and as you know many people answer that by just saying as, as superficially as possible, "I just want to get through it, I want to make money, I want a nicer car," and I hear you not saying those aspirations are necessarily wrong but there is something else that is more important, more enriching.

KORNFIELD: I don't know any poets who have that as their main aspiration.

FOX: A better car? [laughing]

KORNFIELD: Yeah, exactly. I mean, they might want to live nicely, but what you said in some way is not the life of a poet. Hafiz again: "The mind is ever a tourist wanting to touch and buy new things, then toss them into an already filled closet." So, yes, there's the dry life of accumulation, but that doesn't feed the soul, it doesn't feed the hungry heart—and I actually, I don't know, I don't really believe in accumulation and consumerism or consumer society as a place of satisfaction for almost anyone. My experience is that if I sit down with someone who may have chosen ostensibly materialistic aspirations and have some time to sit, maybe in the evening with a good bottle of wine, under the stars, and really ask "What matters?" and listen, that there's a hidden beauty and a hidden longing and a hidden love that will come out of that person too. And I think that's my work and it's really the work of a poet, to speak to that level, to anyone, so that there you are, on your shopping rounds and you're walking into the hardware store buying sandpaper and maybe if you're fortunate enough, somehow—or you're going to the post office and there comes a poem in the mail to you and it reminds you of a depth your heart already knows. I loved in this Spring issue of *Rattle*, all the conversations about what it meant to be a poet, and I remember asking my dear friend and editor Jane Hirshfield what it meant to her, what poetry was for, and one of the things she said was she would like to have a few lines that she wrote remain on the tongues of others after she's gone. And then I told her one of my favorite poetry stories. Pablo Neruda, toward the end of his life, was invited to read in Caracas, Venezuela in the great national theatre there, and being the icon and the conscience and voice of much of the Latin culture, it was filled with people celebrating him as only can be done in a society that still loves poetry in that way. And he got up and he read, gracious as he was, for quite a long time, and then he said, "Is there anything you'd like to hear?" and someone raised their hand and said, "Would you please read Poem 19 from *20 Love Songs and a Song of Despair*?", and he said, "Oh, I'm sorry, I didn't bring that with me," and then 400 people stood up and recited that poem to him. And I think, oh, what a culture that is, to have the voice of the poet in the hearts of so many people. I forget what question you asked—

FOX: [laughing] Oh, that's okay. Would you say poetry is more a way to connect with oneself or to connect with others?

KORNFIELD: That's like a koan. If you connect with yourself, do you connect with others, if you connect with others, do you connect with yourself? And the answer is yes. That's the good thing about koans. They can have all these incredible paradoxes. Yes, yes.

FOX: You mentioned before, to play the Devil's advocate, so to speak—

KORNFIELD: Please. I like the Devil. The Devil makes much better poetry, thank you. [laughing]

FOX: Mark Twain said, "I'd like to go to heaven for the weather but to hell for the company." [Kornfield laughs] But in terms of wrestling with the demons, why not just lead them into the dungeon and try to avoid them through your life and escape unscathed in that sense?

KORNFIELD: Because if the demons are locked in the dungeon they always come out at night. And they come out in other ways. The poet John Ciardi wrote, "An ulcer is an unkissed imagination taking its revenge. It's an undanced dance, an unpainted watercolor, an unwritten poem." Something like that. And the fact—staying with the theme of this conversation—that we don't grieve as a nation in many ways for what we've done and so forth that then allows us to continue on destructive courses. Albert Camus wrote, "We all carry within us our crimes, our betrayals and our ravages. Our task is not to unleash them on others, but it is to make them conscious in ourselves that we may transform them." So I don't see that we have a choice. I think that to be an honorable human being means that we have to face *Mara*, which is what our demons are called in the Buddhist tradition, that we have to face our own shadow and only then can we live in an honest way; otherwise we place it on other people. And again, I think it's James Baldwin who wrote, "The problem with people who hate is that once hate is gone, they'll have to deal"—or, "I believe that once their hate is gone, they'll have to deal with a great deal of their own pain." So there's a kind of bravery to the art of the poet to speak that, to plumb that, and to cherish it. I was sitting at dinner the other night with Daniel Ellsberg, the 35th anniversary of the *Pentagon Papers*, and his wife Patricia, and at our table were also Joan Baez and John Burton, who'd been the head of the Senate in California for a long time, and some friends of Dan Ellsberg and my wife. And John Burton was talking about how darkly he sees the political process and system now, and Joan was talking, as a non-violent activist for years, about her concerns about these dark times and Daniel Ellsberg carries certainly a piece of that. And then my wife who is a Jungian spoke—and an artist—spoke up, and she said, "I love the dark." Right into the shadow, you know, and just looked them in the eye. "I love the dark, it's only through entering into the dark and walking in the dark and being willing to tend what's in the darkness that something that needs to transform and grow like the underground of the Winter coming into Spring, it's only in that way that something can grow, grow and bring beauty back into the world." And they started this marvelous conversation that I, as a kind of appreciative husband, could only smile at, in which she was drawing out of them the dark and talking with them about how something was going to get born out of it.

I want to tell another story because it's what I do and it's what moves me and it's kind of cheap to say, but it's at best my form of poetry. So, Rilke writes about being a poet; he says, "which means not numbering or counting but ripening like a tree which doesn't force its sap and stands confidently in the storms of Winter, not afraid that Summer may not come. It does come, it always comes." And there's a kind of planting of seeds in the j—

FOX: Would you start that again?

KORNFIELD: Yeah. Okay. I will, I'll start the story again from the beginning. We were really talking about going into the dark and how there's a certain way—my wife as a painter talks about holding an image or a phrase or symbol in the womb of imagination and tending it the way you would tend a child. And I think poets do that, poets get an image or, entering into the darkness, are willing to tend that and know that by tending even that which is unseen that something luminous can be born. And I read then this passage from the poet Rilke where he writes about being a poet which means "not numbering or counting but ripening like a tree which doesn't force its sap and stands confidently in the storms of Winter, not afraid that Summer may not come. It does come, it always comes." And in these times there's a story that I like to tell—and the story again is, storytelling for me is my own kind of poetry at best—of A.T. Ariyaratne, who is the most successful community activist in Asia that I know of and he lives in Sri Lanka and was a school teacher years ago and took his rich students out to the poorest villages and made a bond between the two, and started an organization called Sarvodaya which has now spread to one third of the population of the country, the poorest third, to build roads, schools, dig wells, not in order to build roads, schools, dig wells, but in order to build community and love between people and the character of the country. Sri Lanka's been in a terrible civil war for the last eighteen years. Several years ago the Norwegians brokered a peace treaty, which is fragile now, and after it was brokered Ari called his followers together to the temple, the great temple at Anaradhapura which is one of the oldest temples in Sri Lanka, nearly two thousand years old. And 650,000 people showed up in a country of only 17, 18 million people, a huge crowd. And he stood up there and presented to them in a way what I would consider a poem. He presented, just in two pages, the Sarvodaya Peace Plan, and it was the Sarvodaya 500 year Peace Plan. He said, "The Buddha teaches that all things arise due to causes and conditions. Those who are foolish look at the current conditions, those who are wise look at the causes. If we look at our current war, we can see that it's taken 500 years to get into this struggle—400 years of British colonialism, 500 years of conflict between the Buddhists and the Hindus and the Muslims, 200 years of economic disparity between the rich and the poor parts of the island, and so it will take us 500 years to undo this. I propose ten years of a ceasefire, where we simply rebuild our roads and take care of the damage. I propose twenty-five years where we learn one another's languages, where we learn one another's cultures, where we school in one another's religions and understandings. I propose a fifty year plan to begin to right the economic injustice and have the richer areas help develop the poorer areas, and I propose that in one hundred years we have a council of elders that meets to see how we're doing and that we meet every hundred years for every 500 years to make sure that we succeed in our goal." And I, I heard this, and I just about wept, because it was the voice of an elder and visionary, it was the really the voice of a poet, of someone who can step back and not worry about the next election cycle or worry about their own small life, but look from the perspective of the cosmos and the common good, and the blessing of the many.

FOX: Well it seems that poets take a much longer view of human existence, as you say, rather than the next election, or the next meal. And yet, most of us are pretty short-term.

KORNFIELD: That's the mystery and the—what's a better word than beauty—the mystery and the, um, dazzle of it, that we're so fleeting and that at the same time we can know eternity. And that's what a poet speaks of, whether, whether it's the taste of a fresh cherry that I bring into San Quentin prison and place in the hand of a man who hasn't had a fresh cherry for twenty-seven years, or whether it's, yes, sitting at the edge of my daughter's bed after we've had some conflict when she was a teenager and she wept and falls asleep and then I sit and I look at her sleeping in her glorious innocence that she had since the day she was born and before and that she can never lose, especially in my eyes as a parent. And that's what we do as poets, and that's what poetry does, it awakens us.

FOX: But it seems to me also as poets, our being in touch with that innocence always remains, whether we are aware of it or not.

KORNFIELD: Mhm, mhm. My teacher called it the original mind, the original beauty, Buddha nature. Here's a passage for you, just to build on what we're saying. This is from Earl Shorris. "There are nine different words in Maya for the color blue in the comprehensive Porrua Spanish-Maya dictionary, but just three Spanish translations, leaving six butterflies that can be seen only by the Maya, proving beyond doubt that when a language dies, six butterflies disappear from the consciousness of the Earth." And part of the work of the poet is to let us see all nine shades of blue and all the butterflies.

FOX: We talked about Neruda and 400 people reciting the poem, and that taking place in his country. That would be less likely in the United States. We seem, as a nation, not to be too much into poetry. Is that—?

KORNFIELD: We're not so much as we should be. Period. And yet, some of our poetry we get through our music. I see the iPod generation walking around and some of the songs are mediocre, but some of them sparkle. Some of them tell truth; some of them open their eyes. And I think that we could have Bob Dylan, who is perhaps one of our Nerudas, come to a colosseum of 50,000, and 5,000 of them stand up and recite a song to him, recite a poem. So I don't think, we don't have the love that the Persians and the Iraqis and the Venezuelans might have for teaching and memorizing poetry but maybe it's there in our songs somewhat, and I hope it comes back in these other ways. It doesn't stop our poets. "In the Chernobyl Nuclear Accident," says Linda Hogan, "the wind told the story that was being suppressed by the government. It gave away the truth. It carried the story of danger to other countries. The wind was a poet, a prophet and a scientist." And there's some way in which poetry will continue because human beings will continue and something in us wants to give voice to the depths of our experience. You know, it may have its crescendos in a culture and its lulls but it's unstoppable.

FOX: What do we have to do to be more willing to express our truth instead of being afraid to do so?

KORNFIELD: I wish I knew. The only thing that I do know is that it's helped a great deal by a few individuals who do so. I think poetry, like love, is self-communicative. We catch some truth from another who is willing to stand up and speak it. So, here is this frail woman about my age in her sixties in house arrest in Burma, Aung San Suu Kyi. She's been there for almost fifteen years, unable to leave the country to go be at her husband's bedside as he died of cancer two years ago, or to be there for her son's graduation from Oxford. She could leave—the dictatorship said, you could leave, but you wouldn't be allowed back. And somehow, she said, I can't leave, I can't leave. Somehow the flame of her spirit and her very simple words—like Nelson Mandela's, coming out of Robben Island—the flame of her spirit is so strong that it gives heart to millions of other people and many of them speak the truth because she is there. And I don't think it's just her. I, we are so interdependent. I think it's the longing and love of all the people around her that made her happen and I think that it's her flame that keeps them, their spirit alive.

FOX: And yet when we have someone like Nelson Mandela, who after twenty-seven years of prison was president of the country for one term and said that he didn't want to set a precedent for personal power so he left office after one term and his successor, of course, took a second term—do you find that distressing?

KORNFIELD: I find it oh so human. [Fox laughs] It's the stuff of poetry. We learn a lesson or we have a noble moment and Ryokan, who was the most beloved of all Japanese poets, writes—this one I know by heart—he says, "Spring morning I hang my begging bowl by the side of the shrine to play with the children. Last year, a foolish monk. This year, no change." And there's some way in which the poem is never finished, or the poetry is never finished, and our humanity isn't finished, and when I think about how I might die, having been a contemplative and a Buddhist teacher and so forth, there are all these great death poems—the last moment, the Zen master crosses his legs and sits upright and with tremendous dignity and graciousness, pens a little poem. And I think, well, that would be a very cool way to die. But it might not be that way for me. I might be kicking my legs and saying, oh, and crying, "I don't want to die, I don't want to die." I don't know. And I think that the honesty about our humanity, and Thabo Mbeki's second term even though Nelson Mandela didn't take one, is part of what we have to wrestle with and it's part of what makes life actually interesting for us. But to know that Nelson Mandela could walk out of Robben Island twenty-seven years later with so much dignity and so much graciousness and be so well-spoken makes me proud to be a human being. . . and there are other things that don't. [Fox laughs]

FOX: What would you like to have happen in the rest of your life?

KORNFIELD: I'd like to be able to give something beautiful more to the world and to the people I love. Nothing else is really very interesting at this point. Creativity and generativity and passing it along is the most satisfying thing. I don't really want anything. I want to be able to give and bless and empower, and I see that, I mean I look at this pile of beautiful books of poetry on the floor here, and they're blessing us, they're empowering us, they're giving us their best in some way, and I hope I can do that for some more years, in different ways. I travel a lot because I love living in other cultures. and I've come to the point where I don't particularly want to travel unless I can do something while I travel. I'd like to go and be part of the project that's connected to Spirit Rock. It's helping in upper Burma bring medicine and build schools and hospices and things that they need. Or I'd like to go to the Middle East and help in a peace project that some friends of mine are doing. That's really what's alive for me. As long as I'm allowed to do it, and when I'm not allowed, I'll say it was a great ride. No regrets.

FOX: That's probably a good place to stop, but I have a few other questions. Five hundred years from now, with the peace plan for Sri Lanka or anything else, would you guess it would be different or is there going to be no change?

KORNFIELD: I'm very hopeful, even though I'm very, even though deeply dismayed at our current world circumstance. One of the great causes of hope for me is characterized by a book I read last year called *Bury the Chains*.

And *Bury the Chains* was written by Adam Hochschild. He also wrote *King Leopold's Ghost*. He was a founder of *Mother Jones* magazine and a fine writer. It's the story of a few men who were sitting in a tavern or sitting by the side of the road in England in the late1700's, contemplating the evil of slavery, and seeing that the whole British empire, even though the whole British empire, ran on the slave trade, as an economic underpinning, and imagining, envisioning that the empire could be run without slavery. And I can't remember the name of the key protagonist in it, I think it was Thomas Clarkson, who got together with a small group of Quakers who were against slavery, and they began a campaign—there were a dozen of them but particularly Clarkson, rode on horseback 30,000 miles around England for several decades, and doing so he brought a couple of ex-slaves who were really well-educated, well-dressed, articulate, who spoke of their experiences and so-forth, into the parlors and the living rooms of good English folk. And by the end of thirty years this small group had got the British legislature to pass a law outlawing slavery in the British empire. And one of the poetic moments of this story is that the Quakers who would not take their hats off to King George or to any king other than God, all took their hats off when Clarkson died in honor of what he had done for humanity. As I read that story, I see that we are limited only by our imagination. Yes, we will always have a shadow, yes, greed and fear and ignorance will be part of the dance, but there are ways we can do it much better, and we're just infants in that inner development. We've got a lot of outer development happening. And I think we can all sense the potential; every one of us can sense the potential for human beings living with more compassion, with more care for one another, with greater wisdom and less prejudice and racism and fear. We all know it's possible. So I'm actually hope—more than hopeful. I envision the possibility as being true for us.

FOX: Well, in our lifetimes, in the past sixty years, I think there have been in the United States enormous changes in consciousness about a number of issues including minorities, women—

KORNFIELD: Exactly—

FOX: All kinds of things that we took for granted fifty years ago—smoking, all kinds of things.

KORNFIELD: And I think we, we will come up with a better—to use a phrase that was used for an organization for a while—I think we will come up with a better game than war to solve problems. I see a tremendous possibility.

FOX: What's the appeal of war? Why do we do it?

KORNFIELD: Hmm. Maybe you could say, what's the appeal of power? That's one part of it.

FOX: Yes.

KORNFIELD: And there's a tremendous appeal to power.

FOX: Yes.

KORNFIELD: And it has all different parts to it, I mean if we look honestly, because each of us looks for power in our own way. I certainly have, do. Some of it's creative power to express and extend ourselves, some of it's power for security to keep ourselves safe, some of it's power over others for pleasure in some way. Some of the most primal and fundamental drives. And then if you read books like Robert Ardrey and *The Naked Ape*, well wait a second, there's Ardrey—maybe it was the *Territorial Imperative*—and Konrad Lorenz, *The Naked Ape*. You can feel the history of our fears and our needs to survive. But I read a wonderful counterpart to that recently. It came from a man named Robert Sapolsky who was part of a large conference in Washington D.C. on the transformation of consciousness and neuroscience with the Dalai Lama where I was also a speaker. Dr. Sapolsky is a professor at Stanford and a primatologist who, like Jane Goodall, spent twenty years in Africa working with both chimps and with bonobos. And the article that he wrote described their two cultures. The chimpanzee culture is a power-based, aggressive, patriarchal, a little bit Gangster-style culture, where young chimps that come in, "you follow the line or we mess with you," and Alpha males run things and so forth. It's very patriarchal. The bonobo society—maybe you can think of the hippies in their best year, the summer of love, or something like that—is based on much more egalitarian principles and sharing. It's a sexually free society where instead of solving relationships through power struggles, they're solved through mutual grooming and lots of sex and lots of a great kind of playfulness. So, it has a whole different way that it works and it's also more feminine and matriarchal in some ways than the chimp society. Those descriptions I knew; what was more interesting was that he cited some studies where in chimp societies the most aggressive males were taken out, or died off for various reasons, or they had contact with a more playful and cooperative society and they were able to learn that, and not only were they able to learn it but they were able to pass it on to successive generations. And he described in some detail how this happened. Now as humans, we have the same number of shared genes, probably 98 ½ percent, with bonobos as we do with chimps. So I found that a terribly promising story. Maybe we can learn to live more in the bonobo way. But the contradictions will still always be with us. I'm holding a translation of Constantine Cavafy, the great Greek poet, and his poem *Ithaca*. Just a few lines: "If you find her poor, Ithaca has not defrauded you. With the great wisdom you have gained and so much experience you must surely have understood by then what Ithaca really means. Ithaca has brought you the journey. . ." and there's this whole—you know the poem. And in some way I see the life of a poet as, as that. It's not that one accomplishes or gets, but that it's in the living of the journey. And the poems of the ages, these hundred and thousand year old poems, are really exchanging notes on the journey in the most beautiful way.

FOX: It seems to me that being a poet is more a state of being than what you write down on paper.

KORNFIELD: I like hearing that, it gets me off the hook a little bit. [laughing] And I do agree with it. When Martin Luther King said, "If a man sweeps streets for a living, he should sweep as Michelangelo painted, as Beethoven composed music, as Shakespeare wrote his poetry," that's his way of saying just what you're pointing to, that it is a way of life and a way of being. And sometimes we have reclusive poets, bless them, we have, oh, Wendell Berry on his farm—he's not so reclusive, but he's down there, the mad farmer, and I just praise, I bless him for being on his farm, and sometimes we have the poets who go into the middle of the fray.

FOX: Yes.

KORNFIELD: Here's that poem I wanted from Hafiz. "A poet is someone who can pour light into a cup, then raise it to nourish your beautiful, parched, holy mouth."

Li-Young Lee is the author of three critically acclaimed books of poetry, his most recent being *Book of My Nights* (BOA Editions, 2001). His earlier collections are *Rose* (BOA, 1986), winner of the Delmore Schwartz Memorial Award from New York University, *The City in Which I Love You* (1991), the 1990 Lamont Poetry Selection; and a memoir entitled *The Winged Seed: A Remembrance* (Simon and Schuster, 1995), which received an American Book Award from the Before Columbus Foundation. A new volume, *Behind My Eyes*, is forthcoming by W.W. Norton in January 2008. Lee's honors include fellowships from the National Endowment for the Arts, The Lannan Foundation, and the John Simon Guggenheim Memorial Foundation, as well as grants from the Illinois Arts Council, the Commonwealth of Pennsylvania, and the Pennsylvania Council on the Arts. In 1988 he received the Writer's Award from the Mrs. Giles Whiting Foundation.

Born in1957 of Chinese parents in Jakarta, Indonesia, Lee learned early about loss and exile. His great grandfather was China's first republican resident, and his father, a deeply religious Christian, was physician to Communist leader Mao Tse-Tung. After the establishment of the People's Republic of China in 1949, Lee's parents escaped to Indonesia. In 1959, his father, after spending a year as a political prisoner in President Sukarno's jails, fled Indonesia with his family to escape anti-Chinese sentiment. After a five-year trek through Hong Kong, Macau, and Japan, they settled in the United States in 1964.

Through the observation and translation of often unassuming and silent moments, the poetry of Li-Young Lee gives clear voice to the solemn and extraordinary beauty found within humanity. By employing hauntingly lyrical skill, and astute poetic awareness, Lee allows silence, sound, form, and spirit to emerge brilliantly onto the page. His poetry reveals a dialogue between the eternal and the temporal, and accentuates the joys and sorrows of family, home, loss, exile, and love. In "The City In Which I Love You," the central long poem in his second collection, Li-Young Lee asks, "Is prayer, then, the proper attitude/for the mind that longs to be freely blown,/but which gets snagged on the barb/called *world*, that/tooth-ache, the actual?" Anyone who has seen him read will add that Lee is also one of the finest poetry readers alive.

He lives in Chicago with his wife Donna, and their two sons.

# Li-Young Lee

March 10, 2003

FOX: Do you remember the first poem you ever wrote?

LEE: Yeah, I guess I do. It was, "Here is a fish, make nice dish," or something like that. I caught a little fish for my mother and I wrote that, I was just learning English, and I was just so amazed that words rhymed.

FOX: So your first poem was in English!

LEE: Right.

FOX: And how do you find writing in English? I assume it's not your first language.

LEE: No, it isn't. It's like my third language. But I keep forgetting languages. My first language is Bahasa Indonesian and I learned that from my nursemaid. My mother was absent a lot in the beginning because she was trying to get my father out of jail, and so after we left Indonesia I started learning Chinese and I lost all the Bahasa. Then I began to lose a lot of my Chinese when I was about fourteen so English became much more comfortable. I guess it's buried under there, I don't know. I don't know how that works, Alan, I don't know if you forget it, or is it a buried language?

FOX: It's probably different for different people. I assume you don't use the other languages now, or do you?

LEE: Oh, I do. My mother only speaks Chinese, so I only speak Chinese with her. And I had a brother who recently died and he didn't speak any English, so I used Chinese with him. But after he died, it dawned on me that the people that I use Chinese with, there's less and less of them. So I feel as if that language, my use of it, is getting less and less.

FOX: Have you written poetry in Chinese?

LEE: No, no, I used to write letters in Chinese to my mother. Up until college, I was still writing letters, but they got more and more elementary and so I don't even write, I can't even read, Chinese any more. But I was back in China about 10 years ago and within a week I was dreaming in Chinese. I was answering, my wife is Italian-American, and I was answering her in Chinese, so it must have been just natural for me. And I was suddenly able to read a little bit more every day, signs and things, so I think it's under there somewhere probably.

FOX: How is the process of writing poetry for you? Do you write every day, or when you feel like it, or what?

LEE: I don't know, Alan. I feel like I actually am on the job, I feel like I'm on twenty-four hours a day. I'm always listening for or trying to feel, just to get a sense of that field of mind that you're in when you write, when a poem happens, so I'm always feeling around for that. I'm doing that twenty-four hours a day, and I'm ready to put everything down to write the poem. I got up this morning about four because I thought there was something happening. I wanted to sleep in because I went to bed late last night, but I thought no, no, no, 'cause it doesn't always happen. So I got up and started writing—nothing came of it, a couple of lines. It's so haphazard for me. I don't have a system. I just feel like I'm doing it all the time. It's really inefficient, you know. I've tried to sit down and do it but it doesn't always work.

FOX: Do you have an idea of what tends to inspire you or the spark that starts the process?

LEE: I don't know, Alan. I've been thinking about it a lot. Lately I've been noticing that any situation I'm in, for instance, this interview—I'm aware, I'm more and more aware of the fact that so many things had to happen in order to make this meeting possible. Not only the phone calls and the invitation to the interview and my flying here in the airplane, so I think, well, somebody had to invent the airplane, right? And then I think, well, *RATTLE* had to have happened for this interview to happen which means, Stellasue, your life had to have a certain trajectory. Alan, your life had to have a certain trajectory to make all of this happen, right? And I think about the cab driver who took me to the airport and somebody—I just think it's almost too much to disentangle, the myriad things that have to happen to make any situation occur. So I came to the conclusion that everything makes everything happen and it dawned on me that that's the way a poem happens. So I don't know if there's a particular cause. But a poem somehow is a version of that condition. And I think that's part of the joy of reading poems. We read a poem, we start to notice how words refer to each other from the beginning of the poem to the end of the poem. There's this kind of manifold or myriad field of reference going on, of connections. So I don't know what it is that ever makes me write a poem, you know, the sound of a bird or the smell of leaf mold, my hand, the coffee I had or the coffee I didn't have or the ache in my left knee. There's just so much, so I suppose for me I can hardly tell what it is. That's part of the frustration for me too because I feel as if at any moment a poem could occur because that condition of *allness*, of *everythingness*, is occurring all the time. And so what is so special about when it yields itself or manifests itself in language? I don't know what that is, but I've been thinking about that. So I guess I don't know what inspires me, would be the answer.

FOX: Do you ever have an idea or a wish for what will happen to a poem, how it will be received, or what impact it might have?

LEE: I do, [pause] I suppose that something in me—I wish the poem would last, would last forever, but I don't know what I mean by that. I hope that it contributes to the, I don't know, the evolution of humanity, I hope it contributes to that. That sounds arrogant or claiming too much, doesn't it?

FOX: No, I wouldn't think so, if that's a wish. For me, I would have an idea of where I want it to go, what I want to have happen, perhaps unconsciously.

LEE: And I guess it's happened to me, Alan. You know, I feel as if reading poetry has helped me in my own evolving as a human being, so I want to return the favor?

FOX: When you read poetry, what touches you the most, what has the greatest impact on you?

LEE: I guess the doorway for me is the emotional doorway, if there's emotion in the poem, if it's authentic or authentic feeling. If there isn't that, the poem can be I think intellectually really wonderful, but I'm not interested. I can appreciate it, I can respect it, I can stand in awe of it even, but if I'm not stirred, I don't take it to my heart.

FOX: And what emotions do you like the best when you find them in a poem?

LEE: I don't know. Maybe, maybe it's not even emotions. Now I'm thinking a little more, a little harder about that. Maybe what it is, what I really love when I read a poem is the visceral experience of a sense of wholeness, that somehow the poem I've encountered is a reflection of a psychic wholeness, that when I'm reading the poem the poem is—it dawns on me, Alan, that every poem is a portrait of a speaker, right? So if my experience of that speaker is a kind of integrated, a deeply integrated but at the same time a highly differentiated psyche—I'll use that word, I'm not sure what I mean by that—but then I get a real sense of satisfaction, a sense somehow that in the poem the emotional function is well informed of the intellectual function and the intellectual function is informed of the emotional function and they are both informed of the erotic function and the erotic function is informed of the spiritual function. Sometimes I have a problem when I read a poem that's just the mental function, it seems uninformed of the physical functions or the emotional functions or the spiritual functions. Or even a poem that is just the spiritual function working overtime but uninformed of the other functions. So what I love is a poem that somehow posits, proposes, a condition of wholeness.

FOX: When you read poetry, do you find the emotional part often when you read, or is it rare?

LEE: I think it's very rare. I would say, I can't tell, Alan, if it's rare because it's really difficult, right? It's difficult. Or whether for the most part it's disallowed, because we don't allow it, won't allow it into our lives. I don't know, it may be disallowed in the culture at large, and I feel maybe it's not allowed in poetry, either, or we don't trust it or something like that. But maybe we haven't evolved enough. Maybe our emotional function is retarded.

FOX: Maybe poetry is an acceptable way of conveying emotions.

LEE: Yeah, but then you think about all the poets who we consider great, Eliot or Pound, I don't think they're particularly emotional poets. I see on your shelf there, Yehuda Amichai. I love him because there's a lot of emotion in those poems, it seems to me. And so I think that's really rare, and it's emotion that feels to me that it's not uninformed, that it's of his intellect, but the intellect is very informed of the emotions, and they're both informed of their temporality and their eternity. Amichai, I would say, is a poet that really gives me that. But I think that's rare in the English language.

FOX: I tend to agree with you because when we read submissions to *Rattle*, one rule I have is if when I read the poem if I'm almost in tears [Lee agrees] or if I'm laughing, it's in. And that doesn't happen too often, either one.

LEE: Right, right. Why do think that is, Alan?

FOX: I think we look for emotional connection and I think poetry is a way of doing that. . .

LEE: But then why are the people who are writing not doing that?

FOX: Ah! I think you've put your finger on it. I think it's tough to do.

LEE: Yeah, it's tough to do.

FOX: Do you find that you're inhibited in what you write? Do you ever censor, because you might reveal too much of yourself? Is that an issue for you?

LEE: No. Maybe it is an issue, but it's kind of a backward issue because what I'm trying to do is reveal more and more. And I do recognize that there's something inside of me that resists it. For instance, Stellasue has given me this new strategy into a poem. But I do find that there's something that resists being revealed, so for me the problem isn't that I'm revealing too much and I'm trying not to—no, the problem for me is that I'm trying to know myself, to self-reveal, to uncover. In this way I think I feel poetry is apocalyptic, uncovering, as opposed to ecliptic which is covering, right? And in the same way I find that poetry is disillusioning in the best way—it frees us of our illusions. But there must be something inside of me that resists disillusionment, that wants to hold onto all my illusions, all my narrow definitions of what myself might be.

FOX: What have you written which is successful in conveying emotion in your own work?

LEE: I wrote something just recently I feel as if that has a lot of emotion in it, but I can't tell, I haven't shown it to anybody yet, but I feel like it has a lot of emotion.

FOX: Do you typically show your work to anybody before you send it off for publication?

LEE: Well, my editor, but no, I don't have much of a, which is a real problem, I think, for me, and a handicap, maybe. I wish I had some readers—I show it to my wife when I'm ready to show it to her. . .

FOX: Is she helpful?

LEE: She's very helpful because she has a really good bullshit detector. I just read something to her over the phone. She said, "No, no, no, no, Li-Young, you don't mean that." [Fox laughs loudly] And I tried to convince her, you know, I'm so defensive. [more laughter from Fox] I tried to convince her, "I did mean it." And she said, "Now think about that. Did you really mean that?" I thought, all right, I didn't mean it. It was just, it was a device or something. So, yes, she's tough, she doesn't mince any words, she doesn't pull any punches, [laughs] so that's tough.

FOX: Is that a good thing for you as a writer?

LEE: I think it's good. I think it is good to have somebody who's not a writer. She comes from a coal mining background, and she doesn't particularly value literature. She values a hundred other things, but not literature. But I think it's also valuable to have fellow poets reading which at the moment I don't have.

FOX: It's an interesting issue, the impulse to reveal and yet the contrary impulse to protect.

LEE: I don't know what that's about. I thought about this a little bit and it dawns on me that it's part of the whole difficulty in writing. I feel when I'm sitting in front of an empty page, part of my problem is I feel like the poem could start anywhere. So there I am sitting in front of an empty page and I feel like the page is almost a symbol of pure potential. I could start with the window or the bird or my feet or my shoes or my socks or my nose, my thumb, anywhere, I could start anywhere. But the minute I put the pencil down on the paper, the minute I start it, then the potential closes down. Then it starts to be about this particular poem. And even though you try to move that poem into a kind of spaciousness, you try to say as much as possible, but even so, it does feel as you're closing down into this particular poem. And so for me, the experience of writing one poem is saying goodbye to the 999 other poems that want to get written. So sometimes I do have the sense as if I'm like a little doorway and there are 10,000 poems that want to get through. So for me to pick one poem is to say goodbye to 9,999 other poems and that grief just makes me crazy, because I have to pick one. And so sometimes, it doesn't make sense, because what I do is end up closing the door and saying "no" to all of them. It's weird, right? I don't know. So it's a kind of neurosis. I'm probably talking about my own neurosis here, you know [laughs]. But I don't know. There's a kind of loss. The whole thing about revealing is so interesting to me because I do believe that the practice of poetry is a viable path to self-knowledge. If we study the things that human beings have made, it's a way to study human beings, right? So then a poem is a product of the psyche, and it's a way to study the psyche. So it seems to me that it's a way that we can know ourselves better, right? When we write the poem, we can say, well, here's where I am today. So it's a form of divination. So we don't even need to do the *I Ching* to find out what's going on, we can just write a poem and say, this is where I am.

FOX: What reward do you get from writing poetry?

LEE: For me it would be the experience of the *all,* which is so strange to me because it seems to me that that's our perennial condition, that's we're always in the *all.* I don't know why we need a piece of art or the writing of poem to remind us. Because when you're in that state, if you're writing the poem, that trance state, it's almost as you're omniscient, you know things you didn't know you knew, and you see connections you didn't think were there. And that condition of seeing all those myriad connections at once, I guess it's just that experience of the *all.*

FOX: How would you compare poetry as an art form with other art forms, music or sculpture or painting?

LEE: I think of poetry as a score for the human voice, so I guess the voice is ultimately the thing you're scoring. How does it differ? I'm not sure it's different. I think all art forms are revelatory. All art forms reveal us to ourselves so all art forms are viable paths to self-knowledge, to knowledge of our, well, I'll use this word—primordial condition—our original condition which is our interconnectedness and interpenetratingness with everything else. So I guess all art forms lead us to that.

FOX: Do you do many poetry readings?

LEE: I've been doing a lot lately, well, for the last ten years I guess I've been doing a lot.

FOX: Is that something you enjoy?

LEE: I do, I do enjoy it when I remember what it is I'm trying, or what I would like to do. Because it seems to me that the most a poetry reading can be is the imparting of a kind of inner richness. I think the worst, the least it can be, and I hate it when it becomes that, is when—I guess this is what I feel—if I do a reading and the audience feels, boy, he's really smart, or he's really deep, or he's really interesting, I feel like I've failed. But if I do a reading and the audience goes home and thinks, wow, human inner life is really rich, my inner solitude is really spacious, and maybe a second or even a third or fourth thought, they think, hey, he's pretty good, then I succeeded. If that's the first thought, that they are rich or that the quality of their listening is really spacious and rich, then I feel that it's a successful reading. Again, I'm just returning the favor, because I've gone to readings where that's exactly what I felt after hearing the reading I feel like, wow, I felt an inner richness or richness about life, or just being alive, and only almost as an afterthought I think, wow, that person gave that feeling to me. God bless him, or her. But a lot of times when I'm listening, and I can't tell whether this is my problem as a listener or the poet's problem when I'm listening, and I feel, boy, that person's really smart, or that person really knows how to use language. I feel as if psychic energy has been drained from me but not given back. Then I feel that's not different from TV. I mean, the TV just drains your psychic energy and doesn't give you anything back. I think real art, somehow, the more psychic energy you put into it the more you get back. It's weird. You get it back tenfold.

FOX: Well, that is interesting because to me you're saying that showing off is not helpful but self-revelation on a deep level, true level, is.

LEE: That's exactly how I would say it. That something else is going on. It's not about a bunch of people listening to somebody else or looking at somebody else. I think something deeper is going on. If the poet is a great poet, I don't know, I never heard Frost read but I would suppose, or Emily Dickinson, but I would suppose if I heard them read that they would reveal me to me, as opposed to revealing themselves to me. Somehow by revealing themselves to me I have been revealed to myself.

FOX: I would think that's one of the most important benefits of poetry, to allow the reader to reveal him or herself to him or herself.

LEE: Right, yeah, so it's a real mysterious and wonderful thing that happens between the reader and the poem. Yeah.

FOX: Do you find that audiences differ a great deal at your readings?

LEE: They do, in terms of age or gender or class or race, but ultimately I'm trying to hit something that is the same. We're all mortal human beings, part spirit, part matter, dying and eternal, male and female, dark and light, good and bad, so I guess I'm trying not to pay too much attention to the surface quality of the audience. I'm just trying to pay attention to the heart that's afraid, that's jubilant, sad, happy, clapping, singing, grieving. It seems to me that it's all the same heart. It's inflected differently with races and gender, but I never try to tailor the reading, and that could be my downfall, too.

FOX: How do you mean?

LEE: I don't know, I just read to a high school audience and maybe, I walked in there thinking, well, I don't care, they're eighteen or seventeen or sixteen, they're human beings and I'm a human being, so there must be some common ground here, but maybe I was wrong. They were so quiet I thought maybe, did they all go to sleep, man, or what? So I can't tell whether, or maybe they were just listening well. I don't know. But maybe I should have tailored it a little more to like a seventeen-year-old, eighteen-year-old audience instead of trying to. . . I don't know, Alan, I really don't know, but that doesn't seem fruitful to me. That seems like a bankrupt thing to do, to try to guess your audience. I believe in a universal, or in a common ground.

FOX: Do you ever teach writing?

LEE: I tried that. I tried it a number of times, just enough times to come to the conclusion I can't do it. It's like sainthood. I don't even have a little bit of a saint in me. [Fox laughs] You go in, you open a vein and sometimes the student catches it in a bucket or a cup or a thimble or they don't catch it at all and you're bleeding all over the floor. But that's what it felt like to me. It felt like, I don't know, it is an incredible service that one is doing and I wasn't, what am I admitting? That I'm too stingy of spirit to do it? But that's can't be true, because not everybody is meant to be a teacher, right?

FOX: Absolutely, but look at it from the other point of view. What has helped you the most in terms of learning from others?

LEE: I think being around poets helped me a lot. Being around them, seeing how they function in the world. For the most part, I would say how they somehow embody the condition of that *all* in a world that isn't completely friendly to that condition. So the poets that I have always loved, who are living poets that I've loved and been around their presence, their presence has taught me so much about poetry. They way they react to things, the way they see things, they way they are.

FOX: Who are some of your favorite poets?

LEE: I guess ones that come to mind, Gerald Stern, Philip Levine, Galway Kinnell, John Logan, Hayden Carruth, there are so many of them. Emily Dickinson, Lucille Clifton, Robert Bly, Robert Frost, Lee Bai, Du Fu, Jack Gilbert, Linda Gregg, Michael Palmer, Allen Grossman, boy, we're living in such a good time. There are so many great poets. I think we're living in a really special time. There are more and more poets. Somebody told that there are more poets now in North America than there ever has been in the whole world. And I thought, wow, that's a lot. That's really wonderful.

FOX: Do you find that there are cultural differences in the writing or response to poetry in the United States in comparison with other cultures, other countries?

LEE: I was in Indonesia and I saw this crazy poet. Boy, their idea of a poetry reading was very different than our idea. He had an ax hanging from the ceiling of this place we were in and the ax was swinging back and forth, just missing him. He was ducking and he was chanting and shouting these poems.

And I thought, wow, that is like nothing I've ever seen. It was an ax head, it wasn't the ax, and it would sometimes stop and he would swing it again and it was just swinging around. He was drinking, had a bottle of beer that he broke, and he was lacerating himself with the broken bottle, and chanting poems, and he was in some sort of weird trance. I couldn't tell whether it was theatrics or real, but the other people seemed to me like they were in this trance with him, they were really into it, and shouting, and clapping, and responding gutturally, grunting when he was, and so I thought that was kind of interesting. But there must be some sort of cultural background for that, right? If we did that in this country, it would be just . . . sensationalism?

FOX: Probably.

LEE: So I guess it's just different, and I've noticed in Indonesia the kind of possessed quality of poetry had not gone out of favor yet. I think maybe in North America or in Eurocentric countries we are suspicious of that, if somebody believes that poetry is a form of possession by higher powers. I happen to believe that it's the *all* speaking through the singular *one* so I'm all into that.

FOX: Do you think that over the past twenty or thirty or forty years poetry in the United States has become more popular, less popular?

LEE: I think it's more popular. There are more poets writing, more books published, more magazines, more MFA programs. I guess there might be a downside, and I sometimes think the downside could be when we forget that it's ultimately about spirit, or it's ultimately about soul, and we think it's about other things. The upside would be it's a sign of our evolution as human beings. In my most hopeful moments, I think it could be that it's ultimately a sign of our evolving.

FOX: Do you think that writing of poetry can be taught?

LEE: Taught? I suppose. I hope so. I feel as if I'm teaching myself. Can it be taught? Maybe, not taught from the outside. It can be taught, I think, as a road to the interior. I think it can be taught that way, but I don't think it can be taught like this writing scheme or this meter, or something like that.

FOX: What suggestions do you have for a new poetry writer?

LEE: Boy, I feel like a new poetry writer, Alan, so I don't know. I guess, just keep doing it, believe in yourself, remind yourself. It's the deepest thing you're probably doing. Well, that's not true. I mean, there are deeper things, such as raising children. Just remind yourself of that and keep believing in what you're doing.

FOX: Do you like to hang out with poets?

LEE: I do. Some of the poets I mentioned, I love being in their presence. They always teach me to be more expansive, more welcoming, more accepting, compassionate. Maybe I've been lucky because I've heard the other thing, too. I've heard poets are terrible, they're stingy and they're self-aggrandizing, but that hasn't been my experience. The poets I've known have all been extremely capacious in their emotional range, in their acceptance, in what they love and what they'll tolerate. Now those are the poets I've known, maybe I'm just lucky. So I love being around them, but I don't get to be around them all the time because of my conditions of work and family and where I'm at. There aren't that many in Chicago.

FOX: You mentioned compassion. What's the role of compassion in poetry?

LEE: I'm almost embarrassed to talk about this stuff because it's so murky. So I can't even account for it. I feel as if it weren't for poetry I would be a worse human being than I am even right now. I know I'm pretty bad in so many ways, but I can remember the day when I discovered not just reading poetry, the idea of writing it—reading it I appreciated it and this and that—but the moment I started writing it I started to think, well, wait a minute, I have to change. In order to write these poems that I love so much, in order to write like, for instance, Emily Dickinson, I thought I'd have to change, because I don't think what she's doing is a technical issue at all, I think it's about her being. [Fox murmurs agreement] And for me to write like that, I would have to get to that place, that complete openness and self-acceptance and self-forgiveness that's going on. I know there's a lot of pain in those poems but she's willing to forgive what she's doing in those poems, that is, be irrational, to defy probability, all that stuff. I never thought for a second it was some sort of technical device she was doing. I thought, well, okay, I'd have to be that, how do I be that, how do I get there? Or when I read a Gerard Manley Hopkins poem, I would think, that sort of appreciation for existence? I don't think that's a technical device. I think, how do I reach that place in order to write like that? In order to earn the authority to say that? So I thought, I have to change.

FOX: Wonderful insight. So what did you do when you had this realization?

LEE: I don't know. I just started thinking about why. It made me more self-reflective, noticing how I'm not consistent with what it is I'm saying or whether somehow my saying, the poems somehow live ahead of me because they're a paradigm for what I want to be, they're a paradigm for the consciousness or the love or the compassion or the tenderness that I want to embody. If I read a Roethke poem, the tenderness he has for the natural world, I feel like I would have to ask myself, well, how do I get to that place, to be that tender? Unless I believe, which would really just feel nauseating to me to think, well, how do I affect that device? I'm not interested in that. I'm interested in how do I make my heart like that. But see, and I know Roethke was a real asshole, that's what I've heard, I don't know. Or John Logan, I was just reading his poems, and I know a lot of people think he's sentimental and overwrought—I don't. I feel he's tender and I think he's a master of the line. I just ask myself, how do I get to that place, to be able to say those things with authority. And I don't know how. So I guess maybe making the poem is self-making. But I think Yeats said that. He said, "I'm not making the poem only, I'm making myself."

FOX: That's a very interesting way of looking at it. I think that, for myself, when I was young I wanted to fake it better, have something—I remember a speech in high school and my instructor said, "Why'd you write this speech? It's not to entertain, it's not to educate, it seems to me you wrote something just to impress people, and it's hollow." I think that to be a really good writer you have to access yourself in a true way.

LEE: Yes. I think ultimately, Alan, what I've been trying to say so clumsily for this past hour is I don't think the poem or the poetry is the final opus. I don't think the work is the poem or book of poems or the novel or the painting. I think it's the self and that the making of the art is a way toward that total presence that one is trying to achieve. And how do you do that? You can't just go through the world and try to be. I think art is a viable path toward total presence.

FOX: Yes.

LEE: That took, what, three seconds to say. I should have said it in the beginning. I guess that's what I feel, so that the total presence is the grail. The poem is not the grail. The poem is a kind of divination. You write a poem and you look it and you go, wow, I'm really dark today. And you say, why? And you look and you go, that's a really incomplete unfair view of existence. And then you realize, oh, well then, you have to work through something. So I look at the poem as a kind of looking into the mirror. How do I look today? How does my soul look today? But then, of course, you have to have some sort of ideal as to what a total poem that manifests total presence, what that would look like. And I think we do have models of that.

FOX: Such as?

LEE: I would say certain great poems by Robert Frost, like "Directive," "West Running Brook"—boy, that poem just breaks my heart every time I read it. That poem, "West Running Brook," is just amazing. The need of being versed in country things, poems like that that give you feeling of, an experience of total presence. Or even in Neruda's poems, in "Residence on Earth," even in their translations, somehow the presence gets translated. So for me it's about presence. And so the work is not even the poem, the work is the self, without making too many claims on poetry.

FOX: I think, poetry is—you used a good word—the mysterious.

LEE: It really is.

FOX: The process, the result, it's very mysterious. I think it calls upon the poet to really look at himself or herself.

LEE: Yes, and I think it's ultimately a kind of alchemy, Alan, because I've been thinking that, even a metaphor, we could think of it as a literary device—that's just so bankrupt to me, when I think about it that way. I literally feel when I think of it as a literary device, it just feels nauseating to me. But when I realize that ultimately what a metaphor does is it marries two seemingly incompatible psychic contents. It marries them in an image that's a metaphor, so it's alchemical, right? You're trying to happily integrate parts of your psyche that resist integration, maybe it's feeling and thinking, but then you find an image and image is like a perfect marriage of thinking and feeling, right? Whereas a statement would be all thinking. Do you know what I mean? But an image or a metaphor is that composite of thinking, feeling, everything married together. So it's ultimately alchemical and I think that it's good for us to do that with our own psychic energies, to marry them, to make them admit each other, to encounter each other, to integrate each other.

FOX: Why do you write poetry instead of novels or short stories or something else?

LEE: I have this theory, Alan. I notice, for instance, a poem is the scored human voice. Voice is speech and all speech is done with the exhaled breath. You can't inhale and speak so you have to breathe out. Unfortunately, or fortunately, the exhaled breath is the dying breath. When we breathe in, our bodies are full of life, our muscles have real tone, our blood is full of oxygen, our bones actually get very compacted, they actually get harder. There's some proof for this, and we feel full of life and very comfortable. And when we exhale, our bones get softer, our muscles lose their tone and it's the dying breath. Now when we speak, we're using that dying breath, so I think that gives writing a particularly tragic undertone, overtone, what's the difference? What is undertone and overtone? Let me just use *tragic color*. Because what you're doing is you're using the dying breath, you're inflecting or figuring your dying breath. The interesting part, though, is meaning gets born. The more you speak, the more meaning gets revealed so that meaning grows in opposite ratio to the vitality of the dying breath. So as meaning gets bigger, the breath gets less and less. Which seems to me a paradigm of life—that as we die the meaning of our lives gets born, and that seems tragic to me. There's something melancholy about that thought, that meaning can't even get made unless I expend the breath, right?

FOX: Unless you die.

LEE: Right. And so part of that is, I think, because one feels so sharply that one is engaging in one's own death, one's own dying, when you're scoring the human speech, you try to ransom that breath, you try to make it count as much as possible by packing it with as much psychic content as possible. The language that most approaches that state is poetry. A sentence of poetry is more packed than any other form of speech, I think, with psychic content, emotional content, intellectual content, spiritual content, visceral content, because I think more than with any other form of speech, you're more aware of the fact that I have to spend this breath to give birth to meaning. Robert

Frost knew that. He said, "Well spent is kept." Right? So you get to keep the meaning, but you have to spend the breath. Did that make any sense, Alan?

FOX: I think so.

LEE: I've been thinking about it and trying to find a clear way to articulate that.

FOX: I think what you're doing now is like the process of writing a poem.

LEE: I'm also thinking there's all these weird trajectories of force that go on when we write a line of speech or a sentence of speech because while vitality decreases meaning gets born and yet potential decreases, right? Because we go from a state of, the beginning of the line is pure potential, before you even put a word down you're in a state of pure potential, but as the line proceeds, you close down, the potential is closed down. But then the poem keeps bringing your hand or your thinking back to the beginning of the line so it enacts this desire to return to pure potential all the time. Does this make sense, Stellasue, to you? You're actually enacting in the writing of a poem the deepest laws that govern the universe. I don't know why that should be a surprise, because ultimately if a poem is a paradigm of psyche and if psyche is a paradigm of cosmos, well then, it's obvious, it would be that a poem would be a paradigm of the *all,* that seems obvious—so why is every time I think about it, it seems surprising or novel? I don't know why that would be. So I think one writes poems because of that. You're trying to ransom that dying breath. You just can't stand the thought of death, so you try to pack everything in as much as possible.

FOX: Would that have anything to do with the reason why many people have an aversion to poetry . . .

LEE: Yes! Of course! They can't stand that density, the total presence. It is too much. Why is it too much?

FOX: Ah.

LEE: I think this is a weird time we're living in, Alan, because I've noticed, for instance, people's reactions to certain words. We're living in a time where the word "sincere" and I didn't know this, is suddenly a bad thing. I don't get it. I heard a poet say to me, "Oh, I hate sincerity." And I thought, oh, what do you like? Insincerity? I don't get it. [Fox laughs] What do they mean by that? And then I was talking to a poet and I said to her, "Well, for me, poetry is a form is disillusionment, right? It frees you of your illusions in order to uncover the condition of the *all* which we are constantly in the midst of." And she said, "Well, I don't like to be disillusioned." Why? You want to be illusioned?" [Fox laughs loudly] I mean, Hollywood gives us illusions. *People Magazine* gives us illusions. TV gives us illusions. But I think art gives us reality. And the reality that's uncovered is so rich. Maybe that's what it is—it's not only rich and beautiful but it's terrifying, too. Because it's so vast, it's so limitless and so overwhelming, it's overwhelming. So maybe we can't stand abundance. We can't stand abundance and so we keep making models of scarcity. I feel as if we keep living by models of scarcity. And I feel like somehow horizontal models are all based on scarcity. But I think vertical models are based on abundance. And maybe we can't stand abundance. We can't stand the fact that ultimately this condition of the *allness* is what is our real condition. And so we'd rather live, we don't want to be disillusioned. I want to be disillusioned. When I first read the poets that I love, I thought, wow, you mean, this is real existence, this is somebody speaking truthfully about my own experience of the *all*. And I just don't want to live in illusion. And yet I'm my own worst enemy. I do recognize that I keep creating little illusions I can function inside of.

FOX: How would you say your work has evolved in the past ten or twenty years?

LEE: Well, I hope it's gotten better, deeper, truer.

FOX: What would you consider to be better?

LEE: [pausing] Fuller, fuller, more, the word that comes to mind is "naked," less, less dressing, more the thing, the true speaking directly, what it is, is exactly my experience, less dressing, fuller, more differentiated and at the same time integrating more psychic contents. I hope the presence of the poems, the presence that those poems impart is fuller, deeper.

FOX: And what would you like your work to be remembered for?

LEE: Oh, man, I don't know, just, I don't know. I just want to write a good poem.

FOX: Well, I think that's a good spot to end at.

LEE: I think I was rambling a lot, Alan, all over the place. I don't know what I was . . .

FOX: It was very interesting.

LEE: Okay. I hope it wasn't too weird, too [lost in Fox's laughter]. . .

PHILIP LEVINE was born in Detroit, Michigan, in 1928. He is the author of sixteen books of poetry, most recently *Breath* (Alfred A. Knopf, 2004). His other poetry collections include *The Mercy* (1999); *The Simple Truth* (1994), which won the Pulitzer Prize; *What Work Is* (1991), which won the National Book Award; *New Selected Poems* (1991); *Ashes: Poems New and Old* (1979), which received the National Book Critics Circle Award and the first American Book Award for Poetry; *7 Years From Somewhere* (1979), which won the National Book Critics Circle Award; and *The Names of the Lost* (1975), which won the Lenore Marshall Poetry Prize.

Levine has also published a collection of essays, *The Bread of Time: Toward an Autobiography* (1994), edited *The Essential Keats* (1987), and co-edited and translated two books: *Off the Map: Selected Poems of Gloria Fuertes* (with Ada Long, 1984) and *Tarumba: The Selected Poems of Jaime Sabines* (with Ernesto Trejo, 1979).

Levine has received the Ruth Lilly Poetry Prize, the Harriet Monroe Memorial Prize from *Poetry*, the Frank O'Hara Prize, and two Guggenheim Foundation fellowships. For two years he served as chair of the Literature Panel of the National Endowment for the Arts, and he was elected a Chancellor of The Academy of American Poets in 2000. He lives in New York City and Fresno, California, and teaches at New York University.

# Philip Levine

June 20, 1998

FOX: What factor has been most influential on your writing?

LEVINE: I think that the thing that influenced me most was, curiously enough, the work I did as a young guy in Detroit. I started doing industrial work when I was very young. It was wartime Detroit; anybody could get a job. And at the time I didn't know that this was not what I was going to be doing with my life. I hoped it wasn't going to be because I didn't like it. But I met a lot of extraordinary people doing that kind of work, the kind of people I don't meet when I teach at the University of North Carolina or Vanderbilt or Princeton or Brown or Columbia. And one of the things that struck me then was that they were not in our literature. I couldn't even find them in the movies. We didn't have television back then. Their lives just seemed ignored. And yet they were the people who really were building America, or tearing it down, however you look at it. And I thought, what an opportunity to transform these people or some aspect of them, to memorialize them, to grab them before they faded into their mediocrity, which some of them did, but I knew some of them when they were young. I also knew their sadness and the sense of isolation and alienation. A lot of them were southerners, Black and white, and a lot of them couldn't make much sense of Detroit, which was then not the city it is now. It was a very thriving, busy, rich city during the war with so much industry going on. I loved it, I loved the city. It was a kind of carnival to me.

FOX: Do you regard your work as political in any way?

LEVINE: Yeah, in the way that Orwell would probably, if he read it and liked it, that it is a record of lives that a lot of people would just as soon weren't looked very carefully at, because they represent a critique of capitalism. To see people of promise going under year after year is a very painful thing and to talk about it is, in a way, a political act. Also to rescue these people, which is my hope, to rescue them from anonymity and make them appear as human as they were. I have some sort of faith that if readers see that this guy doing this sort of work is actually quite an extraordinary person, that he or she, the reader, might say he or she deserves more, she deserves better, her kids deserve better. So, yeah, in that sense, I feel an obligation to break down stereotypes and to present actual occurrences and move people about these lives that they'd just as soon not be moved about.

FOX: Some readers find a significant difference between academic poetry as compared with the poetry of the streets. Do you see a distinction?

LEVINE: Yeah, I see a distinction. I remember once in class I used a curious phrase. I said, "This is a real indoor poem." The class all looked at me, and I said, "It's an indoor poem. It's written by the light of the library. It's all about Wittgenstein or somebody like that. I mean, it derives its impulse, its energy, its inspiration, from books, it never had to go out and meet anybody to be this poem." I said, "How about a little outdoor poetry? How about getting out there and sort of meeting other people?" So I see certain poetry today as very academic, that its sources are literary and its impulse is to comment on the literary and to be taken back into that literary fold. I don't see William Carlos Williams as a poet like that. He was an extremely well-read man, too. To a degree I see Stevens that way, and I think that's why they are the two great forces in American poetry right now, the Williams side which also has a great allegiance to Whitman which is a poetry that wants to be born out of daily life and how people actually live. And then I see a much more elegant poetry born of Stevens.

I read a long poem by someone I won't name; it since got published in a book. It was a poem in several parts. For example, one part was about a bad romance with a woman who was a heroin addict. Another part was about a certain wandering minstrel type, a guitarist who sang in cafes and was out to meet a woman of means; these are young people. And there were writers and painters and people like that. And the guy gave me the poem and asked me what I thought of it. And I said, "I'd like to see a plumber in here, I really would. I'd love to see a plumber, or maybe an out-of-work carpenter, somebody sitting on his back porch and thinking, 'Oh shit, I deserve better than this.'" It seemed to me that all of the characters were literary clichés or cinematic clichés.

FOX: What you have been talking about seems to involve teaching. What role does teaching play in your life?

LEVINE: It's the way I've lived. I mean, it's how I could afford to eat and raise three kids. The first couple of years of teaching I felt were a kind of cruel punishment from the Creator, but I fell in love with it. I really got to like teaching, as long as I didn't have to do too much. Now this school here, Fresno State, where I did a lot of teaching, was really a pretty second-rate school. I may be being kind to it when I call it second-rate. It depends on how many rates we have here now. I have also taught at places like Princeton and Brown, Columbia and U.C. Berkeley, but the students I got here were fantastic, the reasons being, one, is that these kids could learn. They were not horrified or offended by the notion that they weren't writing well. They didn't expect to do things [snap of fingers] like that. When I taught at Princeton, everything they had done in an academic setting they had done efficiently and very well; why wouldn't they do this well? Well, it's hard to learn how to write poetry. And when I brought that news to them, they were outraged. They were really angry. And my attitude became screw you. "I don't give a shit whether you're angry. They didn't hire me to make friends with you-they hired me to try to teach you how to write poetry and you're not doing it. Goddammit, you think just because you described your grandfather gardening that that's some kind of miracle."

I remember the whole class turning against me and saying, "But the grandfather is sixty-seven years old and he's still gardening." I said, "I don't give a shit, my grandmother's eighty-something and she's still working. That's not a miracle. Poetry is language, and the language here is clumsy. You haven't got three words here that are happy to be in the same line." Also, they didn't have anything to write about. They wrote about their ski trips. I'm not kidding you. We'd have the Easter break, we'd come back and they'd all have gone skiing and I'd get all these poems about skiing. I said "this is silliness," and so I taught there one semester and that was enough. I never wanted to go back. The students at Fresno State work for a living. Not every semester were they terrific, but I'd get a student who was really good and knew poetry and knew him or herself as a valid human being and therefore knew that what happened to him or her was of some significance. You just needed one person like that in the class and the others would say, "Oh, I don't have to write about the difference between time and eternity, I can write about what it's like to work in a drugstore, or what guys say to girls in their cars." They could write about how they can't get along with their parents or who knows what. And so I got wonderful work out of them. I don't know how many I had that went on to become quite successful. But they were the best I ever had as undergraduates. I prefer teaching undergraduates.

FOX: Why do you prefer undergraduates?

LEVINE: Because they haven't discovered that poetry is a business and consequently they're interested in learning and they're interested in doing better and they haven't been bitten by some sort of bug that has to do with renown or fame or what have you. They also haven't learned how frustrating it can be, so they're still full of hope [laughs]. And you're teaching them to read at the same time you're teaching them to write or trying to teach them how to write. The one thing you know you're teaching them is how to read better.

Last fall I taught at the University of Houston. I taught a graduate class and it was incredible. These young people, I suppose the oldest was probably in her thirties, were really ferociously committed. I'd start talking about a poet they hadn't read and off they'd go to get the book and read it. They were nice to each other without lying. I mean, if they didn't like something, they'd say so, but they'd do it in a tactful way. It was the best graduate class I'd ever had. And I teach in the fall usually at NYU; I'll be there again this fall. I took one year's vacation from it this last fall. There again, students are good. They're serious. Most of them work in New York City and I really like their spirit.

FOX: You mentioned that the young people haven't realized about fame, etc. Of course, you've achieved a certain measure of fame. How has that affected you?

LEVINE: Not much. I remember when I won the National Book Award the second time. The first time I was sure I wasn't going to win so I didn't even go to the ceremony and I sent my son instead. They offered to fly me to the event, but they wouldn't tell me whether I won or lost. I was sure that *The Selected Poems of Stanley Kunitz* would win, so I said the hell with it. It was a fancy affair with a terrific dinner at, I think, the Plaza Hotel, so I called my son. I said, "You interested in going?" He said, "Yeah." He loves good wine. I said, "I'm told the wine will be terrific." "Great," he said. So he went. I said, "Stanley Kunitz is going to win, and he should win, and when he wins you go up and say, 'My father congratulates you.'"

So my kid sits there and drinks and eats and gets plastered and suddenly my name gets called and they push him up from the table. He's sitting with the people who publish me, and they push him up there. He goes up there; he doesn't know what to say. So finally he looks out at the audience, and it was Stanley who told me this, and he says, "My pop said Stanley would win," with this befuddled look. When he called me later that night after he sobered up, he said, "You'll never guess what." I'd forgotten the date. "You'll never guess what happened tonight." I said, "What happened?" He said, "You won the National Book Award." I said, "You're kidding." "No," he said "you've got a check for $10,000 and a sculpture by Louise Nevelson." I couldn't believe it. And I didn't deserve it. And then the second time I won, I was sure I was going to win and I did win. And that time I got the money again and sculpture by Joel Shapiro, which was very nice, and for a week I just thought I was hot stuff. The Pulitzer cost me a month, there was a month where I walked around feeling, boy, have I arrived, whoo, is this hot stuff.

I was living in Wilmington, North Carolina, in the spring, teaching there, just one course. I only teach one course at a time now that I'm in my advanced years, and anyway, people would recognize me. I was quite amazed. I mean, I'm in a restaurant and a waitress comes and hands me a little folded up note. I open it up and it says, 'I love your work'. I thought, wow, this is amazing. At another restaurant the waiter said, "I'm coming to hear you read next week." And in Fresno, of course, I'm recognized all the time. And in New York, occasionally, people will know who I am.

I remember being with Allen Ginsberg once in San Francisco. He had trouble walking down the street. I mean, everybody wanted his autograph, everybody wanted to talk to him, he was so recognizable. I don't know what you would do with that. I'm amazed that he was able to keep writing through that storm of renown. I know when Saul Bellow won the Nobel Prize, he said, "That's it, I'll never write again." Well, he was wrong; he did go on to write.

But, it's fun. My mom, who died recently, when I would get some sort of an award, she'd be just thrilled. And I would remind her always of a remark she made when I was twenty-three or twenty-four. She was very proud of the idea and very pleased with the idea that I'd be a poet, and she said, "Someday you'll be famous and I'll be your mother." I used to remind her, "You know, Ma, even if I ain't famous, you're going to be my mother. You're stuck with me, even if I go to jail."

FOX: Do you have any inkling about what more you have to say?

LEVINE: Yes and no. For example, I have written very little about romantic love. Whether I will take that on, I mean I have maybe four poems on the subject. I have only one poem about what was a powerful experience in my growing up which was anti-Semitism. I have only a single poem. I have no poem that really takes seriously the idea of growing up Jewish in America. And then there are a lot of people who have meant a great deal to me, who don't enter my poetry. I think that's the most singular thing that I'm aware of, that I have not found a way in poetry to present these people. I've written about some of them in prose, but I haven't found a way to write about them in poetry, and I wish I would. I want to find some sort of avenue into what they meant to me. Because they were real models of what I would call heroism. Sort of like Kierkegaard's knights of faith, they were people of immense goodness and generosity, who nobody but I seemed to realize were that valuable.

And I didn't merely meet them when I was very young, either. I met some of them in my thirties and forties. None of them were teachers in the literal sense; they were all my teachers in another sense. I hoped to learn from them. I think that's the thing that I most want to write about. Say romantic love, for example, if I didn't write about that, it wouldn't be a big deal. I mean the world is full of love poems, good, bad and terrible, but some of them are fabulous. So it isn't a subject that has been ignored. Whereas these people, if I don't write about them, they're not going to enter American poetry.

FOX: Do you find in your writing that you ever hold back for fear of offending the person you want to write about?

LEVINE: Yes, I do. I don't hold back so much as I create a mask. For example, I have four poems about sisters. I don't have any sisters. But I have had what I would have to describe as a relationship between a woman of either approximately my own age or a bit older in which I functioned as a brother. One of them is an aunt who I lived with for a while after my father died and when I was a kid. She must be about eighty-eight now. My relationship to her was very much like an older brother though I was in my teens, no, I was younger than that, I was about nine. And, I mean, if the phone rang, she'd say, "Get it, Phil." She knew she didn't speak too well so she would rather that I answered the phone and quarreled with the finance company. She thought I could do a better job of holding them off so they didn't repossess the car. I really loved her. At the time she did not have a boy child. She had two daughters. She was very much taken with me. I wanted to have her enter my poetry, but I didn't want to have her be offended by it so I transformed her into a sister and she appears in several poems as a sister, at least four.

As a young guy, I once wrote a poem which offended my mother and I thought, well, it wasn't worth it, and I'm not going to offend anybody that I care about in my poetry again. If Zbigniew Herbert and Czeslaw Milosz could live inside communist Poland and not have their poems censored, they had to figure out ways to say the things they had to say and befuddle the censors. I said to myself, the censor is in me, it's Freud's censor, and so I've got to mask that in some way and it shouldn't take that much ingenuity to do it.

At the same time, there was going on in America this whole thing of confessional poetry which began more or less with W. D. Snodgrass' *Heart's Needle* and then Lowell's *Life Studies*, Ginsberg's *Kaddish*, Ann Sexton's work, Sylvia Plath's, and I thought, well, these are people with different temperaments. I don't want to talk about my wife the way Robert Lowell does. Lowell takes lines from her letters and puts them in his poems, and they don't make her look too good. He's left her for a younger woman and she's upset, naturally, and so he takes lines out of her letters. And the book is called *For Lizzie and Harriet*. Well, Lizzie was his wife, Harriet is his daughter. I think to myself, why don't you leave those people alone? Wasn't it enough that you abandoned your daughter and your wife and went to live in England with Lady somebody-or-other?

FOX: What advice do you have for young poets?

LEVINE: Well, there are two avenues I think you have to talk about because we live in two poetry worlds. About a year ago, I had a terrific argument with a guy who administers a book prize. He had chosen a committee that I thought was just hopeless, and I, being a fat-mouth, told him so. I said, "You shouldn't have these people on this committee. They shouldn't be giving prizes. These are people with very narrow agendas and so they are going to be fighting amongst each other to push their agendas." I said, "You should choose people with much broader tastes who can accommodate each other and who care about a great variety of American poetry." And the guy said to me, "You don't think I know anything about poetry, do you?" I said, "I didn't say that." "No, you think I just don't know my ass from a hole in the ground, right?" I said, "No, I didn't say that. You obviously don't know who these people are." He said, "I studied with Robert Creeley.

I know a lot about it." I said, "I'm not talking about that, I'm not talking about poetry eternal." I used the classification of the Catholic church. You have the church eternal and the church temporal. In the church eternal, the priest is Jesus Christ's shepherd on earth. In the church temporal, he may be trying to make time with the little boys. To the altar boys he may be a real creep, but in the church eternal he has a function that is an eternal function. I said, "I'm not talking about poetry eternal, you know a lot about that." I knew because I had read a book he'd written about William Carlos Williams. I said, "You know a lot about that, but you don't know anything about poetry temporal, which has to do with making out, getting ahead, pushing your agenda, pushing your friends, earning points from other people, getting renown, fame, jobs, all that crap." Then there's poetry eternal where you draw strength from Milton, Dante, Shakespeare, Chaucer, Keats, and you encapsulate it in your own words and you pass it on to the generations to come.

I try to get my students to focus, and young poets to focus, to forget about all this temporal crap. If they were my students at Fresno State where I taught for years, they were already so behind the eight-ball. They're going to send their poems to *The New Yorker* and it's going to be from Fresno? They'd say, "From Fresno? Oh shit." [both laugh]

Whereas if the student is a student at Columbia or Harvard, the poetry teacher gets on the phone and says to the poetry editor at *The New Yorker*, "I've just found this wonderful, talented young man (or woman), you must read." "Of course I'll read it, send me the poem." So I try to get them to focus on poetry eternal. I didn't even know there was a poetry temporal until I was well into my twenties. I didn't know poetry was a business. I had no idea. I didn't even bother trying to publish. I didn't even know how you would go about it. I didn't even know it was important. I was just trying to write and to become a better writer. Then at a certain point when I had two children, my wife was about to have the third child, I realized I was going to have to go to work [laughs] and I didn't want to go back into industrial Detroit. I began sending my poems out and I was lucky enough to get a lot of them published, and then I began to have to have truck with this poetry temporal. And it hasn't been such a pretty sight. In that arena, poets are no better than anybody else. So my central thing is to try to get the students to focus on the eternal aspect.

I also try to convince them not to waste time defending what you write, just forget it. If you show it to a friend and the friend doesn't like it, thank the friend, because you're getting candor and whenever you can get candor in America or probably Britain or France you're very lucky. But don't let anybody, anybody, suggest that you don't have the material to be a poet, that you don't have the experience to be a poet, because it seems to me that everybody has the experience to be a poet.

I remember a young poet, a very successful young poet, Li-Young Lee, very good poet, saying to me, "How did you get permission, how did you give yourself permission to write?" I said to him, "Li-Young, I never had a notion you needed permission. I thought I was unique, that no one who had ever lived was quite like me, and if I didn't get this writing done, I would pass from breath without the world ever knowing that there was such a unique little character as me. I gave myself permission. Nobody gave me permission." And Li-Young was astonished by this. Li-Young is a far more interesting person than I and a very handsome man, a very charismatic man. Why he would be asking this question puzzled the hell out of me. I mean, I would think just being Li-Young would be plenty. But I guess he has been someone struggling to find that permission to write.

FOX: How do you know when a poem is finished?

LEVINE: Well, very few of them are finished. Most of them are abandoned, even the ones that are in the books. Sometimes I'll write a poem and I'll say, "Oh, son of a bitch, I got that one right." But, usually, I see little passages that are compromises. Well, that's as good as I can make it. There's a lot of sewing and stitching going on to simulate this flawless flow that goes from here to here, but I can see and remember where I did the pruning and the altering, and then I get to a point where I'm not making it any better and I just say, "Well, time to move on."

I have seen people, both men and women, who are just stuck on a thing and say, I have to make this perfect, forgetting that you're John Jones or Emily Jones and not John Keats or Emily Dickinson, and you ain't going to make it perfect so move on and maybe the next one will come out right. I mean, you do the best you can and then don't waste your time. I have rewritten poems, older poems. I have a book called 1933, the title poem is "1933," and when I went to put it in my *Selected Poems*, I rewrote it. I took about 30-some lines out and rewrote two passages to create a transition from here to there. The book came out, no one noticed the difference. [both laugh] I waited for someone to say, "Boy, you really changed that poem." I took at least 30 lines out and no one noticed. I thought, well, I guess I did it for myself, or for the poem. I did it for the poem. I very much believe in doing it for the poem, I want the poem to be as good as I can make it.

FOX: I understand that Larry Levis died unexpectedly and willed to you his poetry. Could you tell us about that?

LEVINE: He didn't really will it to me. Larry died in May 1996. I had talked to him probably three or four days before he died and he said he was coming out here. He comes from Selma, California; his mother's still there and he was going to come out here in June. We were going to go over this manuscript which he described as almost complete. We had looked at each other's books for maybe the previous twenty years. We have been useful to each other, I mean, he was my guru and I was his. He was certainly as good a critic as I am. And then he died and so his sister, who's the person he was the closest to in the world, called me. I know her well, a wonderful woman. She said, "Larry's got this book that he wrote me about. He said it was almost done. Would you put it together for him"? I said, "Sure, yeah." I felt I owed it to him. I also felt it was going to be easy, I mean it was almost done.

Well, [laughter] it comes in the mail, a carton like this [gestures] full of drafts of these poems, some dated, some undated, some handwritten. He had written me, oh, I don't know, probably a couple of hundred letters over the years. They're now, his letters to me and mine to him, in the Berg Room at the New York Public Library. He was a wonderful letter writer. Most of his letters were typed, but maybe one of five was handwritten, and I could always read his handwriting, but obviously he had made some effort to have his handwriting communicable to others, not so when he wrote for himself. I got this box in the beginning of July. I didn't finish the manuscript until sometime in October. It was a lot of work, it was awful work. I mean, it's hard enough to make decisions about your own work, but to be making decisions about somebody else's—I hated the job, frankly, I just hated it, but I felt obliged to do it. I never had any doubt about that. You stare yourself blind at this stuff, which version is better, and some of them are so different from each other. I enlisted two other poets to help me, David St. John who teaches at USC and was a good friend of Larry's, and Peter Everwine who lives here and was one of Larry's teachers, and they helped me a lot, so by no means did I do it by myself. And then the book was published and it received terrific attention and notices. I think Larry was an incredibly gifted poet. I think he was the best. I think some of the stuff he was writing in his last three books was as good as anything anybody in America was writing. Anybody. He was a remarkable poet.

FOX: What would you like to be remembered for?

LEVINE: [laughs] Oh, my good looks, those movies that I made late in life [laughing] or my singing late in life, yeah, my crooning. I don't know. I guess two or three things. I think I'd like to be remembered as a decent guy. I'd like to be remembered as a good teacher and a good father and a good poet and a good husband and a good brother. There are a lot of things I'd like to be remembered for, come to think of it. But I suppose chief among them would be as a good poet, or somebody who advanced American poetry or somebody who took it into areas where it hadn't been.

I was in Washington, D.C. in April, near the end of April, and I went to the White House. There was a sort of to-do at the White House, a poetry to-do, which was more interesting than you might suspect, and Hillary and Bill were our hosts and they were charming. I mean, they could talk a dog out of his fur, you know [both laugh]. They were amazing.

But, then afterward, I went with group of people, we had a drink, and there was a woman there named Lorna De Cervantes. She's a very nice woman. I think she lives around San Jose. She said, "I've always wanted to meet you." And I said, "Well, thank you. I know your work. I'm happy to meet you." She said, "I always wanted to meet you because you're the father of Chicano poetry." I said, "I'm the what?" She said, "Yeah, you're the father of Chicano poetry. That's your reputation in the Bay Area." I said, "Really? But, I'm not a Chicano." She said, "I know, but all those marvelous Chicano poets were your students." And she rattled off their names. She knew all their names. And she said, "We've kept up with what you've done. We think it's just terrific." And then I remembered when I retired here, they were going to pick someone to teach poetry writing and the Chicano students got together with the dean and made a big fuss, "We want another LEVINE; hire a Hispanic." And I said to the dean, "They don't really think I'm Hispanic, do they?" He said, "No, it's complicated. I can't explain what they mean. They mean somebody who's sympathetic to what they're doing, is what they mean." So that's one of the things I was most proud of. I mean, the whole White House thing paled by comparison to this little remark that this woman made, which really just made me feel wonderful.

I remember when they opened a Chicano art center here in Fresno and the first year they gave an award, they gave it to me as this great friend of

Chicano art. I think of all the awards I got it was the one that I liked the most. I mean, it just felt terrific.

And I remember I was in New York once, it was a couple of years ago, and they were giving the National Book Awards out and one of my students won, a Chicano, Victor Martinez. You can't imagine how good I felt. I just felt, wow, that's incredible, one of my kids won the National Book Award. I went to see him read at Barnes and Noble the day of the night he got it, just before. He was reading with other nominees at Barnes and Noble, I came in, and he recognized me. "Phil, what are you doing here?" I said, "I came to hear you read." And he said, "All the way from Fresno?" I said, "No, no, all the way from Bleeker Street." He said, "Where's that?" I said, "About a mile in that direction." "Oh," he said, "thank God. If I screwed up and you'd come all the way from Fresno, I'd feel awful." But the next day, I picked up the *Times* and he'd won. So that was terrific.

When I came here, maybe the second or third semester, I had a very brilliant Chicano student. I forget his name now, but he was also interested in acting. I know I had a profound effect on the way he wrote by what I was giving him to read. I mean, the stuff he originally wrote was just nothing and I was pushing things like Dylan Thomas at him, lyrical stuff, because I had the sense that he had a lyrical impulse. He began writing this very lyrical work and it was just terrific. He gave up poetry to pursue his career in acting, but at that time he was serious about writing. One day he was in my office and we were looking at one of his poems, and he looked at me and he said, "You think I could really be a poet?" I said, "I think you're practically there." And he said, "You know, when I was in high school, my teachers said that I couldn't write because I didn't have a language." And I was struck by that. It reminded me of my mother's ambition to be a writer. My mother was foreign-born, and I think she was discouraged in much the same way, that her English wasn't good enough. But her English was terrific. She spoke English without an accent, she was very well read, but she was not encouraged.

FOX: So, would it be fair to say that what really turns you on is giving voice to those without a voice, as workers, as writers, as individuals?

LEVINE: It's a simplification, but it's certainly not inaccurate. It leaves out something and that is it leaves out the beauty of language and the beauty of language lyrically used which I'm also addicted to. There's a lot of poetry that I love that doesn't truck with the voiceless, that is really kind of Byzantine and elegant and marvelous. One of my favorite poets in the 20th century is

Yeats. If you had said to Yeats, "Would you like to give voice to the voiceless?" "No, no, no, they're voiceless because they have nothing to say [laughs] and who'd want to listen to them anyway?" But he's a marvelous poet.

I'm enthralled with the medium itself. John Ashbery is a guy I read. When he's good, I think he's just dazzling. I love some of Merrill's work. He's very elegant and very beautiful. It's very different from anything I'd write. Also Richard Wilbur's work; these are contemporaries who really do it beautifully. I remember Ashbery being shocked once when I told him how much I liked a certain poem of his. He said, "What! You read it?" I said, "Yeah, I read it." And then he said to me, "You know, Philip, sometimes I get serious and I read you." [both laugh] I said, "Yeah, well, sometimes I get frivolous, John, and I read you." But I don't think it is frivolous. I think when he's really on his game, boy, is he good. And he's a more gifted poet than I am. I don't have any doubt about that. His command of language is extraordinary. When I read Charles Wright, who I just think is a marvelous, marvelous poet, very clearly that is not his aim, to give voice to the voiceless. So I think we each find our own niche and I think the great health of American poetry right now is how many different directions it's taking.

Sharon Olds was born in San Francisco on November 19, 1942. She earned a B.A. at Stanford University and a Ph.D. at Columbia University. Her first collection of poems, *Satan Says* (1980), received the inaugural San Francisco Poetry Center Award. Olds's following collection, *The Dead & the Living* (1983), received the Lamont Poetry Selection in 1983 and the National Book Critics Circle Award. Her other collections include *Strike Sparks: Selected Poems* (2004, Knopf); *The Unswept Room* (2002); *Blood, Tin, Straw* (1999); *The Gold Cell* (1997); *The Wellspring* (1995); and *The Father (1992)*, which was shortlisted for the T.S. Eliot Prize and was a finalist for the National Book Critics Circle Award.

Olds's numerous honors include a National Endowment for the Arts grant and a Guggenheim Foundation Fellowship. Her poetry has appeared in *The New Yorker, The Paris Review*, and *Ploughshares*, and has been anthologized in more than a hundred collections.

Olds held the position of New York State Poet from 1998 to 2000. She currently teaches poetry workshops at New York University's Graduate Creative Writing Program as well as a workshop at Goldwater Hospital on Roosevelt Island in New York. She was elected an Academy Chancellor in 2006. She lives in New York City.

Sharon Olds (photocredit: © Catherine Mauger)

# Sharon Olds

November 15, 2001

FOX: When did you first consider yourself a poet?

OLDS: Last year.

FOX: Tell me about that.

OLDS: Well, I figured, a plumber is a plumber. You don't have to be a great plumber to call yourself a plumber, if you are a plumber each day. But what the word poet meant to me when I was a kid, those faces in the little portholes of the Oscar Williams anthology that I carried around with me—those creatures, those beings, were so special, they are so special, they are kind of like angels in some way, whose power of speech extended over time, who were helping us long after they had gone, and delighting us. So I didn't feel comfortable using that word for myself. But then I figured, that's what I do, that's what I do, so that's what I'm going to call myself. But if I'm ever asked, like, on an airplane or something, what do you do, I always say I'm a teacher.

FOX: Because?

OLDS: I'm a teacher! [Fox laughs] And it's an identity, I don't know. That's a good question. Maybe I'm more confident in myself as a teacher than as a poet. I haven't worked harder on teaching than on poetry, it's no easier to do, and it's nothing less important to me. When I was a kid growing up, my teachers sort of saved my life.

FOX: What is the most important thing you can teach your students?

OLDS: One of the most important things that I can do, I think, is keep them company as a fellow writer. Remind them that I do not speak as an authority, that we're all in deep and anxious hope of the next day's poem

[Fox laughs, murmurs agreement], may it come to us from wherever it comes. We know that hard work won't do it; though we work very hard, hard work won't do it. So I'm in the grip of magic and hope and prayer, and I love to have companionship along the way. That's not really answering what can I teach them, but it's more like the atmosphere that I feel is accompanying us. In the classroom, it's my job to try to see that we take good care of each other. It's nobody else's job but mine, and they are so smart, and they are so sweet, and they are so gifted—what can I teach them. I love them. Is that a form of learning? Does that make sense to you, Alan, what I'm saying?

FOX: Definitely, yes. How do you feel your reputation affects your students?

OLDS: [laughs] Do you have those things in the interview where you say "wild laughter." [still laughing]

FOX: Well, there is laughter and there's more loud laughter.

OLDS: Well, I can't laugh louder. [both voices blur in laughter]

OLDS: I don't know, I have no idea. When I used to, if I were fortunate enough to be asked to give a reading and I'd arrive at an airport, the people who were going to pick me up would never pick me, and then when I would finally say, "Are you looking for me?" they would look a little startled [Fox chuckles]. So I finally learned to say, "You know, when you pick me up, I'm tall, I wear glasses and I look like a school librarian." [more laughter from Fox] And they came for me in a moment! So that made me feel as if they had thought I would look ferocious, furious, fire-breathing. Reputation. Each one of us, in whatever our sphere of life is, has many different reputations. We're thought of one way by one person and one way by another. I don't know what my students will have heard about me, who they will have read. There are poets I respect deeply who don't respect my work. They may have read them. That's okay. I'm a teacher. Because I am, along with them, a first-draft writer, that's our main vocation. Our good fortune, our gift, our passion. I can speak from that perspective to them as fellow first-draft writers and revisers. So in a way, it's doesn't matter what we've heard of each other before we gather. They don't tell me, and I don't ask them. So, I just don't know. There was so much anger in my early work, and I wasn't really aware of how much there was. What I'm like as a person, which is not very angry, alas [laughs]. . . I'm trying to develop it in my later life! But reputation,

reputation—we're going to be working together, and by the time we've been doing it for a month we're going to start to know each other, and trust each other, and so, as you can see, it isn't a question that I've really thought of. It's an interesting question.

FOX: What satisfies you the most when you elicit it from your students?

OLDS: I guess what I love is when they are listening to each other so closely that they can describe so accurately to each other and usefully what it is they feel they're hearing, and seeing. There's nothing like that. And, of course, they bring in these new poems that are just astonishing, and so that's thrilling, but I think it's that concentration, the listening. In my class we don't look at the poem until we've heard it twice. I'm big on ears! So that attentiveness, and the development of more articulateness about what it is we feel and think, and what happens to us when we hear this line of the poem or that word of the poem—developing those skills, which I want to do along with them, is what I think helps us as writers.

FOX: So you find, I imagine, when you teach you also learn.

OLDS: Oh yeah, oh yeah, we keep each other company. And I'm there to take care of the room, to try to make sure that nothing goes on that's going to harm anybody. And then I listen, and then they tell me how we're doing and then the conferences, the one-on-one, are a huge part of the work, too. I'm blessed to be at N.Y.U., a creative writing program led by a director who is just the smartest, the sweetest, and most sensitive person. Do you know Melissa Hammerle?

FOX: No.

OLDS: She used to be at the "Y". She's now our Heart and Soul. So I know that there are a lot of other people around, the other teachers and Melissa and everybody, we're all in the work together of receiving the honor of our students wanting to come and work with us.

FOX: How do you know when a poem is finished?

OLDS: Well, what I say about that is a little odd. This is how I put it to myself, that it lets go of me. What does that really mean? That I'm done, that

I feel I can't help it. The way I experience this is that I can leave the notebook closed. If a poem doesn't feel finished to me, I know it doesn't feel finished by my going to the notebook and opening it. I think, uh-uh, no, no, or I think, ah, maybe, mmm, it almost always has to do with the ending—always, I would say, has to do with the ending of a first draft. So it won't let me go because it's not finished yet. It's lying, not that poems can't lie—there are brilliant lies in poetry. But for me, there's a certain kind of falseness that just wrecks a poem, especially at the end, as if I had been forcing it to arrive at some place of my choice. The poem didn't want to go there. It wasn't heading there at all, but I had had it in mind that it should arrive there [Fox chuckles]. Then the poem just, it calls me back, and then once it's done, it's a relief. Once I feel that I have gone with it as far as I can, and not into false territory, okay. Then maybe a day later, a week later, a month, a year, or ten years later, I will type it up, and then I see its faults in a fairly objective way. Ah, I mean what I think are its faults. Usually I don't get to the faults that some other people see as faults. I think, no, I've got to go with this, I've got to go with this. I don't know if it's a fault or not, but this is it, how it's going to be. And then once I type—I write by hand with a pen, a ballpoint on grocery-store notebooks, and I type on a Lettera 22 portable manual that I carry on my back. I've been using these crafts of writing and typing since I was, I don't know, seven or so. It's a long time by now. I'm used to that method.

FOX: Could you talk about falseness in a poem?

OLDS: Yes [sigh], it's interesting, isn't it? I think it would mean different things to different people.

FOX: What does it mean to you?

OLDS: Wishful thinking [pause], salvation addiction, especially in the last line, idealization of my characters, my stuffed animals, my muses, these poor people I write about—not seeing what you're seeing, your brain not daring to see what your eye is seeing, or your heart is seeing, or your pen not able to write what you know you're seeing or what you don't know you're seeing [laughs]. I think for me, I think that would be it, trying to look good, that's a kind of sentimentality, idealization and lying, whatever good means, it means different things different days probably.

FOX: Then do you have to write without thought of the audience or how others will react?

OLDS: Yes, oh, I would think so. Another kind of falseness for me would be wrong language, too elevated, too de-elevated. Like my will wanting to choose instead of letting the poem choose. You know, it sounds so weird and mystical, but I really think it could be studied electrically with brain waves, when you get to certain levels of concentration other connections blossom that are more, a little more unconscious. So when I say letting the poem do it, I don't really necessarily believe Allen Ginsberg's "first thought best thought," and I revise a lot, a lot, but I suppose choice of vocabulary does have something to do with imaginary audience. Because if there are lots of difficult words that seem difficult, I'm not comfortable with that—as he says on TV, who's that guy, he says, "I'm not comfortable with that." [Fox laughs] I love that guy [laughing], oh, oh, I feel I'm looking at myself when I see him—you know the guy I mean?

FOX: No [laughing].

OLDS: He plays a lawyer on *Ally McBeal*, or he plays a shrink, maybe, on *Ally McBeal*. Anyway, now we've got my cultural level established. [Fox laughs loudly] I like clarity in poems I read, but there are a hundred kinds of clarity for every hundred poets. I don't mean accessible, I don't know. If I go back and see that there's what I would consider too high a diction in a first draft, or the second or the fifteenth, I will bring it down, and if it's too, oh, curse-wordy or anti, what is it called, counterphobically crude, I don't know what I'm comparing it to, an ideal self of the poem. I don't understand these things at all; it's as if there's something to be true to, and it isn't I, and it isn't any particular reader—it's as if it's to be true to the poem. And what is the poem? Often, in my case, it has a story, of some ordinary thing in life, and so maybe I partly mean, like, say that painting, it's not photorealism, it's emotionally evocative. Whatever I want a poem to be, I want it to be true to some kind of combination of experience and feeling and thought. I want it to be dancing to its own music.

FOX: You were talking to me about magic. Can you elaborate on that in terms of your own writing or thought processes?

OLDS: Oh, we're in the grip of magic!

FOX: Yes, exactly.

OLDS: Maybe sometimes I feel that the best of what we do is the least in our control. Like metaphor, we can't go to the icebox and pull out the ingredients and make a metaphor. We're helpless. If we focus a certain way, and give ourselves in a certain way to the writing of poems, they happen, they seem to just happen, they spring up out of the earth of the brain. Who has ever made one up by force of will? They seem like a gift from the unconscious or whatever—that kind of magic is what I mean. Again, I bet we could measure it in electricity! They could map it. I've been reading Oliver Sacks' book about the postencephalitic Parkinsonian disease that he treated, *Awakenings*, and at the end he shows electrical graphs of states of emotion—so it's not really magic, but I guess what I mean is something you don't have control over. You can, if you want to make metaphors, you can behave in a way that might make them more likely to arrive. I think of it sometimes like putting little dishes of food on the sill if you wish a dog to visit you, or bird-feeders like the feeders in Central Park. When you want to see some new species, you say, "Let's go to the feeders," and you go and there are these amazing thistle-socks and all these great things that bird lovers have put up, and the birds will come or they won't, but you have more of a chance for them to come if you put the feeders up. I would say, to extend that metaphor, that I believe in things like exercise and sleep and sobriety—not, in my case, perpetual and uninterrupted sobriety, but most of the time, and always when writing—to take good care of oneself, physically and spiritually or emotionally, whatever. To me that's like the preparation for writing as well as we can.

FOX: How does your inner life of writing intersect with your real life in the world?

OLDS: I have no idea. [Fox laughs] I mean, which is our real life? I can't even remember. I don't really know. Ask me again, Alan. Can you say that in a slightly different way? Or tell me how that works for you. How does your inner life intersect with your work life?

FOX: For me, in a more pragmatic way. Most of my real life, much of it is business and real estate, so I will have a fantasy of how things should be and then try to impose that on the real world to make it happen, so it's sort of a goal-oriented thing.

OLDS: Cool. Is that a good way in your work to make it happen?

FOX: Yes.

OLDS: Yeah, it's almost the opposite of what I'm saying, isn't it?

FOX: Right, exactly.

OLDS: Yeah, isn't that funny.

FOX: I don't think it would work that way with what you do.

OLDS: In a way—as a teacher, I can't be passive in the way that I am as a writer, not that I'm very passive as a writer, but I try to be enough, passive enough, so that it's an inspiration, so that the metaphors might come. I don't know how it intersects. I like to live in the moment. Someone told me recently that they could tell, a month ago, that an experience we were having was going to become a poem of mine. I was zero thinking of poetry, zero, because I zero think about poetry when I'm living, like would this be a poem? NO, for me that would be strange. But someone who knows me well knew that, and it was true, it was quite true, the poem was actually forming as the experiences were happening and I wasn't aware of it. Then, when I was alone on a bus or an airplane, then I saw a poem, or "a poem came to me," as I put it. So many poets work in notebooks, and gather, I think maybe most poets work that way, but for me it's noticing that there is a poem there and then writing it out, just finishing it right then. And then, as I said before, working on it later.

FOX: For the first draft of the poem, does the poem follow some inspiration or does inspiration follow from the work of doing it? [Olds laughs] For me, I can't sit down and say, okay, I'm going to write a poem now, and just do it. I have to say, oh, wow, this poem is coming, I'd better put everything aside and write it.

OLDS: Me too, totally, exactly, exactly. I think it's maybe more fiction writers who sit down every day, from what I can tell from my friends. In my case if it isn't something I care a lot about, a LOT, and if it isn't free in some way, it won't come to me. It just won't, it will not do it. There's no way I can make it do it. But then sometimes a poem will come to me when I have to be out of the house in twenty-five minutes, ooo-ooooh!

FOX: [laughs] What do you do then?

OLDS: Oh, then I'm late. [Fox chuckles] I'm usually an on-time person, and if it's something I can't be late for, which it often is, like teaching, or a conference, mainly what happens is, most of the time I can't be late, so I'll try to make a few notes, brief enough that they don't start the whole thing going, which if you do that, it wants to reach its end fiercely and it's a mess, because I'm only going to have one chance at actually writing it.

FOX: What kind of impact do you want your work to have?

OLDS: [laughs] Hmm, we could call this heh-heh laughter [both laugh more].

FOX: If the questions were easy, I'd answer them myself.

OLDS: [still laughing] Ah-ha!

FOX: I do the easy part, you do the hard part.

OLDS: They're good questions, Alan. They're great questions—of course, I've managed to totally block it out because it was such a scary question.

FOX: What kind of an impact would you like your work to have?

OLDS: I wouldn't like anyone to be harmed because of it, that's for sure. That's the first thing that comes into my mind, first thought best thought—first do no harm, *primum non nocere*. That's what the doctors say. It doesn't look in my early work as if I'm avowing that. When I wrote my younger poems, I never thought anyone would read them. Who was ever going to see them in a million years? And then I had good fortune. That's the first thing that comes into my mind. Muriel Rukeyser used to say poets think their families will die if they read the family poems. She said it's like being gay. You think that if your parents find out, they'll die. But they don't. We've tried to think of cases where people have been harmed by poems. I cannot think of one at the moment. It's a very negative answer to what impact you would like to have. That's my answer, maybe. That's kind of consuming for me, the idea of what impact you would like it not to have.

FOX: It seems to me, your answer is consistent with the view that you seem to have an affinity with the art of writing itself and that's more important to you than what happens later. Would that be accurate?

OLDS: You mean its fate out in the world, when I am done revising? Yes. If I could only have one or the other, absolutely! Oh, oh, that's a feeling like, [deep inhale], such a good feeling, a kind of a balance, a very intense focus, a freedom from being yourself almost, freedom like you get in hard work and other things. But the sending out and getting back, the offering—Muriel said, stop saying "submit." [Fox laughs loudly]. "Offer, offer." Offering and receiving back, I think many of us feel ambivalent about that. The world life, the worldly life, like when you're about to give a reading, fear, anxiety, unease, excitement, worry, and you really want, you thought you really wanted to do it but now it's time [laughter], yes.

FOX: So if you have a reading three months from now that's wonderful and if it's two hours from now it's not so wonderful?

OLDS: Two hours is still not as bad as it's going to get; it's three seconds, you know, three minutes, oh, God! That's just nerves, that's nerves. But it's not a pure pleasure. It has all the anxiety, energy, excitement of a performance. And the writing itself is not like that. No one's there, nobody's there. Of course, every poet you've ever read is there—they're like a tureen to be drunk from, for refreshment and elation, as we're trying to do whatever it is that can be done with our pen.

FOX: When you're doing a reading, does your anxiety persist throughout or dissipate once you've gotten into it?

OLDS: Once I'm almost done, and nothing bad has happened, I'm very relieved! And it's much better than it used to be. I used to always have nightmares and I used to be really quite sick before I got up there. My mouth remains dry and my hands shake and my knees shake, those just seem perpetual, but I'm thinking about the audience more than I used to. I'm not thinking so much about how am I doing or how badly am I going to fail. And I feel close, in theory, to most of the people there, because most of them are writers. I'm having my turn, and next week it'll be their turn, and my heart will go out to them for the fears that come over us when we're separated from our group—often not a very safe position to be in our species. But then the older I get, the younger they get, and I'm not as afraid of people younger than me as I am of people older than me, although if there are cool high school kids sitting in the front row at a reading, my heart will absolutely sink at first, but then—it's a phobia, and a desire to see if I can make contact with other people whether I know them or not. It makes me so nervous to think about readings. Let's not think about readings anymore. [Fox laughs loudly] I'm getting that anxiety as I talk about it; I'm starting to feel it! Can I read you something?

FOX: Yes, please.

OLDS: I read this and wrote it down; it's in the deli window downstairs. "September 12, 2001: Dear New York City: We are shocked to hear this news. I hope you are all right. I am sorry if someone died. Here is a poem: You are as sweet as a hart / we have met your soll / you are very nice / Love, Michael Bodker." Heart is spelled h-a-r-t, soul is s-o-l-l. He wrote this letter to New York City and it came to the Del Monaco Deli and it's up in their window.

FOX: Hmm. [long pause] You know, in *Rattle*, we focus on a group of authors, like poetry editors, Pulitzer Prize winners, inmates in prison, and one of my favorites was when we published school children, kindergarten through twelve.

OLDS: There's not a bad poet in first grade.

FOX: Yes.

OLDS: None of them are anything but fresh and original. Why am I saying that? Surely, they sometimes just write "roses are red, violets are blue," but when I've done a little in schools, they aren't old enough yet to know that they're supposed to be worried. I mean, we're all so worried about what other people think of us, this is just a part of being a human being, awfully rare to not feel that. But in first grade, it's different, it's not so big as it will become. So I think, they don't know how to avoid being original. They will learn. [Fox chuckles] We all have learned.

FOX: It seems to me that you may be talking about self-consciousness and you're saying that when you write you are not self-conscious and when you approach a reading you are. Is that. . . ?

OLDS: Probably so. I mean, I can't really say I'm not self-conscious when I'm writing, but I want to enter a state that is as little self-conscious as possible, that is focused on some kind of image, or feeling, or story, with some kind of truthfulness and accuracy, and then the language, the whole language, is available to me! Born the year I was, [Fox laughs] and I can use any word, from that whole place, in a poem. There's so much going on that if I'm really concentrating there kind of isn't room for being self-conscious. And then there's the physical deep pleasure of the ball-point nib flowing across the grocery-store notebook which has—I think they've got more plastic and less paper, less fiber, more glass, less trees, now, and it makes it sail, you just sail, the medium point with the octagonal handle. I don't find that the round ones sail quite as well. Remember in Wordsworth's poem where they're skating at night, whush, whush, whush, such a pleasure physically to write. I love to draw, so writing is a little like that. Yes, so I'm having physical pleasure from writing and seeing the homemade cursive coming out. And that's why when I type it up—a lot of great poets, Lucille Clifton herself, types first drafts! But for me, to have the flow and the shapeliness and the kind of animal/vegetable/floral/faunal shapes of the letters, rather than striking a key and having it God-knows-how appear. . . I don't really understand how the ink comes out of the pen [Fox chuckles] instead of all falling out. Oh—ballpoint! Yeah—there's some little ball bearing in there. I guess that's how it works, isn't it?

FOX: Yes.

OLDS: Cool.

FOX: Well, it seems that what you're saying is that for you the act of writing is really an all-encompassing process; it's physical and visceral and mental and emotional and all of that. Is that. . . ?

OLDS: Yes, and then whatever I'm seeing, while I'm writing, might get in the poem, which might be a good idea and might not be. I write on airplanes a lot, and so I'm seeing the ground, and clouds, and my study window sees a park, so I might see a hawk hunting. So what I'm actually seeing is—each one of us tries over the years to find the setting or settings, right? that will limit us the least. Well, I think it's a great joy to do anything with one's whole being rather than, as is so often the case, being divided. Right now, the sirens [heard in the background], before September 11, they affected us differently. I wouldn't have noticed them much, or I would have played with them like when you're dancing and then someone puts on another radio with another kind of music on and then you try to dance actually to both of them at once? But now I hear sirens and I'm . . .

FOX: Yes.

OLDS: There—they've stopped [deep breath].

FOX: You seem to be very sensitive to your environment. Is that true for you, what's going on around you?

OLDS: Don't you, I think we are that way, you know, writers. Don't you feel that?

FOX: Yes.

OLDS: Yeah, I don't know if it's one reason that we become writers, a gift, a burden, high maintenance. Yikes, omigod—vigilance, that's what it's called, vigilance. Yes, not the most appealing human quality, but many of our friends in the forest have sharp senses.

FOX: You talked about truth. Can you talk about the most important truths that inhabit you or your work?

OLDS: Hmm . . . I almost feel as if with each of our poems there's a different truth and it's local and different from the day before. It's funny, I think of it as not lying—accuracy—that's really my favorite word, whether it's accuracy of imaginative vision or of an actual fact, either way. My truth is someone else's lie. Truth, truth, truth, I don't know. I don't think there are any ideas in my poems, they seem perfectly innocent of ideas to me, anyway, but then I wouldn't know how to find an idea. Anyway, I don't really think in terms of ideas. I'm not very strong on abstractions, so I don't know. If my poems had a voice, what would they say? [laughs] Probably different books would say different things, some of the earlier ones would have to say something about not understanding things and being afraid and angry, and so the book could say, "I'm pretty pissed off, but I love this life, I love these people." And then maybe *The Father* would say, "How are we going to do this, both hate and love someone, and lose and not lose, and age and grow and try to understand and remain ignorant." These aren't truths that I'm saying, they're more like conditions: bafflement, joy. But then, when I think of someone else's work, then it gets interesting, because then you could talk about the truths, like in Lucille's work, and, in a different way, Brenda Hillman's work, and Yusef's work, oo-oh-oh, what could you say? [Fox laughs] You'd just have to fly around the room, filling it with flowers here and there. My God, amazing, amazing. So I don't think I have any truths. But I think I would love for the—not the evil to be sufficient for the day thereof—but the accuracy to be sufficient. That would be great, but then there are all these things that pull one away from that. It's an impossible, you know, we can't, we wish we could be really good.

FOX: What pulls you away from accuracy?

OLDS: Um, habit, maybe, like habitual line breaks. I mean something that's new and then next week it's not new and you're still doing it. I'm getting tired here! Your view is so beautiful out here, Alan. The Citibank is almost all silver now. It's like this pale, pale, celadon stripes and there's a big rose-colored finger, rosy-fingered sunset, rosy-fingered [Fox laughs] evening, vespers, what's the opposite of dawn, day, night, dawn, dusk, rosy-fingered dusk. So much for ideas.

FOX: Stealing from Shakespeare, but that's okay.

OLDS: Oh, [laughing] did he do rosy-fingered dusk?

FOX: Rosy-fingered dawn, I think, [murmur]. . .

OLDS: Oh, right, right.

FOX: You talked about your early work coming out of anger and that it has dissipated. What's replaced it, if anything?

OLDS: I don't think it has dissipated. It may have concentrated, but become a little more conscious, somewhat more conscious—it has to be more conscious than it was then! I don't know what I thought I was doing. It was some kind of accuracy, I guess, at that time.

FOX: It seems that you're saying then that it was an unconscious accuracy because you weren't aware of the anger . . .

OLDS: Not how much, not how striking it was. What might there be more of now? It's easier to think about this in terms of other people's poems, but trying to think of mine, more of? Irony!! Slight irony! Two instances of slight irony in the last couple of years. I never had one ounce of it. I didn't even know what it was. I had to look it up every time I heard the word. I could not even hold the definition in my mind. There's not a lot of it, but there's more than there was.

FOX: You've talked about other people's work. Who are some of your favorite poets to read?

OLDS: The people that I tend to immediately think of are the people about a generation older than I am. Stanley Kunitz, Gwendolyn Brooks, Muriel Rukeyser and Ruth Stone—these are parents, parents of mine. Going further back, I've been reading some Arabic women poets from the seventh century, beautiful, touching, strong—funny! And I was looking at John Donne's "Elegy to His Mistress on Going to Bed." I felt better sharing with Mr. Donne a desire to write about sexual love. It's hard to do and it's easy to do it badly, and I certainly trip up in that regard, but I felt very at home reading that poem of his. I've always loved the metaphysical poets. And then I was reading some Navajo religious chants, we call them poems, they're not poems in the same way that maybe Donne's poems are—I don't even think in the same way Herbert's are—well, getting too close to ideas there [Fox laughs loudly].

FOX: When did you start writing?

OLDS: My first poem, I am proud to say, is inscribed in stone on the main Post Office here in New York City. When I heard that people wrote poems, I didn't know that you had to make them up. I thought you just wrote them down, so my poem went, "Nor rain nor snow nor sleet nor gloom of night delays these couriers from the swift completion of their appointed rounds." But then I was told that you couldn't say you had written a poem unless you had invented it as well as written it out. Then I wrote some fiction, from about ten or eleven through high school, and lots of poems, and then there was college, poems and stories, and then there was a period of ten years where I was trying to write like George Oppen. I do love grammar, but I don't have any ability to be abstract, and yet that is who I wanted to write like, Oppen and Gary Snyder. And then when I was thirty I started just writing my own stuff. What were you saying before, Alan, what was the question—I got away from it.

FOX: It was when you first started writing.

OLDS: Right, when I first started writing. So, actually, at seven I started copying other people's stuff and then at 30 I stopped copying. There are all those writers in the half generation above mine who started to write about children and family. It was clearly what part of the landscape, part of what could be done. I didn't know how recently that had arrived, because I'd read Whitman and Dickinson, and it seemed poetry had always been very personal, intimate.

FOX: Is poetry for you a means of being intimate with others?

OLDS: Huh, I never thought of that. Probably, yeah, yeah. But it doesn't really feel like a means, it feels like a great place that we go to, that we visit. I know that probably that place is in the human soul, it must be, but I think of things, I tend to think of things in outward terms, so to me it's like a safe house for the whole world, for anyone writing now or whoever wrote or ever will, anywhere. And then all of us can go there and read what they've written. So I tend to think of it like a holy place, secular / holy, profane / holy, but definitely a place of creation, not destruction, and so it's a little almost too big to be a means? In a certain way, but I'm sure it's true, that one of my loves of it is that it isn't just about trying to build a little edifice that won't be full, where the floors will hold, the doors will close to the jambs. A few people, Liz Brooks, Seamus Heaney, for people who make poems that ring like bells, every board is true. Then there's a lot of poems with more rough edges. In a way there's a truth to rough edges, also. It isn't only the wish to make something, to create something, but it's a gift that you want to give someone, true. You don't really think about that while you're making it, but surely that's one of its great beauties. It's a social art, we're a social species, poor us, God help us. [Fox laughs] You know, you wouldn't know it, you wouldn't know it, but you would because social means murder and passion and the whole thing, unfortunately.

FOX: Yes, they're all there.

OLDS: ghuuuuuh [harsh expulsion of breath] How do you do that noise? [repeats sound several times] Growl. [both laugh] [transcriptionist tears out handfuls of hair]

FOX: What pushed you toward poetry as opposed to fiction or some other kind of writing?

OLDS: Oh, my fiction was such trash. I mean, my poetry has its trashy side, but my fiction was, it was just lying. It was lying. It was, oh, there would be a heroine in a story who would receive much anguish, discomfort, and somehow in the end would either triumph or die. It would all be very, oooh. But I found that when I got to poetry the line and the line breaks and the rhythm, the mixture of troches and iambs and anapests and dactyls, the big mix, but a lot of troches, I don't mean I tried to write in troches, just if I look I see that I'm doing that. There was something almost a moral force that form and craft in poetry exerted so I was less inclined to bullshit. Was it that I was afraid? Something was slowing me down and also I can't make anything up. I don't have any imagination. Not that I'm saying that my work is autobiographical, of course, I'm not saying that. Why would I ever say that? 'Cause I've never said that. [Fox laughs continually through this statement] But there are people with imagination. I know a bunch of fiction writers and it just astonishes me. And of course, many, many, many, many poets are extremely inventive and imaginative, most, but I couldn't do that. It just showed what I was trying to do. Also the description or the adjectives, I deeply did not understand the form, profoundly didn't understand fiction. When you read it, you go into that world, oh, it's terrifying, actually, it's very frightening. Like, I'm in the middle of *Desperate Characters* and the cat bite is getting worse and worse and worse and I'm partly anxious because of that. Sophie's cat bite in Paula Fox's novel is swelling as the novel goes on. I'm halfway through and, is she going to die? I mean, I'm longing for her to get some penicillin. The rabies shots, I don't know. It's as if my best friend is sick. It's not really as if my best friend is sick, it's really much less than that, but it's very, very powerful. What was I trying to talk about?

FOX: Actually, we were talking about when you first started writing. . .

OLDS: . . . write fiction, right. Can't do it. Can't do it.

FOX: So it sounds to me like what's you're saying is that as a writer you've stuck with sharing your personal truths rather than making stuff up or inventing . . .

OLDS: Well, I don't dare say that because I believe so passionately in invention and I'm always, since I'm always using this word truth, I always want to say, whether I'm at NYU or at Goldwater Hospital or visiting a high school, that we can lie all we want in our art. I love the imagination. I love it. It comes to me in metaphor, so I don't know how I could put that—Ah! I could say that one of the things I love best about poetry is that it has the sentence, not all of it does, some of it does, mine does, what I'm used to does, it has the sentence and it has the lie. Oh! So it has in the air a shapely stopping and starting that is not water flowing into the channel that is a set channel. It's water gurgling over ground that is dry and wet and porous and not making it some shape and that is precious to me a lot because of dance, 'cause I love to dance. And so it makes a shape on the page like a body, to me, an amoeba's body or who knows whose body, but that mirror of an irregular shape that I see when I see a poem on the page, or mirror of regular shape, Brandenburg Concerto shape, that kind of, whuuu, excitement within stringent beautiful laws. So maybe that was my thing about fiction, maybe the line controlled me away from being a big liar. I was a big liar as a kid. And I quit lying when I was, I forget when, eighteen, I think. I think I quit lying when I was eighteen. Also I write in formal stanzas of four-beat lines in four-line quatrains, however disguised this is, however little I knew I was doing it until a few years ago. That is the rhythm of the church hymns that I grew up with in the fundamentalist; there are very few fundamentalist Episcopalian churches [both laugh]. I don't quite know how it worked. I think it was a combination of what was said in church and how it was interpreted at home. So being a formal writer, I didn't think I was, but I turned out to be, I didn't want to be, I am. And having it be the church's form, maybe that's that moral force, fear of hell, that the liar feels when writing that helps me try to be accurate. At least it works, don't you think? [laughing] I'm just making that up. I never thought of that. I have no idea if that has a grain of truth in it. I think it has a grain, but I'm not sure if it has two grains.

FOX: Why did you decide at eighteen to stop lying?

OLDS: Because one night when I was going to sleep I was remembering something, and I suddenly thought, did that happen or did I just wish it had happened? And it scared, what is the bejesus? What form does the bejesus take? Does the bejesus wear a long white robe? It scared somethin' out of me. It truly frightened me. The way drugs frighten me. I was taking something, something, oh, God, so young, my brain not even formed, and I wasn't able to write. I couldn't write my name for like about a week, oooh. So I quit lying at eighteen and I quit drugs around the same time. Not that I'd been doing a lot of them, but in the place where I was and in those days, it was not unusual for us idiots to be destroying our brains left and right. And I don't want to not be able to write a sentence. And I don't want to not know whether something actually happened to me or I just thought it happened. I want to be able to speak and understand at least one language. American English is such a great language.

FOX: Yes, yes.

OLDS: Ain't it a beauty.

FOX: Absolutely, yes. Do you find any gender differences in the writing of poetry?

OLDS: That's so interesting. It's so hard to tell. There's so many genders, first of all. And then there's so many other circumstances that are leaning on all the various genders in one way or another. How would we know? Do you have any instinct about that? Do you think that it is or isn't a powerful factor in craft and tone and all kind of things like that, besides subject?

FOX: Well, I believe there's an essential difference between the male energy and the female energy. However, I also believe that females can carry a lot of male energy or males can carry a little or a lot of female energy. The male is more striving toward stuff and the female to me is more gathering in somehow, nurturing.

OLDS: Hmm. It's so interesting to think about that in terms of poems. I guess that I would be 50/50 male and female as a poet. That drive. So then I wonder is it human drive that in some women predominates and some men, see now, there are women who are born men. I just can't keep up with it. I think there's a bisexual, I'm saying human bisexual. I would have to say, looking at my writing and at how I feel about it, that I feel like 50/50, in terms of the definition in that way. I guess I'm more, I feel I'm on slightly more secure ground to think about human drive and human gathering, since we're going to find guys with more gathering, gals with more drive. And then we're going to just find people in whom it is so mysterious, we just have to bow down and kiss the earth. We don't know what else to do with ourselves.

FOX: Do you have any clue as to how your work might change in the future, for the rest of your career or life?

OLDS: Well, is this wood? [knocking sound] Yeah. [Fox laughs] Like everyone else, I'm in kind of a state of constant prayer, now. Oh, what's going to happen to the Earth, and its people? I know that when I started at Goldwater Hospital and there were people who could not move and could not speak, the possibility of writing poems with them, learning the methods, eyes up for yes, to spell out letter by letter the words for the first line of a poem, I want that for more people all over the earth. It's funny, I couldn't be more in love with New York City, I couldn't. I was in love with it from the first moment I heard of it and I love it with a huge tender love, as we all do, but I've become like a citizen of the Earth much more than before. At the same time, I love my precious town, village, the neighborhood, the neighborhood. And all the unfairness here, all the kids in the city who can't write their poems, mmph. So I tend to want more people to be able to write more poems, that's kind of—I totally forget the question.

FOX: That's okay. How would you encourage more people to write poems?

OLDS: I would think that if each of us who's sending out poems spends as much time on some neighborhood project with poetry as we're spending on sending out our poems. I think every poet is a potential, many, many poets are potential teachers and just teachers in the sense of keeping company with other people who would like to write poems. And not going about receiving those poems with mostly a critical air, but with mostly a joyous air. I know a lot of poets think so differently about this, but this is how I think, this is how I feel about it. Any hospital, any prison, any grammar school, any high school, any hospice, any ward. NYU now has a writing program on a children's cancer ward in a hospital, an oncological ward, and a lot of the kids don't make it. They write poems and their parents, with their parents, and our graduate writing students are the teachers there. At a women's prison, at a high school for the, what do you call them, challenged by being gifted, at the hospital. I was just crazy when I was New York State poet laureate for those two years, crazy to try to set up a national program of every creative writing program being given bunches of money to have outreach programs. Now a lot of the programs wouldn't want that because they don't believe that poetry is some kind of birthright that everybody out to have the chance at. And I respect these varying views of our arts, because I don't know what it is. I just know what my feeling is about, what I would like to help do with it. So those are, I guess those are the things I think of, is that kind of grass roots, and any one of us who has ever been in any group where poems were being shared could go start another such group. That's what I think. And then look at this, Michael Bodker's poem here in the deli window, here's a poem, "you are as sweet as a hart / we have met your soll / you are very nice."

FOX: That's great and that's a good place to stop.

Gregory Orr was born in 1947 in Albany, New York, and grew up in the rural Hudson Valley, and for a year, in a hospital in the hinterlands of Haiti. He received a B.A. degree from Antioch College, and an M.F.A. from Columbia University. He is the author of nine collections of poetry, including *Concerning the Book that is the Body of the Beloved* (Copper Canyon Press, 2005); *The Caged Owl: New and Selected Poems* (2002); *Orpheus and Eurydice* (2001); *Burning the Empty Nests* (1997); *City of Salt* (1995), which was a finalist for the *L.A. Times* Poetry Prize; and *Gathering the Bones Together* (1975). He is also the author of a memoir, *The Blessing* (Council Oak Books, 2002), which was chosen by *Publisher's Weekly* as one of the fifty best non-fiction books the year, and three books of essays, including *Poetry As Survival* (2002) and *Stanley Kunitz: An Introduction to the Poetry* (1985).

He is considered by many to be a master of short, lyric free verse. Much of his early work is concerned with seminal events from his childhood, including a hunting accident when he was twelve in which he accidentally shot and killed his younger brother, followed shortly by his mother's unexpected death, and his father's later addiction to amphetamines. Some of the poems that deal explicitly with these incidents include "A Litany," "A Moment," and "Gathering the Bones Together," in which he declares: "I was twelve when I killed him; / I felt my own bones wrench from my body." In the opening of his essay, "The Making of Poems," broadcast on National Public Radio's *All Things Considered*, Orr said, "I believe in poetry as a way of surviving the emotional chaos, spiritual confusions and traumatic events that come with being alive."

Orr has received a Guggenheim Fellowship and two poetry fellowships from the National Endowment for the Arts. In 2003, he was presented the Award in Literature by the American Academy of Arts and Letters, and was a Rockefeller Fellow at the Institute for the Study of Culture and Violence, where he worked on a study of the political and social dimension of the lyric in early Greek poetry. He teaches at the University of Virginia, where he founded the MFA Program in Writing in 1975, and served from 1978 to 2003 as Poetry Editor of the *Virginia Quarterly Review*. He lives with his wife, the painter Trisha Orr, and their two daughters in Charlottesville, Virginia.

# Gregory Orr

March 9, 2005

FOX: When did you realize you were a poet?

ORR: Realize I was a poet . . . um . . . I have several different answers to that. One is there was a certain moment when I realized that all I ever wanted to do was write poems. And that was certainly the turning point in my life, in a sense of direction. My sort of hilarious self-definition of being a poet came a lot later. I remember thinking, when I publish my first poem in a magazine, then I'll be a poet. And, when are we talking now . . . We're talking something like 1967 or '68, something like that. And I'm still in college. And I had this idea that if I publish a poem in a magazine I'll be a poet. And that there needs to be something to sort of "mark" that. And I got the idea that I would buy a briefcase. [Fox laughs] And I thought, what? I mean, I'd never had a briefcase. I don't even think I'd ever seen a briefcase in my life at that point. But I somehow had the idea that this would be something that someone would keep important papers in, like poems, if you were a real poet. Maybe I thought poets also smoked pipes [Fox laughs] and I didn't like to smoke, so that wasn't going to work. But the other answer, the real answer—about knowing that writing poems was all I wanted to do with my life—that came senior year in high school in a really small, rural school, upstate New York. We had a high school librarian, Dorothy Irving, who decided to take about seven of us from the senior class and teach this honors English class, which was a term no one had ever used or heard of in Germantown, New York before. But she took seven of us out of this senior class of thirty-six and we met in a side room of the library. But we also did things—she would take us forty miles away to Albany to see a ballet or 120 miles south to New York to see a play. And these were incredible expansions of the horizon for all of us in the class. Physical horizons, cultural horizons. And then the other thing that she was doing was also having us write every day. All different kinds of writing—prose, sketches, haiku. And somehow it was that inner landscape of writing that was truly liberating for me. And, in fact, there was just one day when we went for a walk outside the school for about half an hour, and then we came back and she said, well, you should write a poem about this. And, for some reason, I wrote a poem about somebody standing on a rock by the ocean. Now, we're in upstate New York [laughs], we're not talking reality. We're talking the world of imagination created out of language.

FOX: Mm-hm.

ORR: And maybe that language was magical, that you could create a world out of language. For me, that was so exhilarating and liberating. It was incredible, I thought. I'd always had a kind of vague idea of being a writer, but I thought writing was prose. I thought that was like you describe reality, here's the chair with wooden legs and a blue seat and stuff like that. I thought, well, that's what you do with language and that's how you become a writer. But I also thought: how boring, you know? I mean, in a sense, the chair's bad enough, but to describe the chair and make people see the chair? I just couldn't get it. And it wasn't, there was something that needed to be done inside me, and it was only going to be done with a magical, liberating use of language and that's, to me, what poetry was.

FOX: You mentioned an interior landscape. Can you tell me more about that?

ORR: At one level it's the landscape of dreams and nightmares. It's the landscape that your brain sort of spontaneously generates in dream-sleep each night. And that's certainly a different landscape than you inhabit in the world. And within that landscape you also operate by different laws than the physical world uses. In dreams, things are always turning into other things—metamorphosis. That's wild. That doesn't happen in this world, but it does in dreams. And the interior landscape, for me, is also the landscape of emotion, which is, until you give it language, without shape or substance. And even though it's the landscape of your being, you can't move through it until you can give it some form. I think, for me, as a poet what you do is you give it form through language. Which is kind of a highfalutin way of saying that there were things inside me that needed, that were so real, that they needed some form of expression. The, sort of, classic biographical turning point for me is my brother's death when I was twelve and was holding the gun that killed him in a hunting accident. That precipitated enormous emotional consequences and catastrophes inside me, none of which I could make real. I couldn't speak about them.

Who could I speak about them to? My parents? I mean, to who? Who can you talk with about something like that? And we lived, as I said, in this little village where I'd lived my whole life. So I lived with this terror, guilt, shame. All of this material inside me. And I always had, in the back of my mind, a kind of desperate hope after my brother's death, I thought, well, someday I can talk to my mother about this, someday I'll talk to her and she'll forgive me, or whatever we could do in the way of human transaction. And when I was fourteen, she died, pretty much overnight.

FOX: Wow.

ORR: And so, I thought, wow, this is it. That was the one person I thought I might be able to talk to. And, of course, being a fourteen-year-old kid, it was clear to me that her death was really one more consequence of my brother's death. So the irrational logic of the guilty was making me more and more trapped inside that story. It was agony. Poetry, for me, was first, as it is for so many people, I think, both release and escape. I mean that rock by the ocean that I wrote about, well, it was the landscape of isolation, but it was also a dream of somehow being released from this world I was trapped in, inside myself.

FOX: Mm-hm.

ORR: And it was a long time before I was able to realize that, yeah, a poem can be a release, but it can also be an assimilator of all that chaos and confusion. And, in fact, the most powerful and significant poems, I think, are not poems of escape but poems that understand you can take in all that emotional chaos and still order it to coherence.

FOX: You talk about the impulse to write and the importance of that. What happens to you after the poem is out there in the world? Is the response meaningful?

ORR: It certainly is now. I love reading my poems to audiences now. I love the idea of communicating with people in the sense that what I really enjoy is that if I read my poems to people, we somehow start talking after the reading. Those things where they say, will you take any questions after the reading? They're terrified to even ask you that. And I'm thinking, the hell with the reading, let's just have the questions, let's just have a conversation.

So, I've gone from this person who was in terror of other people and, again, I'm describing the first several books and stuff. I had no pride, no pleasure in sharing, in confiding. I was still so far inside myself, working out my own self-absorbed, anguished story.

FOX: Mm-hm.

ORR: I like to think that it had some significance or interest for other people, otherwise it's really a waste of paper. But I wasn't personally capable of admitting to those poems and the person who wrote them, being interested in a human exchange, which now seems to me the glory of poetry. The first glory of it is that there's a place where a person can go who has emotions and experiences. They can go to the page and put them on the page and make a poem. And that's the first glory. Or the first survival, the first joy of it all. But then there's this second joy, which is that people can pick up that page and read it and be moved or be interested. Be affected. Because that's what I was with poems that I read when I was a kid. And all of us have had the experience of reading a poem and saying, oh my God, wow! It just goes inside you and you think, well, that's got to be a miracle. Reading a poem that somebody wrote twenty years ago, it moves you. It moves you to tears. My God, this is speaking my soul! You know, is there anything else like that in the world? I don't think so!

FOX: So, it's a way really of knowing another person on a very intimate basis.

ORR: Absolutely! The most intimate basis, because it would feel as if, pardon the word "soul," let that word stand for whatever we can't really name, but you can feel that connection. And its power to affect a reader, to give a reader . . . I apologize if these words seem really simple or simplistic, but to me, when you read a poem that really, really moves you, you get both hope and courage from it. You really do. I know these words are hard to work with. Because they sound naive. But they're not naive, they're fundamental. I think when I read a poem that deeply moves me, that feels beautiful and moving, I feel as though I've been given more courage to live. It's true, right? I mean, it's just true.

FOX: Mm-hm.

ORR: What happens, even if it's a heart-breaking poem, is you think, my God, you mean a human being went through this? Or, experienced this? And they made something beautiful and coherent out of it? And they're giving it to me? It's inside me now? I mean, you read Whitman or Dickinson, and, my God. . . . There's this line in Whitman, he goes, "long enough have you timidly waded, holding a plank by the shore. Now, I will you to be a bold swimmer. . ." And then there's something, I can never remember the next part, but it's something about swimming out there and dashing with your hair, some nice gesture that Walt would like. But what I see is this, look, now, long enough you've been timidly wading, holding a plank by the shore, and now I will you to be a bold swimmer. And that's about life! That's not just about somebody being afraid to go into the ocean. And you feel that, you feel, well, Whitman, I feel him willing me to be a bold swimmer. Come on! Go out in the water! I love to recite that when I visit the ocean. There's a certain moment swimming where, if you get out past the waves, I like to just swim straight out. Not very far, I'm not a strong swimmer, I'm not crazy or anything—it's not a death wish. But, it's so much fun to recite that while you're swimming out in the water. I mean, you think, oh man, Walt's right here!

FOX: So you make poetry useful, very useful in your life.

ORR: Totally useful! That's what it's there for. I mean it was invented—okay, to me, personal lyric poem, song, this "I" poem about experience—it was invented by culture to help you live. To help you survive. If somebody dies that you love, you fall apart.

FOX: Mm-hm.

ORR: Well, how do you put yourself back together again? People might say to you: Go to a priest, go to a rabbi, read this book of philosophy. Okay, so religion and philosophy, they might help. But also they say (I say): Make up a poem about it, or a song. Write it down on a page. And that, to me, is just as important as any other way of putting yourself back together again. Let's say you fall in love. You fall in love, and pretty much in any culture, no matter how you define it, you kind of go crazy. You go crazy. You're knocked off balance with joy. And insecurity, and this and that and the other thing, and what do you do next? And, you get the love poem. And it's the same kind of thing, it's like trying to . . . I mean, the first thing you do in a love poem, it's not, I think maybe people think the first thing you do in a love poem is you try to charm the other party, you know? But I think really the first thing you try to do is get a grip on yourself. You say, my God, what's going on here? And then once you get that first poem written about I'm crazy in love and this is how I feel and I'm trying to put it down in words. Maybe once you finish that poem, you can then write a poem of charm or seduction or something. [Fox laughs] But you've got to stabilize first. And again, that's what poetry is. How do you survive this? Love and death. Those are the great lyric poems, the great lyric themes, the great crises of human life.

FOX: Mm-hm.

ORR: And you write the poem. Well, it could so happen that you yourself don't feel articulate enough to write a poem or make up a song. But then there are all these other poems and songs that you can use. And you can use them first to stabilize yourself. The poem we read when we're grieving, it consoles us. Remember after 9/11, remember how important Auden's "September 1, 1939" poem was? That poem is an amazing poem. But it was a poem that, to some extent, had been in mothballs. No one had been reading it. Yet, it's among Auden's top ten poems. But, but that's all. That's what it meant. It meant it was one of his best poems. But it didn't really mean anything urgent. It didn't plug into central emotional life. But after 9/11, that poem, people thought: my God, you know, this poem is so important. It speaks to us. "We must love one another or die." That amazing ending. That poem, which was written at the onset of World War II—all that fear and darkness and despair. And then, that tentative affirmation.

FOX: Do you think that in the United States we integrate poetry in our lives as much as we could or should?

ORR: I think we do. But there are a few tangles. If you are a professor at a university (which is what I am), you're supposed to believe and teach that poetry is in the keeping of the high-culture people, which I think is basically not such a great idea. Because it fundamentally misrepresents the nature of poetry, at least as I understand it. Which, as I say, is just basic human, it's your human right just like it's your right to turn to philosophy or religion for comprehension or contemplation of the meaning of it all. You have the same right to turn to poetry and song. And, of course, we do. It's just you have to adjust the definition of poetry; you have to add popular music. You have to add the fact that rock and roll, like it or not—and by rock and roll I mean everything, all the way from hip hop to alternative to blues to Gershwin—when you add all that to the notion of what poetry is, you see that poetry is absolutely central to American culture. Also central as a help in processing that most emotionally tumultuous time in our culture, which is being a teenager, right? I mean, who the hell could have gotten through their teenage years without rock and roll? You know what I mean? You couldn't. And when I say rock and roll, maybe it was Gershwin, you know, that was your time. But remember what it was like. I mean every six months or so, this song comes along that just knocks you on your ass. And you think, oh my God. And you can't get enough of it. You know what I mean? It's just a song on an album, it made it to the top twenty or it didn't. But that status has nothing to do with how it affected you personally. The way it affected you is it obsessed you. You just couldn't . . . you're singing it all the time; you're thinking about it, you can't hear it enough times. And, to me, that means that song is speaking to you. It's working the way a poem does. Somehow it is you. It's channeling you. It's making your existence comprehensible to you—and to the world if they'd only listen. That's real to you. You know, as I say, it's not a top twenty hit. It's a song that really affects you. And if you think of it that way, if you think of how many songs there were like that. I can still remember The Beatles' "She Loves You." And I can remember pushing that on a jukebox in upstate New York when I was sixteen and thinking: Now I can live, this much joy is going to help me live.

FOX: Mm-hm.

ORR: It's a ridiculous song, but it didn't feel that way to me. You wouldn't want to put it on a page, you wouldn't want to write out the lyrics to "She Loves You" on a page and analyze them like a poem, and say, this is as good as a sonnet by John Donne. No, it's not. [Fox laughs] But, the point is, language is channeling feeling. With popular song it's also doing it through melody and everything else.

FOX: What's the relationship between poetry and music?

ORR: That's a good question. I think, in a poem, I think the musical possibilities of language, the patterns of sound and incantation—which is something I love the notion of, repetition of sounds and phrases—I think that because the language is compressed—again, it doesn't hurt that I'm talking about lyric poetry here, I mean, that's all I really know anything about—because language in the lyric is so compressed, the rhythmic possibilities in language become heightened. And we're moving towards incantation, we're moving, in what I consider to be wonderful poems, towards chant, towards a heightened sense of rhythm. You're only steps away from singing it.

FOX: Mm-hm.

ORR: Rap, hip hop, the way that the voice is used as a musical instrument. If more of us had courage as readers to exaggerate the rhythm of a poem when we recited it, I think we would be releasing more power. I think there's a lot of evidence that there's something about music that powerfully affects people emotionally, and we as poets, we're sort of exploiting that. Exploiting, I don't mean in a bad sense. Trying to maximize that intensity, again, for purposes of connecting intimately, emotionally. And irrationally. It's not . . . how music affects us, it's not logically, it's totally without logic.

FOX: When you mention courage, in terms of reading, how does courage enter into your writing? Do you censor yourself out of fear of anything?

ORR: Well, sure. [both laugh] Uh, I censored myself a lot early on, out of shame. I mean, shame is one of the great destroyers of human spirit. I also, for instance, again, the story I was carrying about my brother's death, I felt had to be carried in silence. I felt it was my duty to never speak of my brother's death, just to carry it as a kind of shame in me. To the extent that had I a religious background, it would have been kind of hard-core Protestantism. The bigger cross you lug to the grave without complaining, the better a person you are—that sort of strange thinking.

FOX: Oh!

ORR: That's a hell of a definition of a human life. I mean, when you add to that the fact that I wasn't particularly confident there was something on the other side of the grave, it really made life look pretty grim. And yet it was the way my family had trained me to live. Even when you then enter a kind of family dynamic—again I'm only mentioning it because it's not unlike other family dynamics—with my family dynamic, I had profound shame about my brother's death. The day my brother died, my mother came into my room and she said, something exactly like this happened to your father when he was your age.

FOX: Wow.

ORR: He killed his best friend with a rifle. And I really couldn't say anything. Because, how could this be? I'd never heard of it, never could have conceived of what had happened. With my brother's death, never conceived that that could happen. And now I was being told: Oh, your father did that, too; that happened to him. I had never heard this about my father before, and I would never hear about it again. My mother would never speak to me about this again. My father never said a word. Ohhh. Eight years ago I called my father's sister and said, is it true that this happened? And she said, oh yes.

FOX: Wow.

ORR: My aunt said to me: "Charlie Hayes, your father's best friend when he was a kid. That's the first thing everybody thought of when Peter died, when your brother died." And I thought, everybody thought of it, but nobody said anything about it. I mean, my mother did. It seemed this staggering, impossible coincidence. I thought the day of my brother's death: "This must mean there's some horrible, strange curse going on." My whole life, my father would never talk to me about this. I would periodically try to talk to him, and he just wouldn't speak a word about it. I finally, towards the end of his life, he was even dying at this point, I said to him, I said, "Dad, do you think there's anybody in the world who could know as well as I do how you might feel because of what happened to you? Think about it. It happened to me. Forget for a moment that you think it's your fault that it happened to me. Just think for a moment that the same thing happened to me. You could probably say a few things about this." But he couldn't say anything. So, two things. I finally wrote a memoir about it, trying to transform it. When my father started dying, I thought, if my father and I are linked like this and he's dying, I don't want to die with him. And I just, I need to get through this. I'd written about my brother's death in poems, but I hadn't, couldn't write about the coincidence, my father's experience and my own experience. You can't put that in a poem. You couldn't put it in a novel. If you put it in a novel, people would say: "I'm sorry, that's a ridiculous and unbelievable coincidence." You know? No one's going to believe that. Well, of course they won't! As a contrivance, it's not true. The real thing is, and we all know this, that reality has more bizarre coincidences than would ever be acceptable in fiction.

FOX: Is there a difference between poets and non-poets, and by that I mean the willingness and the need to be known? Which competes with the need to not be shamed, to be secret, to be private?

ORR: I think you're absolutely right; it's both a willingness and a need. It's courage. At one level, you can say it's courage. At another level, writing a poem can be an application to rejoin the human race.

FOX: Hm.

ORR: To be reintegrated into the human community. This is who I am, this is what I feel. This is what I experience. Am I still among you? And I could never have said, I could never have spoken directly about those things. Let's face it, the experiences I had were really quite strange and deeply discouraging for a person. I could never have spoken directly about them. But I learned, ultimately . . . I couldn't write about them in my first book. In my second book, by then I had both the courage and the skill—and this is the other thing, the shaping skill is what you need also—I think I knew from the very beginning that I would have to write about this experience, my brother's death. Because I knew that if I didn't, it was going to exist inside me as a deathful thing. Whereas I feel strongly, that if you write something it's both a release and even a transformation into something maybe not deathful. You discover that. When I wrote my poem about my brother's death, it's extremely rare that someone would come up to you and say, oh, I had the same experience. But on the other hand, many, many people come up to me with experiences that are similar, and that have led them to a similar sense of despair and shame. A dear friend of mine, Jane Kenyon, wrote a wonderful poem called "Having It Out with Melancholy." And it's about being manic-depressive. And it's a lyric poem in seven parts, a wonderful poem. And, for her—God forbid this term "confessional," you know, because that term is an attempt to put shame back on the normal human impulse to express who you are and what you felt—so, no, it's not confessional, it's expressive. It's self-expressive. And that's wonderful. Who else are you going to express but yourself? It's who you are. Thoreau says something like this: "My book *Walden*—it's going to be the same as every other book you ever read, except you're going to see the first person singular in it more often, you're going to hear 'I' a lot. We commonly forget it's always the first person who's speaking." I love that insight: It's always "I" who's speaking. Who the hell else can speak? It's always "I." So, forget this "confessional" nonsense. You know? So, Jane writes this poem, and she's giving expression and form to her personal experience. But how many people in the audience used to come up to her! They didn't even say anything, she said, they just looked at her with tears in their eyes. And she can see it in their faces: "Someone has said what it's like to be me. And someone has given form to what it's like to be me." What a sense of relief and release! And that gets turned into some nonsense talk about therapy and stuff, as though somehow it's therapeutic. It's about healing. There's something wrong with this? Healing's not a good thing? People don't need to be healed? What are we talking about here? I have to tell you, there's a lot of nonsense about poetry.

FOX: Go into that. What are some of your . . .

ORR: Pet peeves [laughs]?

FOX: Your favorite nonsense in poetry.

ORR: I . . . oh. Hm. Don't get me going.

FOX: You can edit it later, so, feel free.

ORR: Yeah. [Fox laughs] I love colleges and universities because they're places where young people go to be reborn. And that happens. You see it all the time. Not all the time, not to everybody. But when it does happen, it's incredible. I mean, for me, I was lucky. As I say, my high school librarian, that's where I was reborn. And, in fact, when I got to college I didn't learn . . . the first college I went to, and the second, I wasn't reborn into poetry. And it already had happened for me. The teachers who taught me there, in college—that's a place where poetry is, in theory, valued. And it's taught. And in many cases there are even creative writing courses and so forth there. And all these things that are wonderful. Right? But then there's also this other part of colleges and universities. And there's something that happens to poetry in our culture that I simply cannot accept, which is that it became part of the cultural elite, part of that. You know what I mean?

FOX: Yeah.

ORR: It's like there's somehow a kind of pyramid. And at the bottom is everything that the professor doesn't want. The pyramid gets narrower and narrower as you go higher and higher. Presumably you're getting closer to God, right? [Fox laughs] I mean, that must be part of the metaphor. And sure enough, there you get to the peak of the pyramid, and there's Wallace Stevens poised on the tip of it. Wallace Stevens and basically, your students are reading his poems and saying, "Huh?" [Fox laughs] And so, they need somebody next to Wallace to say: "Here's what he means." And that's the professor. So you've got this figure of the elite poet who's somehow gotten close to God and the angels, and you've got the professor up there as the pyramid guide. You know, there are always different pyramids, with different people at the top and different professors shouting at each other from one pyramid to the other about how your guy's not really as good as mine. [Fox laughs] So, I hate . . . I'm honestly convinced that poetry is something simpler and more basic than that. That it belongs to human beings regardless of how sophisticated their taste is or has been made to be. I talk about this in *Poetry as Survival* [University of Georgia Press]. There's no human culture on the planet, no society where, if somebody is feeling blue or feeling in love, they don't have the option of writing a poem or making up a song about feeling blue. And if they can't make one up, there's one hanging around that they heard down the street, and they can sing it and it helps them.

FOX: Yeah.

ORR: That's what poetry is. Poetry is this human birthright. By way, not of nature, but by way of culture. But not high culture. This high culture, that's got something to do with so many human beings needing to feel they're better than other human beings.

FOX: Yes.

ORR: Superior. And so you get the hierarchy. Oh, you know, you're stupid, you think so and so is a good poet, when you read more and take more courses and listen to me more, you'll realize that so and so is a jerk. I mean, right, like Whitman was a jerk, right? You know, Whitman's still a jerk to the professors, because you don't need a professor to read Walt Whitman. That's a real problem for professors. [Fox laughs] Nobody can read Wallace Stevens without a professor standing there to help them out. I mean, poor Wallace Stevens, I'm really picking on him. But it's just that's how it happens for me.

He's kind of someone I go to. When I first started teaching, maybe thirty years ago, he was just the darling of the English department. Now there are other darlings. John Ashbery's a darling. I like John as a person. But the way that his work is made to function in this system of hierarchy and superiority, it's nuts. It's nuts.

FOX: I have to agree with you. I think poetry belongs to the people, not to the professors, the priest elite who has to explain it to us.

ORR: Blake, William Blake, he said: Man, forget the priests. To him priestcraft was just a way of making people feel badly about themselves, messing with their heads. And I think the same thing often happens with the teaching of poetry.

FOX: What are the more important messages you try to get across to your students?

ORR: One of the things that I try to say to my writing students is that poetry . . . I guess what I love about poems, one of the things I love is that they seem to me, as I said, to have been invented as a place where you can bring your human confusion, emotional distress, joy or despair. You can bring that inner burden, translate it into language, turn it into words. You bring it to poetry. And poetry's just there waiting for you, and it says, okay, you got some material, you got some raw material, great, you know what I've got? I've got these shaping principles for your story. You got this strange experience? Try and tell it as a story. When did it start? What happened next? Story! That'll give it a little order. Now, that's not so bad is it, you know? You were really confused. Your favorite dog in the world died? Why don't you tell us a story about it? There it is, you know? Or symbol, you know? Which is another great principle. We don't know why these things called symbols affect us, why you focus on this single object and it seems to be mysteriously filled with multiple meanings in a way that's gratifying, and they're all sort of brought together in some strange way and concentrated in a single object. Or incantation, like when you sing a lullaby to a child, it's full of that incantatory repetition. Hush a bye, don't you cry. Or magic spells—these are also incantations. Incantation has amazing consoling powers. Incantation can make you feel better regardless of what's being said. That's what you're doing with a child with a lullaby—in a lullaby it's not the meaning of the words that is helping, it's not the content of that lullaby that's useful. The child is responding to the consoling power of repetition. So, poetry's there with these ordering principles and you as a person bring your disorder to poetry. And you meet and any really exciting poem has got both that disorder and the order in it. And the disorder and the order are both alive, vitally dynamic, alive together. The poem is alive. I can remember when I was a kid and I thought this was really impressive at the time, someone said: "Well, a poem—that's where we turn chaos into cosmos." And I thought, damn, that's so cool, I can see that. But since then I've come to feel that Chaos to Cosmos is too simplistic. I prefer to think of a poem as more like the Yin-Yang symbol the ancient Chinese used, especially the Taoists: that perfect circle containing the black and the white teardrop, how both disorder and order are dynamically present inside the wholeness of a poem. If it were just chaos turned into some perfect sphere circle like a full moon, that would be very magical, but it wouldn't be . . . the beauty part is that a poem brings the disorder into the order. And the disorder is still present; it isn't abolished by the act of the poem. Because if your poems say: Oh, everything's okay, there is no disorder, there's no chaos in the world, that's nonsense. That's an untruth. Some people might find that a consoling untruth, but I don't. Whereas if you keep the disorder alive—that's one of the things that's exciting about the deep poems, the really important poems: that the disorder is still present. It's not abolished. Because we don't live in a world where disorder can be abolished or where suffering can be abolished. What we do have is this wonderful thing called poetry that can take in experiential or emotional disorder, turn it into language and then shape it into the form of the poem—something that can take suffering or confusion and give it form and shape.

FOX: It sounds like you enjoy teaching poetry.

ORR: Absolutely. I get excited. It's not every day that somebody invites you to talk about poetry, right? A funny thing about being a poetry teacher is that my students, bless their souls, are coming to me with their poems. They want me to talk about their poems. And I understand that. It's my job. And I love doing that. But I also want to talk to them about poetry. It's like, there's this incredible thing called poetry. And, of course, it's very hard for young poets to realize, because they're feeling such urgencies and insecurities themselves, it's hard for them realize that poetry is what's really important. The existence of poetry is really, that's the amazing thing. And that poetry itself is larger and more amazing than the poet. But they're so insecure, and we all are when we start out. You know, so many of them, even the calmest seeming of them, are carrying things you don't know about. Needs, anxieties, insecurities, startling experiences. And they're hoping that writing the poem and becoming a poet is going to solve that. Often, it's like "becoming a poet," you know what I mean? That's going to solve these things for them. Well, I'd say no, what's going to solve, what's going to help a lot is entering into an ongoing relationship with poetry, with these huge storehouses of testimony about what it's like to be alive. And testimony about emotional confusions—about the joys and agonies of what it is to be a human being in the world. And that's going to be a lot more important than any individual poem you ever write, no matter how wonderful it is. There's no poet in the world who wasn't really sustained by poetry, I think. Not just by the writing of their own poems.

FOX: What do you enjoy most about what you get from your students?

ORR: I think it's related to the fact that I feel poetry saved my life. Pure and simple. Which is, it didn't solve my life, you know? [laughs] It actually made my life pretty weird. But my feeling is that in many, many different ways, in ways that I can't understand, ways that they may not understand yet, so many of my students have that same kind of feeling and need. And it's kind of exciting to try to be part of the process where they discover what it is that they want and need from poetry. And it's just exciting to be there when they're trying to do that, when they're trying to find the words to make this poem work, or trying to find what it is that they should be writing about, or how they should be writing, how they should be working the language. And feeling like these are all technical problems, but they're really also emotional, spiritual problems related to being a human being.

FOX: Yeah.

ORR: And you can feel that they're tangled together. And you don't really, you know, you don't talk to them. Why would anyone talk to someone about it, about their soul, when they're really trying to write a poem? You talk about the poem, you talk about language, because I love language and my students do also. And yet, there's always a sense in which there's some other incredibly important human subtext that's going on. And again, I'm fifty-eight-years-old now, but when I was twelve and fourteen, I mean, I was headed for death at twenty. And I was lucky. I was headed for death at eighteen when I went as a volunteer civil rights worker to Mississippi. That's where I was headed, I wanted to die there. Well, I love being alive. Like Stanley Kunitz, my teacher, I want to be a hundred [laughs].

FOX: Yep.

ORR: And I wouldn't be if it weren't for poetry and if it weren't for the way poetry goes into life and is about life.

FOX: You mentioned you studied with Stanley Kunitz. Can you share that relationship, what that means to you?

ORR: Well, when I came to graduate school to take an MFA degree at Columbia, I didn't know anything about Stanley's work. I didn't expect to be studying with him. I had never been in a poetry workshop before as an undergraduate, and this is graduate school. I really didn't know what I was doing at all. But maybe about a month after I moved to New York City and I was working at a bookstore, and someone said: "Well, Stanley Kunitz is going to read from this book called *The Testing-Tree* that he's going to bring out next year, just up the street at Barnard. And he's going to be our teacher in the spring semester." So, I went up to the reading, and there were maybe ten people there. And he read from this book called *The Testing-Tree*, and it was the first time that he was writing directly about the central trauma in his own life, which was his father committing suicide when he was still in the womb.

FOX: Wow.

ORR: Yes, a poem called "The Portrait." And this set free and made lucid a kind of theme in his work, the theme of the son looking for the father, searching for the father who will guide him into adulthood. But also, he was writing about the difficulty in living with a mother but without a father. And his mother was a fierce figure. He was writing this material, I think influenced by Robert Lowell and even Ginsberg's "Kaddish," by the confessional poets, in that they were bringing a lot of life material into their work. Stanley had written about these themes before, but in such a disguised manner and so indirectly that no one would really know what was going on. So, I heard Stanley read those poems, and they seemed to me to be handling difficult personal material in a way that didn't feel yucky, that didn't feel like you were learning something about someone that was private. What it was,

was personal and urgent and yet somehow transpersonal. Kunitz had a phrase that was central to his thinking about his own work at that time—he said he was "trying to convert life into legend." His life into legend. So that this kid named Stanley Kunitz, whose father kills himself before the boy is born—this private data becomes in his work the legend of a son looking for a father. It's not just a personal thing, but it becomes something shareable with others—after all, the world is full of sons looking for fathers. That's a kind of male human project. Someone who will teach us, who will guide us, who will show us the way. And he just gave me hope that I could handle difficult personal material which I knew was inside me.

FOX: Mm-hm, mm-hm.

ORR: Um, but I had never, I had never run across anybody that was handling material like that. And I never thought I would ever meet somebody who had. I mean, I didn't even expect to read poems that did that, but to actually have this person as my teacher—it was incredible luck. Because I felt this kind of connection to him. It was a long time before, I mean, I didn't even try to write about my brother while I was working with Stanley directly, because I didn't have enough skill. Emotional skill or linguistic skill. But the fact that Stanley showed that you could write about that stuff, that's amazing.

FOX: Can writing poetry be taught?

ORR: Stanley had something he said: We don't know whether poetry can be taught, but we do know that poets can learn. [both laugh] And so, I don't know whether he goes on to say, so we must. But I think the impulse to poetry is in, I mean, I'm going to say it's in everybody. I like to say that, to ask a group of people: "Hasn't everyone in here either a written a poem once in their life or wanted to?" I mean, do that, ask that question and you discover it's surprisingly true. Whether it's a truck driver or a mailman or an accountant doesn't matter. They've wanted to and maybe, because they didn't feel they could, they ended up buying a card with a poem in it instead. But nevertheless, the impulse was there, the expressive impulse and need. So that the impulse to write is just there. And then, skills about writing, why not? Why couldn't you teach them? And here are all these beautiful poems that have been written, they can read the poems and, God damn, you know, Basho wrote this poem, and look, he just went for a walk in the bamboo grove, and wrote this poem. Why can't you learn that? You see how other people did it. You can learn baseball. It doesn't mean you're going to become a great baseball player, but you can learn the skills.

FOX: You mentioned your librarian teacher in high school asked you students to write every day. Do you still write every day?

ORR: Um, yeah, yes and no. When I was in college, I realized that—and this is the kind of really important thing for me, when I think about my students—we encourage students to write, and we set up these poetry workshops for them to write, and my students in my workshop now, they turn in a poem every two weeks to be discussed, every second week, right? Well, so much of education is sort of brainwashing from outside and, like, sort of, when do you read the book that was assigned for this semester, well, three days before the exam, right? You've got a poem assigned for Tuesday; you have a poem discussion Tuesday, when do you write it? Monday night. And then before you know it you've programmed yourself, you've programmed your creativity into a two-week cycle and it's got an external shame element: Oh Christ, I can't show up at Workshop without my poem, I've got to do something. You're immediately taking that creative person who wants to write and you're training them like a dog, dog tricks, to pervert the impulse instead of internalizing the discipline, you know what I mean? So, some of my best students will come to me and say, "I didn't take the poetry workshop this semester. I've got to get in a workshop next semester because I can't write, you know? I need the workshop to make me write."

FOX: Yes, yes.

ORR: Well, that's no good, really. Then you're writing poems for the workshop, you're doing it for the immediate response of the workshop, the praise or blame or whatever it is. But what you really need to be doing is internalizing the discipline and joy of writing. So, when I was in college it dawned on me that nobody cared whether I wrote or not. I wasn't making friends by being a poet, I wasn't impressing anybody. My girlfriend would have been very happy if I stopped entirely. [Fox laughs] So it became obvious to me that my writing mattered most and perhaps only to me. And so I trained myself to write every day—I felt I needed that self-discipline if I was ever going to learn all I needed to know about poetry. And I felt then that the best way to learn was by writing.

FOX: Mm-hm, mm-hm.

ORR: And I just tried to make myself write every day. I also feel it's great to write bad poems. I feel as though, like, the more you write the better you get. I try to make my students write as often as possible. Because you just get better at it, it's like if you wanted to be a basketball player. What would you do if you were a young person? You'd say: "I love to play basketball; I'd like to be in the NBA someday." Well, the person who wants to be in the NBA "someday," and is actually going to get there, has got to have a lot of natural skills and stuff. But they're also out back shooting baskets six hours a night, you know?

FOX: Yup.

ORR: I mean, that's all there is to it. Nobody's going to get there on natural gifts alone, that's a joke. You don't get, we can't get anywhere at the level that you might aspire to unless you . . .

FOX: And what's the, uh, role of reading for a poet?

ORR: When you're young, you have to read everything. I think you're looking . . . one of the things, when I'm talking about being reborn in college—and it's not just college—I think if you're a poet, you want to be reborn into poetry, into this world of poetry. And it's like, when you're reading books of poems by other poets, that you're reading people. It's like you open this door, and suddenly you're in this big room, and there's Emily Dickinson sitting in the corner by herself, not unfriendly, but pretty much by herself. There's Walt Whitman out there, you know, regaling everybody with his anecdotes. And there's John Keats, and Keats is talking, Keats is kind of blue, because he says in his letters whenever he goes to a party, he has such a weak sense of identity that he becomes whoever is there, loses himself in other identities. And he gets kind of depressed about that. Walt Whitman can't not be Walt Whitman. Emily Dickinson can't not be Emily Dickinson. Poor Keats feels like he can't be Keats, that there is no Keats. And he decides, well, that's part of being a poet. That you're a chameleon, you know? And Shakespeare was a great chameleon, because he could become all those different figures in his plays. But I mean, here's Keats. You read him, you meet him, you know? And when you're at this party, you're meeting these people. But also what you're doing as you read poets is you're looking for your kin. You're looking for your, like, you've got biological parents? You've got a biological family tree, but here as you read these poets, meet these poets, you're looking for your imaginative family tree. You're looking for these poets that you read and you love them so much, you think: "I must be distantly related to them. I must be Walt Whitman's great, great, great nephew or something." You know what I mean? And we make up these trees. I've got a Chinese poet from the T'ang Dynasty in my family tree, and I've got Georg Trakl, the German Expressionist from early in the twentieth century, I sense he's a relative, he's part of my tree, a twisted branch in my family tree. Reading is finding those connections.

FOX: So you really feel a kinship with poets who have an affinity for poetry as you do?

ORR: Absolutely, absolutely. And that affinity, it's like, I mean one dimension of being drawn to poetry to begin with, I think, is a kind of loneliness. And when you read a poet you love, that loneliness and that aloneness is abolished. Maybe not permanently, but why should it be? But certainly briefly and intensely it's abolished.

FOX: I think that's super. A very enthusiastic poet here.

LUIS J. RODRIGUEZ is a leading Chicano poet with four books of poetry, including his latest *My Nature is Hunger: New & Selected Poems* (2005, Curbstone Press/Rattle Edition). He's also founder/editor of Tia Chucha Press, publishing amazing poetry books for 18 years; and Tia Chucha's Centro Cultural, a bookstore/cultural center/Open Mic in the San Fernando Valley section of Los Angeles. A CD of poetry and original music called *My Name is Not Rodriguez* with Luis Rodriguez and the band Seven Rabbit came out in 2002 (Dos Manos Records).

Luis was a leading East LA poet in the late 1970s and early 1980s. He moved to Chicago in 1985 where in a couple of years he became active in the vibrant poetry scene, including poetry slams. He took part in the first "Slam Poetry" tour of Europe in 1993 with such Slam pioneers as Patricia Smith, Paul Beatty, Neeli Cherkovsky, Dominique Lowell, and Alan Kaufman. He's also published award-winning children's books, fiction, and nonfiction, including the international best selling memoir, *Always Running, La Vida Loca, Gang Days in LA* (Touchstone Books/Simon & Schuster).

# Luis J. Rodriguez

October 8, 1998

FOX: How did you come to start writing poetry?

RODRIGUEZ: I don't know. I guess like most kids, teenagers, only my life was more like in the streets and in jail and stuff. For some reason, I started to write. I don't know entirely why 'cause I wasn't very good at language and I wasn't necessarily good in English, but I think it's more like an art that calls you than something you choose. It's more like I was gravitating toward the written word for some reason, just putting things down on pieces of paper and telling ghost stories, vignettes. I was terrible with grammar, I was terrible with syntax, and I couldn't spell very well, but it didn't matter. And to me that was probably more important that it came off that way because learning grammar, syntax and spelling is the easy part. But having that innate drive to want to voice something, to tell a story, to me that's probably the most important end of it.

FOX: Did you experiment with other forms or has it always been poetry?

RODRIGUEZ: I didn't even know it was poetry. There was no formal poetry sense. Somebody told me it was poetry and so I believed him [both laugh]. But when I was about twenty-five years old I decided to go to classes at night and hang with writers and join workshops and that's where I really learned more about the formal parts of poetry and the difference between poetry and short stories. That's when I learned, but I already had a massive amount of work by then, that I was just writing, with no purpose other than to just put it down. So it helped that I could finally know the differences and then dedicate something to say—this is a poem, this is a story, this is an essay, whatever.

FOX: Did your work change in any important ways as a result of going to school and hanging out with writers?

RODRIGUEZ: I think it helped because you're isolated, you're out there by yourself, you don't know what writing is. I read books, but if you don't know what's really going on in the writing world, you're really not going to be a part of it. And nobody could see any "genius" in my writing while I sat by myself, writing this "great work." I wasn't Emily Dickinson who wrote this great stuff and she hardly got out in the world. So I needed to connect with writers, I needed to connect with knowing what the writing world was, what the writing life was like. Pablo Neruda was first introduced to me in a workshop; I never heard of the guy. Then I came to find out how important he is to poetry in the world. So these are the kinds of things that I opened up to. By then I was hungry for it. Then I read Walt Whitman, and everybody else I could get a hold of, like Wordsworth, and I always liked Edgar Allen Poe when I was a kid. I would read these things, even Ezra Pound who, most of it, I never understood. The idea was that I wanted to read Neruda, then Machado, and Paz and all these people. I wanted to really begin to understand what my heritage was, what I inherited as a poet, and this is what the workshops and hanging out with writers and going to performances did; it just opened this world to me. And then, I felt that whatever was inherent as far as me trying to become a writer could connect with something, had a connection with something that was deeper, longer and bigger than I was.

FOX: What is your niche in writing poetry? Is there any special theme in your work?

RODRIGUEZ: Well, it's very much influenced by the life in the streets, the Chicano experience. I think it's more of a migrant experience than immigrant experience. It's more of an indigenous Chicano way of life, a cosmology that, to me, has been formed by all these things, growing up between two worlds and maybe in a third world, mixed in with the borders but outside the borders. And I grew up in the border world. And you were always in between two different things, never part of one and never part of the other, and then there was always a third place where you were creating. I've been formed by all those experiences and I think my poetry reflects it. Now it's about family, now it's about recovery from alcohol, now it's about a poem that I read somewhere that really struck me, or even just sitting in traffic. It still comes from that place of not having a real sense of my country, but also the sense that maybe it's all my country, every bit of it; the borders don't matter.

FOX: Would you say that your writing is universal?

RODRIGUEZ: I think it is just because it is. In other words, I don't think I try to be universal in the sense that I want everybody to understand what I'm saying, so I'm gonna just talk about things that I think everybody will go through. It's very particularized and specific to the Chicano experience, the street Chicano experience, the urban. I don't mean every Chicano has my experience, having been a gang member, drug user, having been in jail, and then transcending that and working in a factory. This is what I write about. But I think the closer I got to that specificity then you bring in the universal because all human beings have perennial themes, their elemental ideas, interests or elemental concerns just keep coming out. So I think they just come out naturally. But the closer I got to who I was I think the more universal it becomes.

FOX: You lead week-long retreats with Jack Kornfield. How does poetry enter into that?

RODRIGUEZ: Very much so. We take maybe 80 to 120 men at a time, but it's not like the men's movement kind of thing. We use ritual, we use map-making, we use drumming, storytelling, poetry. We use people's stories and lives. We have sessions in which we just talk about the issues, whether it's about race, whether it's about gender issues, whether it's about issues between your father and you. Whatever you're wounded by, whatever it is you've gone through in this world, no matter how devastating it may be, art transcends it. Art is the way to deal with just about every aspect of it. You're making beauty out of anything that's ugly. It's like the way that we re-imagine things and then recreate things, like the rebirth out of any crisis. And of course, Jack brings in his Buddhist cosmology. We have Maodoma Sommay who is from West Africa and he brings in his cosmology. Michael Meade is the main person that organizes these and he is a storyteller, but he's also somebody who's studied ritual and mythology for years. I bring in the poetry/Chicano/street aspects of it and I think it's a very interesting mix that seems to work, but mainly because the kind of men that we're bringing in here are men who embody all these things in one form or the other. And if they don't, they learn about things they hadn't even thought about yet.

FOX: What have you learned from the streets?

RODRIGUEZ: When you're talking about the streets, you're talking about people who feel there is no home, even if you have a home. You're abandoned on many levels. The first place you're abandoned is because you have a very race-conscious world in this country, you're abandoned racially or ethnically. Then you get abandoned just by your economy if you're poor. You're not part of the stream of things. You're considered less than that and if you're poor then you have to find a life in the street, you have to find survival, you have to find a means of income, you have to find your art in the street. And that's what I mean being pushed to the point where the street life is where everything happens. And I went through that, and I'm able to draw from that experience even though I've found a home now. Things have changed now where I'm not in the streets every day, but the difference now is that I am in the streets as an elder or teacher and a poet. I go back to these kids; I go back to the streets. I work with the homeless kids. I work with the gang kids. I go into the prisons, because I remember what I went through, and I remember how art and poetry were crucial to my being able to prevail. So if I can go back to these places and help somebody else find that art within them, then I'm giving back what somebody gave to me.

FOX: And people respond?

RODRIGUEZ: Yeah. It's very hard work. I don't run a program in that sense. It's very informal, organic, the way I do things, but it does seem to work. We've now got funding to do workshops with so called at-risk youth. That helps young people develop some leadership and work with art a little bit more intensely. I also get a chance to travel and speak in schools and juvenile facilities, so I do feel there's an impact. There is something that I am shaping as far as the way people think about things, ideas that come out, moving imaginations, getting young people again to feel like they can contribute themselves. Maybe I'm not the best judge of that, but I feel that at least from my end of it, we've really turned around a lot of young people.

FOX: I've talked to many poets who work with young people and all of them say that the worst students in a class write the best poetry. Is that your experience?

RODRIGUEZ: Yeah, because basically that's what I was. I got kicked out of all English classes in high school [both laugh]. I mean, teachers hated me. I was the worst student. I wouldn't do homework. I was very undisciplined for what somebody else wanted. But I was very disciplined for what I wanted. I think the only real discipline to me is self discipline and especially when it comes to art. It has to come from inside of you. It's totally internal. You might have catalysts and support and a lot of inspiration externally, but if it doesn't come from within you, you're not going to do it. It's a kind of discipline where maybe you get up at 6:30 in the morning, 5 in the morning, and work, or you stay late at night, or in the middle of the day. It's a kind of discipline where you sit in the park and you just write. And to me, that's what I had, and that doesn't quite conform to what teachers, some teachers, not all of them, expect people to do—fall into line, do your assignments, make sure that you don't go outside the lines [laughs]. And I'm the kind of guy that would always do that, so I was a terrible student. But I think that there were some teachers, a couple of them, who really could see that I had something, but I couldn't see it. And they were helpful in the sense that they would point out to me, "You have something here, and now you've got to find a way to temper it or bind it up or find your own way to limit it," because I was all over the place and I wasn't going anywhere. But how do you focus this intensity of expression and words that are coming out, how do you find a place where it can become a poem or can become a short story or even an essay? That to me is what teachers helped me understand and helped me try to develop further as I got older.

FOX: I imagine that their confidence and interest in you also was helpful.

RODRIGUEZ: Yeah, it's kind of a funny thing, but it's like people talking about self-esteem. Self-esteem is only one side of the puzzle. You can't have self-esteem if you're not being, how do you say, valued by your community, valued by people in the community who you respect. So you can't just do it by yourself in a vacuum. It's more like an estimate of yourself has to also intertwine with people telling you that you really are of value, you really are important, you really do matter and what you're doing is unique and important. We need teachers that can do that because every kid's different. When they can look at every young person and really see them, I think those are the great teachers, they're the ones that can draw that beauty out of them and say, "You know, you have something to offer that nobody else can do. And here's some skills and tools that might help you get there." But this is something that I think needs to happen more, because most kids that don't conform are pushed aside, they're into prisons, they're alcoholics, they're on drugs, they're raging fools in the street, and you can tell, this is a guy who never found his art or never was conscious of what this art was and maybe nobody in the world told him or maybe it wasn't enough people telling him, "You really have a special unique place in this world and you have to fill it." So I think this is where teachers are vital. And I was fortunate, I think, in my case where there was enough people, not a lot, but there was enough people that could help me see that.

FOX: When you mention the self-discipline, what is your process around writing now?

RODRIGUEZ: Well, now it's very much like a job because I work as a writer. Now, I don't work for anybody else, I'm my own boss, and I worked in factories so long that I got into the thing of 9 to 5, believe it or not, they drum it into you long enough. But, now, I don't mind because now it's for something that I believe in, something that I look forward to, something that I'm enthused about and so I say 9 to 5. I get up in the morning, I work out at the "Y", come back, drink my coffee, eat my breakfast, and then I'm ready to go to work, and I work as long as I can. I get a lot of interruptions, I have to pull in meetings, I have to go and do something, but still my thing is to work. The problem is I don't know when to stop. Sometimes it's late at night and I'm still working. But that's okay. I'm disciplined for that 'cause I believe in this. It is also a very agonizing experience. I'm an intense kind of writer where I really start having these arguments with myself, and I'm writing and I'm getting into it. Sometimes my wife will see me, I start rocking, it's an old thing when as a kid I used to rock all the time, and I'm rocking in front of the computer and I'm just really into this thing and I'm thinking, I may even be talking sometimes to myself, well, what am I doing here? So there's some kind of a battle going on between me and the computer and the words. It's a great battle. I mean, it's a battle that I know I'm going to win, even though sometimes it feels like I'm getting defeated [laughs] all the time. But it's like, it's my high now. I don't drink anymore. I'm glad, too, because I think that takes a lot of energy, a lot of the creative spirit out of you when you're just drinking. I really get into this place, this mode in which I'm just doing battle and it's a great war and I hope it never ends. [laughs] I mean I don't know how other people do it; I'm sure some people just see it as a job. I've heard a lot of writers talk and say, oh, it's a job and a profession and you do all this stuff. That's part of it, that's true, but this other part is bigger. It's an actual ordeal that I go through and I have to overcome it every night when I finish.

FOX: What is the fight?

RODRIGUEZ: The fight has to do with language, has to do with finding the right words, transitions, not getting defeated by simple things—clichés or not finding the expression. Sometimes I want to say something, it's not there yet so I have to really struggle to, how can I say this, the language being condensed, especially with poetry, not letting the words flow all over the place where you're not finding the proper word that really expresses the proper feeling. And so it is a battle, it's a battle to try to create this art out of formlessness. How do you make something specific out of things that are really all over the place? And again, it's a battle that I find very enticing. Sometimes it works and sometimes it doesn't. But I know in the end I'm going to win one way or the other 'cause that's just the way I feel. When I don't, when the day comes I don't win, I'm giving it up. What I mean by winning, it's like eventually I will look at my piece, and I took it where it needed to go. And that to me is what is important. I'm pretty prolific, but I'm not the kind of person who just writes and writes and lets things drift off. I really work them up for a long time. I spend a long time on my poems trying to get them to the point where I'm fairly satisfied. And I can't even tell you what that satisfaction means. It's maybe the line breaks are where they are supposed to be, maybe, who knows, the rhythms are going right, maybe the right words. I don't know, something satisfies me about how this poem is done, and I won't finish a poem until it feels that way. So every poem, for me, every poem goes through this process, where I'm really taking it where it can't go any further.

FOX: Do you work on just one poem at a time?

RODRIGUEZ: No, sometimes I'll work on ten poems at a time. I'll go back to them. Sometimes I'll let some go for a while. Some come fairly easy, some take forever. There are poems that I've spent ten years working with. And then usually, I'm working on ten projects at one time. I've got essays that I gotta write. I'm trying to finish a children's book, and then poems and then, of course, I'm trying to finish a short story collection and have to get back to that. And the interesting thing with me is that I can get to it. People say, "Well, how do you go from a poem to a short story?" I don't know, I can do that. When I'm in the poem, I'm in that poem. But then when it's done, then I think, well, let me see this short story, and I can get into the short story. If I'm going to do an essay I seem to get into it, 'cause there's poetry in the essays and there's poetry in short stories and, of course, there's story in the poems.

FOX: How does a poet earn a living from writing?

RODRIGUEZ: It's very difficult, as you know. You can't really do it by publishing poetry, 'cause I get published and all I get is books for them, which is fine but there's not much money. The money seems to be in readings, it seems to be in grants, it seems to be in fellowships. I've been fortunate that I've gotten a few fellowships. Some of them I didn't even apply for which is great because, I tell you, you get a fellowship, and you say thank you. And I think what happens is you put yourself out there. I have a friend who says that for a poet, the only real currency is acknowledgement, 'cause you're not going to get a lot of money. But, if you get acknowledgement, people see you, they recognize your work, then things begin to happen. "Luis Rodriguez, oh, I read his book, he's speaking here, he's reading over here, he won this award,"—that seems to be the currency that we live by.

FOX: Do you enjoy readings?

RODRIGUEZ: Oh, I love them. I'd probably do them all the time except I need to write, too [laughs]. I need to balance it with family and my other commitments with youth and all my other writing projects. Readings have another dynamic that I get into; it's another kind of a war / battle situation that I love. The adrenaline flows, you're trying, and this time you're at war with an audience, this time it's whether what you work up is going to get over. And you have to find the rhythm, and you have to find the pace and then you have to find the way to express it so that people are really into what you're writing. I love the kind of reading where I just throw it out there, who cares who gets it. I think there's a very important part that lets me read it in a way where hopefully they'll get it at another level, the oral level, cause it's another way to understand the poem. It's different than on the page. And different things happen when you're reading. So I see it as just another way that this poem finds expression.

FOX: How many readings do you do?

RODRIGUEZ: I've cut down considerably. I used to do them two or three times a week here in Chicago. For about two or three years, I was all over the place. I would say maybe two or three a month and usually in other parts of the country and then usually combined with lectures and talks, too, 'cause I talk about the issues, so with the reading there may be a lecture. I cut down a lot because of the fact that I needed to do more writing and because this has become a business now, "Luis Rodriguez Enterprises," and so I have to take care of all that stuff. But, the readings are very important, and I really try to dedicate as much as I can to make sure the readings go well.

FOX: What part of the business do you enjoy the most?

RODRIGUEZ: Writing is the number one thing. It's almost like sometimes I can feel the sense of imbalance when I'm traveling too much, when I'm not writing. It's like something's wrong. I have even set engagements way ahead of time, which I never used to do. Now I tell people, and it's true, I say, I'm booked up to the end of the year. It's not like every day I'm booked up, it's just that there's also times I say I gotta write.

FOX: Do you feel you've already completed your best work, or does your best work lie ahead of you?

RODRIGUEZ: I have the sense that I haven't even tapped into what's possible. And I don't even know if I'll ever get to it. It's like there's a lot more there, and maybe some people get to it and maybe they die before they do. Who knows, but you're always thinking there's more there to be done. It's like there's a big mine that you're mining and you hit one vein and then you think, no, wait a minute, I know there's more beyond this. So you keep going at it and then you might die in the middle of the mine there and you never get to that big huge mother lode, but the point is you have tried. That's the way I look at it. So, no, I think there's much more important work that I still have to do. I'm committed to trying to do it, however long it takes and whether I'll get to it or not, we'll see how far into the mine I can get.

FOX: What advice do you have for young poets just starting out?

RODRIGUEZ: I think the biggest problem with young poets is a commitment that comes, not because there's money in it or because there's even fame in it. It is a commitment that comes to yourself. You have to commit to your own morality, the morality of your own art. It's something that a lot of people miss because they want to have an impact immediately to what's going on, and poetry and writing is not an immediate gratification kind of a thing. It just isn't, it's something you have to really work toward. And to me, the young people have it harder because there's so many things coming at them, and I find that a lot of good writers that I've worked with end up giving it up very young because it's just not immediate what you can get out of it. I remember this one girl who was such a good poet and then she ended up having to work and was going to school but not to become a poet, just to get some kind of degree. I saw her on the bus recently and I asked her, "How's your poetry?" She hadn't been writing and, oh, maybe she'll come back to it, but the point is so many things can pull you away. So I think you have to really see it as something that you have to keep hanging in there with, persistence, and just not give up, and even if you have to get a job here or go to school, whatever you have to do, keep writing, keep going back to it, so eventually when you're at a point where you can say I can dedicate myself to this, you've already done so much leading up to that.

FOX: How do you deal with becoming better known and famous, when people know who you are by your face?

RODRIGUEZ: A really good thing about being a poet is that it's not like being a celebrity. When I go to a reading and I see a large group of people and I know they've read my work and they really admire what I'm doing or they want to know more about what I'm doing, it's a different feeling than if I was an actor and millions of people know you, but they really don't know you, and I think this is better. I think it's almost like I can walk down the street, nobody's going to ask for my autograph, but if I go to a reading and people are there 'cause they've seen my work and they really like what I'm doing and they really want to connect with me. It is a great feeling. It's a sense of, I've accomplished something here because now there's people who can appreciate what I'm doing and maybe get something out of it that might help them and make their life better, whatever it might be. It's just different, and so I think it's a kind of well known that's not so well known, that helps as far as being a writer, because I don't want to be a celebrity. The problem with me is that I'm probably going to write some books or when I do get out there so much, people will get to see me in a certain way. The media, for example, I get to speak and so people see me, "Well, I've seen you on TV," and they don't really know my poetry. So that's the problem, when it's not about what I'm doing as a writer, but I try to maintain the writing end of it so that people get to know me for what I'm writing.

FOX: Do you feel that very many people really get it, understand the fullness of what you're doing?

RODRIGUEZ: I think most people that read my work do. I had a fiction writer tell me that he doesn't like poetry very much, and then he says, "You know what, your poems, I like the first one, the second one after it, the fourth, fifth, the sixth." You know, he really liked them, and I think because it's not that hard to get my poetry. There's also a very surface emotion end of it. I'm not bleeding on the page, but I am able to try to bring out some emotional engagement with the reader and then of course it's successful in the sense that it's performance oriented, it's oral. I'm not trying to get really tricky and fancy with literary acrobatics in my poetry even though I also believe in the power of being able to find interesting ways of saying things. So I think what people get out of my poetry is that there is a narrative drive, there is a sense of the images being familiar enough so they can get to 'em. I do feel like it's more of a poetry that engages more people than maybe some poets who really don't want to reach a lot of people; they want to reach maybe a certain small number of people. I feel like my poetry can reach more people. In fact, I think that the ones that don't get my poetry are a lot of poets who just only read poetry and they don't really seem to know who I am or care about what I'm doing as much as regular folks. I read poetry in schools and kids jump up and dig it. I get good responses when I do poetry in places that nobody will do poetry, at a park, in jail, in prison, and in churches. I've read poetry in churches and people really seem to get into it versus a poetry setting in which you have well known poets who all care for each other, and I'm interested in them, but I don't think they're necessarily interested in me. They seem to be in another place and I think that's where I'm not as well known for what I'm doing. I would really like for them to understand why I do what I do and maybe even to appreciate it as an art, as a developed art that I'm working on, a certain way that I'm putting words together. I would like them to pay more attention. I'm talking about reviewers or some of the publishers or even some of the poets out there. But if they don't, that's fine, 'cause I still have so many ways in which my poetry reaches people.

FOX: It seems that there's a gap between academic poetry and poetry of the streets.

RODRIGUEZ: Yeah, and I kind of feel bad about that situation developing because, again, I don't want to be pigeonholed into the streets when I'm trying to do poetry that takes some thinking and really deliberate use of words, and there is artifice involved. I'm not just trying to be flippant. But the other side of it is that I do think it's a problem when all the great poets can't reach anybody, when poets are saying some great things and very few people are hearing them. I've really got to break through that. I gotta try to talk and read to as many people as possible and really engage them. I think poetry has got to start breaking out of its bounds and I know the publishing world and the entertainment world and all that world could give a hoot, but then maybe it's up to the poets, cause if they're not going to do it, somebody's gotta do it. But we gotta make poetry, I think, central to the culture again. And I think it really says a lot about where the culture is at—where it's missing the poetry, it's missing its soul. I don't think you can have real soul talk between people unless poetry is central to it.

FOX: Would you say that's more true in the United States than other countries?

RODRIGUEZ: Oh, absolutely. I've been to the poorest countries, Nicaragua, land of poets, Mexico, everybody's a poet, you know, Europe, poetry all over the place, Japan, they say that their poetry books sell tens of thousands of copies. Here, if you sell 1,000, you're doing great. So I think other countries appreciate it more, but I think it's changing, too, because the influence in the United States is very great. Basketball and baseball and the latest blockbuster movie is everywhere now, and there's McDonald's everywhere, so, unfortunately, we're transposing or transplanting this antipoetic, unpoetic culture to other cultures that are very poetic intrinsically, have always been. Unfortunately, I think it is affecting them, influencing them, infecting them probably. So I think it's important for us then in the United States as poets to make sure that we push poetry back into the center of the culture because it's hurting everybody that poetry doesn't sell very much and nobody cares about it, that some bookstores don't even carry poetry and if they do they have it hidden away and very few people can get to it. I'm of the opinion of Joseph Brodsky, that poetry should be everywhere: in the hotel, sports events, inaugurations. It should be at high school proms, whatever. Poetry should be happening all the time. It should be constantly on the minds of people.

FOX: Why do you think the United States is so unpoetic?

RODRIGUEZ: Well, it has to do with the fact that the culture is more geared toward money. Unfortunately, this is the biggest, most powerful, money system in the world, and that means you're going to do something else, you're going to have a book by Tom Clancy sell 1.5 million copies because of the money in it. But, you know, Tom Clancy is not a great literary writer. You're not going to get a lot of poetry in there—he might be a great storyteller, I'm not trying to put him down, he's a writer, he deserves what every writer deserves as far as that goes. But, you can tell the difference. Philip Levine is not going to be considered in the same way, and that's a shame, cause I think people like Philip Levine or any good poet are saying something deeper, more meaningful, something more provocative, a little bit more imaginative than any of these other writers that are selling millions and millions of copies. So, I'm even concerned with the self-help fad now, books of self-help, but there's no real poetry in it. I try to read some of these things, I say, you know, this doesn't really help anybody [laughs]. So it's like the real poets are really saying we don't have a place to connect with people. And this is something that we as poets have to try to change.

FOX: What do you think of poetry slams?

RODRIGUEZ: I have always said that they're very important. They're important because, again, it's another place in which poetry reaches out beyond what normally poets do. Poetry slams are not for everybody, though. Some people can get into them. I used to slam. I don't slam hardly at all now 'cause it just doesn't seem to get me going as much as other people. But I attend them. I support them. I think good slammers are great, poor slammers are bad [both laugh]. I think it's another way that poetry needs to keep moving in the culture, going to new audiences. Slams aren't the only way to do it; there's so many other ways of doing them. I prefer personally just a regular reading, just get up and read your story and don't worry about whether somebody's judging you or if you're competing with somebody else. Just read, man, just let it out there, and if you don't get over, well that's fine. Let the other guy get up, maybe he'll get over. That's what I prefer, but there's poetry slams here in Chicago, especially at the Green Mill. There's still 200 to 300 people that show up to them. So that's important, that audiences are still there and we need to keep expanding on that.

FOX: Who are some of your favorite contemporary poets?

RODRIGUEZ: Well, I mentioned Philip Levine 'cause he happens to be one of my favorites, from way back actually. I've always appreciated his poetry. Who am I reading right now? Of course, I like a lot of the Native American poets. I've always liked Joy Harjo, Sherman Alexie who's now getting a lot of attention, and the Chicano poets such as Juan Felipe Herrera, Pat Moyá, Lorna Dee Cervantes and Li-Young Lee. I have a poetry house, Tía Chucha Press. I publish a lot of people that are probably not as well known, but there's Carlos Cumpián. We just did a book by Virgil Suarez. There's a young poet named Terrence Hayes, an African-American, great poetry. I'm interested in these kinds of voices. Cin Salach is here from Chicago, we published her book of poetry. She's a very powerful performance poet who is able to translate that into poetry on the page in her book. So I'm reading all these people. But wherever I can get a handle, find a book in a bookstore that speaks to me, I end up reading it.

FOX: You talked earlier about emotional content. Is that something you try to bring into every poem?

RODRIGUEZ: Well, it kinda comes out of the poems themselves. I don't purposely say I'm going to do this. It's just that there's different kinds of emotions and sometimes emotion is laughter, sometimes I try to be very light. Sometimes if I'm going to be very sad or grieving or sorrowful, I gotta make sure that comes out. Again, it's not like I want the emotion to be crying all over the place. There is a sense of control, a delicate tension. You gotta know how to bring it in. You gotta know when to stop it. But still it's important that it's up to the surface and not just underlying. I make sure it comes up to the surface and hopefully hits another emotional response from people who are reading it.

FOX: You want to combine emotion, I assume, with intellectual interest?

RODRIGUEZ: Sure, all those things. You gotta engage people on all those levels, you gotta engage them esthetically, intellectually, emotionally, spiritually, even other levels, politically. Not that every poem does it but somehow you're bringing all these things in there. In fact, you can't separate any of these issues really. Some people might say, like, here's a political poet. Well, I'm political and then I'm also this, I'm also that, all of these things come into the poems, and they're all part of it. I can't separate myself, saying, "Well, I'm not going to do this kind of poetry." I try to make sure that you're going to get engaged. Sometimes I'm trying to get a spark in your head, or a spark in your heart. Either way, something's gotta [snaps fingers], gotta go.

FOX: Do you share your work with anyone while you're writing?

RODRIGUEZ: Well, mainly, I've been doing it myself, but it's not a good idea. I used to share my work with at least two or three really close poet friends who I trust that when they're going to say something it'll be real, it'll be honest and even if they're critical I can learn something from it. The problem is not to show it to 20,000 people. I used to take my poems to workshops and have 30 people look at them, and then I found out that's not very helpful. Maybe in the beginning it might be, but after a while I said I don't need 30 people telling me what this poem's about. I do need, though, maybe one or two different eyes to look at it differently than me. People who can feed back something to me that I'm missing. But I try not to show it to a lot of a people and, lately, I haven't really showed my poems to anybody. I just keep working on them until I'm happy.

FOX: What would you like to be remembered for?

RODRIGUEZ: I'd like to be remembered for my poetry, and I would like my poetry to be remembered for, the only word I can think of is, honesty. I think there's still not a lot of honesty in writing. I still think there's a lot of covering up, even if the writing is very good. I find a lot of people talk about issues and they're not really getting deep into things. And the ones that do are fantastic. And I'm not saying that they gotta write intimate confessional poetry, I'm just saying even if they're writing things that are not that way, there's an honesty about it that just seems to come through. So I'm looking for being known for that, if at all possible, no matter what I'm writing about, that there's honesty.

ALAN SHAPIRO published his first volume, *After the Digging* (Elpenor Books), in 1981. The next five—*The Courtesy* (1983); *Happy Hour* (1987, winner of the Robert and Hazel Foundation Memorial Award and the Poetry Society of America's William Carlos Williams Award); *Mixed Company* (1996, winner of a Los Angeles Times Book Prize); *The Dead Alive and Busy* (2000, winner of the Kingsley Tufts Poetry Award)—came out with the University of Chicago Press, followed by *Selected Poems* (Carcanet Press, 2000); *Song and Dance* (2002) and *Tantalus in Love* (2005), the latter two with Houghton Mifflin. He has written two prize-winning memoirs, *The Last Happy Occasion* and *Vigil* (University of Chicago Press, 1996 and 1997); a work of criticism, *In Praise of the Impure: Poetry and the Ethical Imagination* (TriQuarterly Books, 1993); and two translations, *The Oresteia* (2003) and *The Trojan Women* (forthcoming), both with Oxford University Press. His new book of poems, *From the Book of Last Thoughts,* will be published by Houghton Mifflin in 2008. Other honors include a Guggenheim fellowship, two fellowships in poetry from the National Endowment for the Arts, the American Academy and Institute of Arts and Letters Writer's Award, the O.B. Harddison, Jr., Poetry Prize, and a Lila Wallace-Reader's Digest Writers' Award. And Academy of Arts and Sciences fellow, he is the W.R. Kenan, Jr., Distinguished Professor of English at the University of North Carolina at Chapel Hill.

Alan Shapiro (photocredit: John Rosenthal)

# Alan Shapiro

February 20, 2005

FOX: Let's start. You were sharing with me a story about the reading at USC. If you could tell it again, that would be great.

SHAPIRO: All right. Well, I read at USC about three years ago and my mother, who at the time lived in the San Fernando Valley, came to the reading, to hear me read for the first time in her life. She was recovering from knee-replacement surgery, and my late brother's daughter brought her to the reading. The reading was set for 4:30. I got there about 4:25. And people were arriving and a lot of friends, a lot of old friends of mine from Southern California came to the reading, so I was saying hello to everybody, and at one point while I was talking to some people across the room, my mother yelled out from her seat, "Alan, we got to get this show on the road!" [Fox laughs] "I thought you said it was going to start at 4:30, it's already 4:35. I'm going to get stuck in traffic on the way home." [Fox laughs loudly] "I made an effort to get here on time; I think you should make an effort to read on time." [both laugh] So eventually the reading started at about ten minutes to five. So my mother, of course, was already agitated. Now I am somebody who gives short readings. I don't feel like it's a wise move to keep an audience longer than they can bear [laughs] to listen to poetry. So, I keep close track of the time and there was a clock to the right of the podium, so after I finished the first poem, I looked up at the clock just to see how much time had passed. Then I read the second poem, and then I looked up at the clock, and then I heard from the audience, "Stop looking at the clock!" [Fox laughs] At first I thought I was hallucinating, I thought I'm just nervous because my mother's in the audience, she couldn't possibly have said anything. But after I finished the next poem, I heard, "Stop looking at the clock! It's rude to the audience. Why don't you get a watch?" And I thought, "Oh my God, I'm fifty years old and my mother is telling me how to give a poetry reading, during the poetry reading." [both laugh] So I hurried through the next few poems—short as my readings tend to be, this was by far the shortest. As I was walking from behind the podium and the applause was dying down, my mother said, "Why don't you wear a watch? You're a big boy, you can afford a watch. Why don't you get a watch?" I walked over to her, and I said, "Ma, this is not the time." And she said, "How would you know? You don't wear a watch!" [Fox laughs] So, that was my USC experience.

FOX: Has your mother ever seen you read again?

SHAPIRO: No. She has not. [both laugh] And she never will.

FOX: You said you like to keep your readings short. It seems like poetry has morphed from *The Iliad*, a book-length poem, to shorter poems now. We do one-page poems, it seems.

SHAPIRO: Well, I read a lot of poetry, I have a lot of poetry committed to memory, I love the oral tradition of poetry, I love hip hop, I love rap music, which I listen to often because of my children, my son, especially. But I do think that the majority of American poetry is primarily lyrical, primarily short, and that the long epic or narrative conventions have been ceded to prose. I think our attention span for poetry has diminished, certainly. I think people can only take in about twenty, thirty percent of what they hear; after about a half hour most people get restless and bored. Now, of course, the receptivity of an audience depends, in part, on the accessibility of the poetry that's being read to them. I also think it's easier to listen to a poem in rhyme and meter than a poem in free verse because formal poems tend to be more appealing to the ear. Which is not to say that some free verse isn't ravishingly musical, but for the most part there are more musical properties to formal verse, and for the most part it's easier to take in a narrative poem than a lyric poem because in a narrative poem you have story to follow. But most poets nowadays write free verse lyrics that tend to be compressed, dense and often fragmentary or alogical. And whatever virtues work like this may have on the page, it is often difficult to listen to in the auditorium for any length of time. It's very different from *The Iliad, The Odyssey*; these are narrative poems that depended on an enormous amount of repetition, formulaic phrases and episodic set pieces. Homer's audience was familiar with the stories he was telling, they knew the plots already. What bards did was riff on stories everybody knew, working their own variations on established material. The metrical properties of *The Iliad* and *Odyssey* were unambiguous and emphatic, which also helped compel and sustain the attention of the audience. I had dinner once with John Herrington, a famous classicist who wrote a wonderful book about the song tradition out of which tragedy comes. After dinner, he recited the opening of *The Iliad* in Greek in a way he imagined Homer would have delivered the poem. The first word of the poem is Menos, "anger," and he shouted it out in a highly stylized manner, like a very loud chant, it was incredibly powerful.

FOX: Mm-hm.

SHAPIRO: The most effective readers of poetry today tend to be the writers of light verse. People like Billy Collins write poems that are very charming and very witty and easy to absorb, easy to take in. He's the Jerry Seinfeld of American poetry. Tony Hoagland, a much better poet, is also really fun to listen to. He does a lot of very serious clowning around on the page, and the humor makes his readings a lot of fun without compromising the importance and dignity of the poetry. I could listen to him for hours. But for most poets, I think, a half hour is about the limit, for me anyway.

FOX: Do you think that's partly a matter of audiences being used to sound bites?

SHAPIRO: Maybe. Yeah. Could be. I suppose our attention span is much shorter than it probably was a hundred years ago. I'm sure that has something to do with it.

FOX: How many readings a year do you do?

SHAPIRO: Well, it depends. I'm doing a lot this year because I have a new book coming out. I just came back from the University of Virginia where I actually read twice in one day, once to the medical school and once to the MFA program. And I have about two or three per month for the next few months. I don't know what an average would be. But this year I'm doing ten or fifteen, that's a lot for me. Unless I have a reason, unless I have a book coming out, I don't do a lot of readings because with a big family and all it's simply hard to get away. So I only give readings when it's worth my while to do so. And that means when I get paid enough and, two, when I'm assured of getting an audience in double-digits. It's never good for the ego to travel two thousand miles to give a reading to seven people. I have a keen enough sense of my own irrelevance; I don't need to have it dramatized to me [both laugh] by having no one show up to hear me read.

FOX: It's a little discouraging.

SHAPIRO: The most discouraging experience is to step off a plane and have the person meeting you say, "Well, we didn't realize there was a basketball game tonight." [both laugh] You know you're in for a long evening.

FOX: Do you have any sense of the popularity of poetry in the United States as compared to other countries around the world?

SHAPIRO: I don't know a lot about other countries. I think that poetry is doing very well in America. I mean, when you talk about poetry, you have to talk about poetries. There's a lot of different kinds of poetry. There is this sort of poetry based in the universities which is often mischaracterized as academic. Just because it's in the university, doesn't mean it's academic. There are great poets in America right now who are making a living teaching because that's the form of literary patronage of our society. The word "academic" has a cold, formalistic, disengaged connotation, and there's a lot of really great poetry that is deeply engaged in the most important aspects of what it means to be alive right now, coming out of the universities. There's also the barroom-based poetry slams, a different kind of work, but very vital and a lot of fun and entertaining. There's hip hop, which at its worst is crude and vulgar, but at its best is just astonishing, I think songs of Eminem or 50 Cent or Tupac Shakur are as good as the poetry of anybody. So, there's a lot of different types of poetry, and I think the diversity of poetry in America reflects the diversity of our culture. And I think that is a good thing. For me, the vitality of American poetry resides in its impurity. We are a mongrel culture. We are a culture that comes from other places, and that is our strength and that is our vitality. I know for me personally that I am nowhere more vital as a writer, and nowhere more American, than in the hyphen that separates "Jewish-American."

FOX: Mm.

SHAPIRO: That's the place of greatest impurity, the place where the worlds collide. And that's where I try to write from, and I think that's what the best work by anybody comes out of. We're a hyphenated culture. And our art is great because it situates itself in or on the hyphen. I feel that my obligation as a writer, if I can paraphrase Coleridge, is to bring the whole soul into activity, and for me that means honoring every aspect of my experience.

Now, I grew up in a lower-middle-class Jewish household in which my parents spoke Yiddish, or Yinglish. So, certain Yiddish inflections and intonations are an extremely important part of my relationship to English. I went to Hebrew school. My teachers were Holocaust survivors, and though I don't have Holocaust survivors in my family, there were Holocaust survivors in the neighborhood where I grew up.

FOX: Mm-hm.

SHAPIRO: I grew up in the '50s and '60s. Rock and roll was an extremely important part of who I was and has greatly influenced the kind of writer and person I've become. As have other forms of popular culture. My brother was a musical-comedy star, he spent most of his life on Broadway, and his last big credit was *Sunset Boulevard* with Glenn Close, before he died in 1999. I grew up listening to musicals; the first songs I memorized were show tunes. That too has influenced my sense of what a poem is or can be.

FOX: Mm-hm.

SHAPIRO: The household I grew up in was not a literary household—there was nobody in the house who read . . . my sister was the first person in my family to go to college. Neither of my parents went to college. My brother didn't go to college; he went directly to New York from high school. He was a professional actor from the age of seven. My brother practiced by singing along to records. We also watched a lot of television. We had a television in every room, and they were almost always on. All those forms of popular and ethnic culture informed my life, and still do. As a writer, I want to be able to find a place for everything. When I went off to college, I immersed myself in higher forms of culture, in the traditions of Western literature, going all the way back to the Greeks, and of course that too has contributed to my sense of what poetry is, and has helped make me the writer I am. I'm never happier than when I can move, say, from high to low levels of discourse, from something literary to something slangy, from something Christian or classical to something American or Jewish-American. To me, that's a way of honoring the impure, mongrel nature of my own experience, which, again, is nowhere more American than in that radical impurity.

FOX: Is there any single influence, a person or a work, that stands out for you personally, to have influenced you?

SHAPIRO: Well, the poetic influences came later, because I had started writing poetry before I had read any poetry, really.

FOX: Mm-hm.

SHAPIRO: I would have to say that Bob Dylan would be my first love, my first poet, the first songwriter who got me interested in language. And particularly "Subterranean Homesick Blues."

FOX: Mm-hm.

SHAPIRO: "Johnny's in the basement mixing up the medicine, I'm on the pavement thinking about the government, the man in the trench coat, badge out, laid off, says he's got a bad cough, wants to get it paid off. Look out kid, it's something you did, don't look now, but you're doing it again." Anyway, that caught my interest. It was in a way the first rap song. [Fox laughs] It was rap before there was rap. Yeah, Dylan was extremely important to me. The Beatles were important, and the Rolling Stones, and then of course, through Dylan I got interested in Beat poetry and was interested in Allen Ginsberg and Kenneth Patchen, and Lawrence Ferlinghetti. I also liked Rod McKuen. Now I know that he's regarded by everyone as the embodiment of the trite and sentimental, the gold standard of bad verse. The majority of American poets who dismiss him have not read him. I have, and I can tell you he is just as bad as everybody says. At the same time, when I was fifteen years old and just discovering what poetry could do, he was a source of pleasure. He was useful, even if what I thought of back then as great work, "Listen to the Warm," for instance, doesn't quite hold up [laughs]. Listen, anything that gets you interested in language and makes you want to use it and express yourself can't be all bad.

FOX: What in a poem does make it hold up?

SHAPIRO: You know, that's hard to say. Part of what makes teaching so difficult, is that you can only teach what you can talk about. And you can't teach what you can't talk about. And there's certain aspects of poetry that are very hard to define, like what makes it really good or what makes it hold up. I would be reluctant to try to define it. Definitions always show the limitations of the definer. Speaking just for myself, I can say that my ambition as a writer is to write something that the reader could not ever forget. I want my poems to be unforgettable. I want each poem to stick to consciousness like a burr will stick to your pant leg as you walk through the woods. I want my poems to have adhesive power. And what gives it that power? I don't know. It's hard to say. Insight, wisdom, a sense of beauty, it has to have all of those things. It has to be musical, it has to give pleasure. Horace says it has to instruct and delight. And instruction on its own is insufficient. And if I had to choose between the two, I would choose delight over instruction any day of the week.

FOX: Yes.

SHAPIRO: But it has to be pleasurable. If there's no pleasure for the writer when he writes, there'll be no pleasure for the reader when he reads. Elizabeth Bishop has a wonderful, wonderful statement that she makes in a letter to her friend, Anne Stevenson. She says that the thing we want from great art is the same thing necessary for its creation, and that is a self-forgetful, perfectly useless concentration. For me this statement describes why I keep writing. It's certainly not for the money. It's certainly not for the accolades which, as my old teacher J.V. Cunningham used to say, have been infrequent and somewhat grudging. Or as Truman Capote puts it, "It's a long walk between drinks." It's not for the poetry readings. It's for that self-forgetful, perfectly useless concentration that I sometimes, when I'm lucky, can reach when I'm in the middle of working. And it's completely independent of whether that something is good or bad.

FOX: Mm-hm.

SHAPIRO: To me, the only thing that has kept me going through the years, as a writer, is that deep, private, self-forgetful joy that I feel when I'm working. When you sit down at the table and it's eight o'clock in the morning and then you look up and it's, God, it's three o'clock in the afternoon. All that time has gone by as if in a single moment. And in that prolonged moment, you were completely given over to the task at hand, you were joyful, even if you were writing about how joyless your life has been. Because you had totally forgotten everything but the poem you were trying to make.

FOX: How do you get into that mode? I assume it doesn't happen every time you sit down to write?

SHAPIRO: No. But, I think the more often you sit down to write, the greater chances of you reaching that kind of hypnotic state. It's the same thing that athletes talk about when they say they're "in the zone." The game slows up, and everything seems like it's happening in slow motion, and the basket is this wide, or the strike zone is this wide, it's exactly the same kind of profoundly in the body and profoundly out of body experience. You feel there's a, I don't know how to describe it except as an intense state of happiness where you feel like all of your faculties are in agreement with one another, and what's inside is in agreement with what's outside.

FOX: Mm-hm.

SHAPIRO: And it's as close to paradise and heaven as we can find on this Earth. That sense of concentration and of, of being somehow completely and utterly present to what you're doing, undistractedly present, is so, it's so joyful that, that when you're not in that state, you're hungry for it and dissatisfied. And that may be partly why so many writers lead unhappy lives. It's not because the work thrives on suffering. I mean, everybody suffers, whether you're a writer or not, everybody lives chaotic lives, bad things happen to everyone. A writer doesn't need to screw his life up in order to feed the suffering machine that is the poetry, not that. But it may be that the pleasure of work is so great that the writer is dissatisfied with every other experience life offers, everything else seems insufficient by comparison.

FOX: Mm-hm.

SHAPIRO: It's like an addiction. And the sad thing about this is that this addiction can make everything else, including family, seem like a poor substitute. Lately, I've come to think that raising children and writing is like walking two dogs that hate each other. Well, that's not always true but it often feels that way.

FOX: Mm.

SHAPIRO: It's just hard to balance those competing claims. By necessity, I've come to realize that it's good for the writing—this is going to contradict what I've just been saying, but I do think it's good for the writing if the writer can figure out a way to board the writing dog now and again and just be with the family dog so as not to feel torn between the two.

FOX: And are you able to do that fairly successfully?

SHAPIRO: Well, I work at it. I've had to recently, because of family crises, I've had to completely abandon doing any work whatsoever, and that has actually been a good thing, to be completely present to my life. To give the same kind of undivided attention to my life that I had given to my work. And it's something that, unfortunately, I have come to rather late in life, to recognize the need for that.

FOX: How successful are you in bringing your students that state of focus, or . . .

SHAPIRO: Well, that depends upon the level of the student. Most of my beginning students aren't interested all that much in poetry, they're just taking a class, and they're just trying to get a grade, and so this sort of discussion seldom comes up—but it does come up with my more advanced students, when they start to think about having a career as a writer. We have great students at UNC; the best of them are among the best writers I've ever had the privilege to teach anywhere, they're really just extraordinary, and they get into the best writing programs. I don't know what it is about North Carolina that produces so many extraordinary writers, but I've been really blessed by having extraordinary students. I ask these kids why they want to write, and they come up with all the usual answers-fame, money, sex, some delusional vision of how cool it would be to live a writer's life. I was the same way when I was their age. When I was starting out, I thought that if I could only get a poem in a magazine I'd feel validated. Then I got a poem in a magazine, and I thought, well, if I can only get a poem in a magazine that pays, then I'd be validated.

FOX: Mm-hm.

SHAPIRO: Then that happened, and I thought if I could only publish a book, and then I published a book, and then I thought if I could only publish a book that gets reviews, and then I published a book that got reviews, and, I thought, if I could only publish a book that would win an award [Fox laughs], and then I won an award, and then a bigger award, and then I realized that none of that was ever going to nourish me as a writer. It's like cotton candy, it looks good and wholesome until you put it in your mouth, and then it evaporates. So, the whole completely human desire for fame is just an illusory source of value. It's not going to keep you going. And then, and then what else? You think you write because that way people will love you for it. Well, most people, particularly people closest to you, aren't going to love you for what you write about them. More often than not, they'll distrust or dislike what you write about them, because nobody wants to give up representational control over their own lives. And, I've found that often love poems I've written for wives or children are often not received in the spirit in which they were written. It's just a complicated thing, and people respond to being written about in understandably complicated ways. Seems like people ought to have the right not to be written about. And then of course there is the wholly admirable ambition to make oneself a great writer. But what exactly does that entail? It entails continual growth and improvement, if you're lucky, but the price of that is that you come to hate all your earlier work. That is, if you're lucky, you're going to get better as you move from poem to poem and book to book. And, as you get better as a writer, you get better at imagining getting even better.

FOX: Ah.

SHAPIRO: So, the discrepancy between the writer you are and the writer you want to become only widens as you improve. So, you're living with a sense of inadequacy and failure all the time, and that only deepens, if you're lucky [laughs]. So, everything about the process of writing is unpleasant, is fraught with frustration and anxiety. The only good thing about it—and it's a big only—is that meditative, Zen-like state of total consciousness, total presentness. And maybe what I'm coming to learn now in my old age is that state of presentness is a good thing on and off the page—that you need to be able to find it anywhere, with anyone, and that if you can't find it in your life, you are less likely to find it in your work. It's not a mutually exclusive relationship, or at least it shouldn't be, or needn't be. The sense of dedication to whatever you are doing, while you do it, should be wholehearted and unambivalent. Of course, if you have been diagnosed with ADD, as I have, you realize part of the reason why I talk so much about concentration, presentness, is because I am a deeply distracted person, and I always have been. And so writing has been a kind of salvation from that, it's been one of the few places where I can go to feel a sense of wholeness. But I'm learning now to do that in other places in my life.

FOX: You mention that when you write about other people in your life, it's not always received in the way intended. Do you find yourself censoring what you write?

SHAPIRO: Nope. Never do. No, never, never censor. One thing that I do trust about myself is that if I'm writing about something, it's to try to understand it better. It's not to get back at anybody, there's no ax to grind, there's no hidden agenda. I am trying to bring as much awareness and moral intelligence as I can to bear on difficult, complicated experiences. My allegiance is always to the truth. To understand my own and other people's experience with as much empathy and sympathy as possible. That's one of the functions of literature, to increase our capacities for moral sympathy, to make moral judgments responsible to the complexities of circumstance. And so I've never written anything with the intention to hurt the person I've written about, though that has sometimes been the effect, it was not my intention, and I simply try to tell the truth with as much sympathy and intelligence as I possibly can.

FOX: Mm-hm.

SHAPIRO: But I don't censor myself, and, as a result, it's made for some uncomfortable moments in some of my relationships, for sure. But there's nothing I can do about it. You know, ultimately, you write about what you can't not write about.

FOX: Yeah.

SHAPIRO: You know? And, and, if you can not write about something, it's probably not worth writing about in the first place. And, so what, what vexes me, what haunts me, what delights me, compels me, is what I'm drawn to as a writer. And I just always trust that I'm doing it in the most inclusive spirit. At least I try.

FOX: It seems to me you've hit on what, to me, is an essential center of life, and that is what I usually think of as the truest truth, what is true and what is important.

SHAPIRO: Right.

FOX: And yet, it seems that many, if not most, people really want to avoid that.

SHAPIRO: Yep, that's right. I think that is right. And that's, of course, why writers aren't good traveling companions when it comes to politics or political movements. We didn't make good communists; we don't make good Republicans, or Democrats, because we have to maintain a certain kind of independence, because our ultimate allegiance is to the truth, however unpleasant and however unofficial, however far it falls outside the boundaries of received opinion. The enemy of truth is the simplifying abstractions by which most people want to live their life. There's a beautiful quote by Martha Nussbaum, in *Love's Knowledge*, in an essay about Henry James. And she says, let's see if I can recall this, um, she says that, um, the role . . . Oh God, something like, I'm paraphrasing, because I don't have it committed to memory, but something like that the role of literature is both to remind the reader of the complicated delicacies of the human heart and to resist the, um, optimistic hatred of the actual that dominates so much of the political discourse of our culture.

FOX: Mm-hm, mm-hm.

SHAPIRO: Isn't that a beautiful phrase, the optimistic hatred of the actual. People do want to, and I include myself in this, hide behind some kind of comforting illusion and it's not because they're stupid, it's not because they're less fully alive, it's just that they're terrified and need reassurance that they have some control over what's happening to them, or that there's some kind of, oh I don't know, some kind of purpose to things that often feel as if they have no purpose. That all suffering can be redeemed. And so I have respect for people's resistances to the truth [laughs]. Because I feel it in myself, but the job of poetry is partly to resist that resistance, and look at the world, the best and worst it has to offer, as unflinchingly as possible. And if poetry transforms experience into beauty, it has to be the kind of beauty that doesn't falsify the reality that it's pretending to represent.

FOX: Well, one truth which we all face, and you perhaps more than most, is death.

SHAPIRO: Right.

FOX: And you seem in your work, and in your life, to confront that head on and get wet with it rather than balk.

SHAPIRO: Yeah. I've had no choice about that. My sister died of breast cancer in 1995, and I nursed her through the last six weeks of her life. And then my brother was diagnosed with brain cancer in 1998, and he moved down from New York to North Carolina while he was being treated at Duke Medical Center and lived with me and my family, off and on for thirteen months, and then at the end of thirteen months he died, at the same time as my marriage fell apart. So, yeah, it's been a rough decade, for my whole family. My fifteen-year-old son is in a psychiatric hospital right now, being treated for severe depression. My aged parents live in Chapel Hill. They're frail as can be and have little money so my wife and I are having to provide them with the care they can't afford. We've been going from crisis to crisis. At the same time, I realize life is life, it's hard for everyone, and my life in many ways is a blessed one. I'm married to a beautiful woman, a wonderful woman; my daughter is healthy and full of joy, as is my stepson, and my son Nat will get better. He's an amazing kid, with a big heart, an extraordinarily talented writer himself. His primary form of expression is hip hop and rap music, and he's just unbelievably good at it . . . he freestyles. Yesterday when I was at the hospital, he said, "I just made up this rhyme, what do you think of this Dad?" And then he said, "My brain can't contain this pain, this hospital is the capital of hell, a spell to compel me to do nothing well."

FOX: Whoa.

SHAPIRO: [laughs] Yeah. I mean, fifteen-year-old kid just made that up off the top of his head and then he said, "My tears see more than my eyes." In any event, I just know he'll be fine. And all things considered we have a great life. It has certainly been a life beset with trouble, but that's just the nature of things.

FOX: And how does your writing relate to what's happening in your life? Is it helpful in dealing with it?

SHAPIRO: You know, the writing is not therapy. In a way it's the opposite of therapy. It's the avoidance of therapy. I suppose that the lowest point in my life was after my brother died. And my marriage ended, and I moved out of the house and had this basement apartment, and I felt as if I had lost everything. Up to that time, I was always someone's brother. All of sudden, I was nobody's brother.

FOX: Yes.

SHAPIRO: I always thought I was going to be my ex-wife's husband, and then all of a sudden, I was nobody's husband. I always thought I was going to be, well, for a long time anyway, I thought I was going to be somebody's son, and then my parents' health began to fail, so I felt I was soon to be nobody's son. I had to ask myself, well, what am I still? What are the sources of continuity still left to me, what aspects of my identity could I consolidate? What's left? Well, I was still a father, I was still a basketball player—I always played a lot of basketball when I was growing up and through my adulthood-so, I played a lot of basketball, I spent a lot of time with my children, and I was still a writer. And so writing was a way of affirming my identity at a time when I felt that it was under siege. Okay? So it was that. The other thing, because I did write about the horrible things that were happening to me, I came to feel that writing, while not therapy was therapeutic in this sense: It provided a way of converting experiences which I had passively suffered into artifacts which I could actively make.

FOX: Mm-hm, mm-hm.

SHAPIRO: So, it's a way of, of creating the illusion anyway, of having some control. At the same time, the reason I say it's the avoidance of therapy is because what I am also doing, while I'm doing that, which I know is very good for me, I am also taking an unmanageable experience and converting it into an aesthetic problem, which the writing of the poem is a way of solving. So, I can solve the writing of the poem, even while I can't solve the life.

FOX: Yes.

SHAPIRO: So, in a way it's avoiding the insoluble, by turning it into something I can at least play with and have fun with, and it sounds weird to say, but writing is a way of being happy. Even when you're writing about how unhappy you are, you're still affirming, it's still an affirmative act. It's still projecting an image of human flourishing, even if, even if you're writing the most nihilistic work. If it's well done, it projects an image of human flourishing.

FOX: I think that's a very good way to look at it. You know, I was reading a little bit about you, and you and I share two very interesting things. One, my brother, at sixty about a year and a half ago, was in my house for a Fourth of July party, and was never heard from again, and we found him in his home four days later, dead of a heart attack. That was probably the low point of my life.

SHAPIRO: I bet, I bet.

FOX: Good health, and just gone. And the other thing was I was touched by your spending the last weeks of your sister's life with her.

SHAPIRO: Yeah.

FOX: And, my mother died in 1990. I was in the room when she took her last breath. What's that like for you?

SHAPIRO: Well, I was there in the room with my sister, I was there in the room with my brother, when they both died. They had very different deaths. I think that you die the kind of death that's consistent with the kind of life you lived. My brother's was very hard and very painful, and there was nothing good about it, partly because he felt cheated out of everything, he was a successful actor insofar as he made a living at it, but he never achieved the kind of fame he wanted. He got ill just when his career was really taking off. He had also just met this wonderful woman and they were engaged to be married, he had all these good plans and desires, and then all of a sudden it was all gone, all ripped away from him, and he was very bitter. By the time my sister fell ill, she had accomplished a lot, and while she still felt cheated, because her daughter was seven years old and she was not going to get to see her grow up, she did find it easier to accept her death, she died more peacefully than my brother did. But to be at their bedside, wrenching as it was, was still an incredible privilege. I felt close to a sacred mystery. I gained a new appreciation for Emily Dickinson and the Congregational community out of which so many of her poems come. It was the custom back then to keep a death watch. The purpose of the death watch was in part to lessen the terror and loneliness of the dying, but it was a moral exercise for the community, enabling those around the bedside to glimpse into the other world, since at the moment of a "good" death Christ was believed to come to escort the soul to heaven. Don't get me wrong, I didn't expect Christ to show up—we're

Jews after all, he'd have clearly come to the wrong address—but I did feel like I was in the presence of the deepest mystery. I was living the experience that Emily Dickinson writes so much about. As if my life had dovetailed with her "I Heard a Fly Buzz When I Died"?

FOX: Mm-hm.

SHAPIRO: "The stillness in the room was like the stillness in the air between the heaves of storm. The eyes around had wrung them dry, and breaths were gathering firm for that last onset, for when the king be witnessed in the room. I signed my keepsakes, willed away what portion of me be assignable, and then there was interposed a fly, with blue, uncertain, stumbling buzz, between the light and me; and then the windows failed, and then I could not see to see." And now, of course in that poem, everybody's waiting for Christ. And all that shows up is a fly. [Fox laughs] Everybody's waiting for the King, and all you get is a fly. And the really blasphemous suggestion is that well, maybe, the king of the universe is the fly. Maybe we only live in a material universe, and that the fly is coming for the body and that there is no afterlife. Because after all, the person is writing in the past tense, "I heard a fly buzz when I died," but doesn't say anything at all about what it's like to be dead, she talks only about what it's like to die. I went as far as I could go with my sister and brother, doing what I could for them, which wasn't much beyond just being with them, holding their hand. But ultimately, like all of us, they had to make the last part of the journey on their own. There's no words for that kind of loneliness. No words for that mystery of transformation, that moment of change.

FOX: Yes.

SHAPIRO: It's that sense of ultimate mystery that made it sacred, that made it feel like a privilege and a blessing, and the hardest thing I've ever done.

FOX: It seems to me that we're born alone, we die alone, and from a certain perspective, we live alone. And yet, we search for . . .

SHAPIRO: But we are, we are creatures of need. We are social creatures. And it is impossible to live a human life that excludes need and relationship. We can't live without others and, therefore, we can't avoid losing, ultimately, what we love, because we're all mortal creatures. And so our grief is the wages of love, there's just no getting around it.

FOX: Yeah.

SHAPIRO: This may seem like a grim and joyless view of life, but it's in fact an affirmative view, because lament is the highest form of praise. I mean, you don't mourn the loss of something unless you valued it very highly. And so, it's an affirmation of life to be willing to mourn. The tragic view is based on the joy, beauty and supreme value of human attachment. Now as far as the being born alone and dying alone, I'm reminded of an epigram by my old mentor/tormentor J. V. Cunningham—I don't know if you know his work at all, and he writes mostly epigrams, most of which are very funny, and here's the one your comment makes me think of: "Naked I came, naked I leave the scene, and naked was my pastime in between." [both laugh]

FOX: Do you feel that poetry helps to bridge the gap between . . .

SHAPIRO: Absolutely. Writing is a profoundly social, deeply communal act, because I'm using words and conventions used by the generations that preceded mine, invented by people who haven't seen the sun in hundreds and hundreds of years. Every time I write or speak, I am in conversation with the dead as well as with the living. I'm using verse forms that put me in conversation with every poet who ever used those forms. I am also in conversation with whoever might read the poem. When you transform experience into words, you're always moving from self to world, from isolation to community, it's the opposite of what happens when you experience great pain and suffering, which turns us inward and away from others. In great pain, you lose the ability to speak; you speak in groans, and then not even that. When you write about great pain, you move from that place of extreme isolation back into the world of other people. In that sense, again, literature is always an affirmation of human relatedness.

FOX: Hm.

SHAPIRO: It brings the self back into connection with a community, whether it's a community of the dead, whether it's a community of the not-yet-born, or the community of language users and poetry readers. But I do think that that's one of the reasons why we write and read, to diminish the sense of isolation and loneliness that all of us feel. It's a way of bringing us into connection with other people.

FOX: You think it's possible to write decent poetry without being real, as a writer, without really putting yourself into it.

SHAPIRO: I guess I feel like the joke is really on those who think they aren't being real, because they always are, even when they think they aren't. They reveal themselves in their very disguises. They reveal the nature of their own imaginings—what could be more personal than that? They're going to stand before the world completely naked no matter how dressed up they think they are. And the work may be the better for the disguise. Good work can come in any form—as direct autobiographical self-disclosure, or as historical monologues, through confession or persona. People can be putting on an act and through that act reveal themselves in ways they aren't aware of but that are nonetheless profoundly moving to an audience. What you need in order to write well, finally, is a feeling for words.

FOX: Hm.

SHAPIRO: Writers are people who happen to write. That's finally all that distinguishes them from everybody else. We all experience the same things, we all experience the same messy lives, we all screw up, we're all imperfect, we all make mistakes. But writers write.

FOX: Mm-hm, mm-hm.

SHAPIRO: And writers don't need to live a special kind of life in order to write, they don't have to suffer, they don't have to cheat on their spouses, they don't have to drink or go crazy. They write because they have the writing gene, whatever that is. And when they're not writing, they're just as schmucky as the rest of us.

FOX: You mentioned the relationship between art and poetry and music. Can you say more about that?

SHAPIRO: I think that, as Walter Pater says, all poetry does aspire to the condition of music. Music, pure feeling, pure crystallizing structure, that's what we all want. But words of course have meaning and refer to a world beyond words, and what I mean by music is just that unforgettable something I was talking about earlier. I want to write poems like the ones I love to read: the ones that make you want to memorize them. I don't think there's a lovelier expression or metaphor than to learn something "by heart"—to have some poem lodged in the heart so deeply it's part and parcel of your body and your spirit. It's finally an utterly sensual experience. To know something "by heart" is to know it in the most intimate way, in the mouth, on the tongue, in the ear.

FOX: Mm-hm.

SHAPIRO: Maybe music is a poet's metaphor for rhythm. I've become truly interested in the music of sentences. I love sentences and the way the shape of a sentence can express the shape of a thought or the shape of a feeling. We think about poetry as being primarily image and metaphor or rhythm. We almost never think of poetry in terms of sentences. We think of sentences as belonging to prose. But, for me, a sentence has always been a musical device, a profoundly expressive instrument. Sentences are like little novels, little novels made of grammar. In all good poems the shape of the sentence bears some relationship to whatever the sentence is saying. In the Old Testament, God's authority is partly a function of his grammar. The Ten Commandments, the reason that's compelling is because they're, well, commandments, imperatives—thou shalt not, thou shalt not, thou shalt not. If God were, say, a Unitarian, he might have written the Ten Suggestions. And it would have gone something like: "Well, thou might consider not killing; on the other hand I could imagine circumstances in which it's impossible not to kill, but on balance, it's probably better not to kill than to kill, but what do I know, I'm only . . . " [Fox laughs] You know, the lack of moral certitude is reflected in a, in a highly qualified syntax that's stopping and reversing itself, qualifying itself then qualifying the qualification. And so, the shape of the sentence is the shape of a consciousness in action.

FOX: Mm-hm, mm-hm.

SHAPIRO: And that's what I read for. You know Robert Hayden's poem, "Those Winter Sundays"? Beautiful opening sentence in that poem: "Sundays too my father got up early and put his clothes on in the blueblack cold, and then with cracked hands that ached from weekday labor in the weather made banked fires blaze." Now, that sentence goes on for four-and-a-half lines.

And, he could have shaped it so that he told us what the hands were doing before he described the hands. "Sundays too my father got up early and made banked fires blaze with cracked hands that ached from labor in the weekday weather."

FOX: Mm-hm.

SHAPIRO: But he didn't. He, he tells us that even on Sunday when he didn't have to, that beautiful "too," the father would get up early. And then, with these hands that have worked all week long and are cracked he makes a fire for his family so they shouldn't have to wake up in a cold house . . . it's only at the very end of the sentence that he tells us what the hands are doing. So, by the time we get to what the hands are doing we realize the amount of sacrifice they've had to make, we appreciate more keenly the father's dedication to the well-being of his family. And no sooner do we register that insight [partly] from the structure of that sentence, that we get the next short sentence telling us, "No one ever thanked him." The power of that sentence is a function of the long sentence that precedes it.

FOX: Mm-hm, mm-hm.

SHAPIRO: It's just so beautifully done. The images in this poem aren't particularly striking. The verbs aren't especially active, but the lines are powerful and memorable mostly because of the syntax and how it varies and how it's drawn through the lines. The artistry resides in the shifting from a long, compound sentence to a short, simple, declarative one. So that's something that I have been interested in for years, the music of sentences and different kinds of sentences, the short sentence, long sentence, simple sentence, compounds and complex, complex compound, periodic sentences. And the different kinds of expressive work that those different sentences can do—I mean think of Whitman's catalogs? Beautiful, long catalogs, in which every detail is grammatically equal to every other detail. He's the democratic bard of the open road, right?

FOX: Yeah.

SHAPIRO: And so he's trying to project an aesthetic, he's trying create an aesthetic that projects an image of human equality, a catalog. No grammatical subordination. And yet every single line is rhythmically distinct from every other line. So you have a beautiful enactment of respect for individuality and a commitment to equality at the same time.

FOX: Do many of your students share your passion for the music of the sentence?

SHAPIRO: Oh, they come to. If they want to do well in the class [both laugh], they better.

FOX: Well, as a senior in college, they forced us business folks to take an English grammar course . . .

SHAPIRO: Which is great.

FOX: And it was one of my favorite courses, it was wonderful!

SHAPIRO: Absolutely!

FOX: And we have these business types sitting there, "Oh God, oh, verbs and nouns . . ." I loved it!

SHAPIRO: Yeah, Yeah.

FOX: It seems to me that in America, at least in our generation, people are taught that poetry is something for specialists and for English teachers. They're kind of afraid of it.

SHAPIRO: Right, unfortunately, yeah.

FOX: What can we do about that?

SHAPIRO: Well, I think hip hop is doing a lot about that. I think poetry slams are doing a lot about that. I think there's a place in poetry for the obscure and recondite, I don't think that all poetry has to be accessible. There's a lot of things in life that we get pleasure from without understanding? Sex comes to mind.
FOX: [laughs] Yes, yes.

SHAPIRO: I wouldn't want to say that all poetry has to be accessible; all poetry had to be this or that. That's what I said earlier in the conversation.

There's a lot of different kinds of poetry. And poetry can do a lot of different kinds of work. I just try to write as honestly and as well as I can about what I feel compelled to write about and hope that it will move somebody else. But I don't worry about that. I do when I go to universities and when I teach classes in other places like summer conferences, and people do raise this question of the obscurity of poetry, and I do say, look, if you can just, if you can just sort of forget everything you've been told about poetry. Forget all the new critical ideas that profoundly influenced the way poetry was taught to us when we were in school, and forget even that it's poetry, and just read it as language. And not think that the meaning is somewhere hidden between the lines or below the words. Instead of asking what does this mean, just say, well, what can I say about this? What does it sound like? What kind of words are used? Are these images appealing? Do they seem pleasant over here, unpleasant over there? I tell my students to assume that the meaning of the poem is patent, not latent. That it's not something you have to dig for, but something that's just right there in front of you. And I think a lot of the difficulty people have with poetry has something to do with the preconceptions they bring to the poems they're reading, and if they assumed that it was just saying what it meant, maybe they wouldn't find it half so obscure—I can remember being in college and reading an essay about Robert Frost's poem, "I have been one acquainted with the night," you know that poem? And it's one of my favorite poems, and at the end of the poem, there's "one luminary clock against the sky, proclaimed the time was neither wrong nor right. I have been one acquainted with the night." I remember reading this essay about that, and the critic was musing on all the possible meanings of that "luminary clock"—he wondered if it was the moon, if it symbolized the indifference of the universe, the lack of purpose or destiny, and on and on. As I read his essay, I kept thinking, "Maybe the clock is just a clock. Then again what do I know. . ." As a reader, and as a teacher, I've adapted the principle of our legal system, of presuming innocent until proven guilty, to this: That we should presume that details in a poem are literal until proven figurative.

FOX: Yep, yep.

SHAPIRO: And I think that might help a lot. I think if people just relaxed and didn't feel like they were being tested when they read a poem, and just relaxed and looked at what was literally there before them, and didn't assume the poem was a riddle or a linguistic Easter egg hunt, they might not find the poetry so hard to read.

FOX: Absolutely.

SHAPIRO: If they relaxed a little bit, maybe they wouldn't find half of it as obscure as they do.

FOX: What I like best is when we get a letter to *Rattle* when the reader says, "I don't really read poetry, but I picked up a copy, and hey, I enjoyed it."

SHAPIRO: Right, right, exactly. That's why it was written, it was written to be enjoyed, if it's not, if there's no enjoyment, there's no art. No matter what the subject is, it has to give to pleasure.

FOX: Do you show your work to anyone while it's still in progress?

SHAPIRO: Um, yeah, I have two readers, two close readers. I have the poet David Ferry—I don't know if you know him—and Tom Sleigh. And C. K. Williams, I think I show them pretty much everything. And those are the readers who see everything. And sometimes pretty early drafts of stuff.

FOX: And how do you deal with their comments?

SHAPIRO: Oh, well. I'm the kind of person who only works on one poem at a time. And, when I'm working on something, I love working on it. When I'm really into it, and I've got it going, and again it doesn't matter whether it's good or bad, just being inside something, inside that world is always pleasurable. And when I get to the point where I show my friends what I'm working on, I feel as though I've taken it as far as I can. And then if they say something that sends me back, that enables me to enter back into it, to continue living in that world, I am grateful to them. Because I don't have another poem lined up to work on. So, if I can continue working on what I'm working on, I'm a happy camper.

FOX: How do your students deal with suggestions, shall we say?

SHAPIRO: Some better than others. But, in general, the ones that really have it, that really, really have talent are really good about taking suggestions.

They also understand, and I make it clear to them, that all I can give them is my opinion. And my opinion may be more informed than theirs, but their obligation is to consider what they're told and discriminate among the comments that they receive, and then act on the ones that make the poem they're writing more interesting rather than less interesting to themselves.

FOX: Mm-hm, mm-hm.

SHAPIRO: And one way of testing how good a particular version of a poem is, is to try it out in alternative ways. They've got absolutely nothing to lose by revising the poem this way or that way, because it'll be one test of how good their initial draft was. If it still seems better than these alternatives, then they've learned something.

FOX: How do you know when a poem is finished?

SHAPIRO: Uh, you don't. You don't. You just get finished with it. You could go on forever, and at a certain point, you just simply have to move on. You're just moving words around on the page and you get to a point where you've gotten as much pleasure out of it, you've learned as much as you can, you've taken it as far as you can, and then you just have to let it go. You just sort of feel done with it, you feel like, I've gotten all the clarity out of this that I can, and then you just move on.

FOX: When you're ninety years old, looking back over your life and career, what do you think would give you the most satisfaction?

SHAPIRO: Oh God.

FOX: Aside from the Pulitzer Prize, of course [laughs].

SHAPIRO: You know, you can think way too much about that sort of stuff. I can remember when my kids were really little and I overheard my daughter and son fighting over who got to use the controller for the television—and I heard my daughter tell my son, "Nat, if you give me the controller, I'll give you a Pulitzer Prize." [both laugh] Wonder where they got that from? But I would like to feel as though I did everything I had in me to do, whatever that is. And by that I mean not just as a writer, but also as a husband, as a father, as a son or friend. What I want right now is to see my children thrive, and if the Devil offered me a choice of either writing the greatest poetry ever written or seeing my children become vital and decent human beings, I'd choose the latter in a heartbeat.

FOX: Mm.

SHAPIRO: No poem is worth more than that. So, that's what I'm hoping and praying for now, is to see my children launched into their own lives in fulfilling ways.

FOX: That's cool. Thank you very much.

Diane Wakoski, who was born in Southern California and educated at UC Berkeley, lived and began her poetry career in New York City from 1960-1973. Since 1975, she has been Poet In Residence at Michigan State University where she continues to teach as a University Distinguished Professor. Her poetry has been published in more than twenty collections and many slim volumes; *Emerald Ice*, which won the William Carlos Williams Prize from the Poetry Society of America in 1989, was reprinted in 2005 by Godine Press; *The Butcher Apron* (2000) is her most recent book. Currently she is working on a big project, annotating poems as autobiography, of which the first volume, *Blue Noir: 1956-1968* is complete. She is looking for a publisher for a collection of her new poems, *The Diamond Dog.*

# Diane Wakoski

May 3, 1999

FOX: You just mentioned that some people feel you're irascible. What would you tell me about that?

WAKOSKI: Well, it's something I myself don't quite understand, but I know that it probably starts from the way I critique other people's poetry, either informally or formally, or in a classroom situation, or if people ask for my opinion on their poems. [Fox laughs] I think I'm a very good reader of poetry, but obviously, like everybody, I have a set of criteria for reading poems, and I'm not shy about presenting them, so if people ask for my critical response to a poem, I tell them what works and why, and what doesn't work and why. For some reason, this is taken amiss frequently. I don't know why you would ask a person's opinion about poets or poetry if you didn't expect an honest reply. And I don't know why you would ask me, since I'm a very serious reader, if you didn't expect me to give a rather serious and sometimes difficult response.

FOX: It sounds like your loyalty is to the work rather than to making the author feel good.

WAKOSKI: Yes, and for some reason this has become what is considered a very unattractive trait in my personality.

FOX: Interesting. How long have you taught poetry?

WAKOSKI: I came in the back door, so to speak, because my highest degree is a Bachelor's degree, but I've taught at Michigan State University since 1976. And, before that, for about ten years, I earned my living giving poetry readings which also included giving poetry workshops, writers' conferences, or going as a visiting writer for anything from a week to a semester, which is where I suppose I realized, one, that I really love to read and critique poetry, that I find it almost as exciting as writing poetry, at least good poetry; and that students are in classes with some vague notion that being in a class will make them get better, but many classes, I don't think, help them get better at all, because they don't get any technical or critical feedback to their poems. They may get something that's as useful as "this is a good line" and "this is a bad line," but they still don't have any idea why. And in the long run, basically, all of us have to read and read and read, and finally figure out the reasons why some things work, whether it's in terms of the prosody and rhythms and the wonderful diction that a poet has managed to create for himself, or whether it's through other devices like just the use of trope that is so accurate that even not very interesting language comes alive in the context of the configuration of ideas or figurative speech.

FOX: Some poets believe that if they read a lot their work will unconsciously become derivative of the poets they're reading. What would you say to that?

WAKOSKI: Well, I would hope that if they read a lot and they read well, they would unconsciously become derivative. I can't think of anything better than being derivative of Yeats, someone whose work that you think is just exquisitely beautiful. I do not mean being a copycat. But, after all, what I feel that I'm teaching, which is why I've agreed to be a university professor all these years, is a tradition. I'm passing on a tradition of which I am part. There's a long line of poets who went before me, and I'm another one, and I'm hoping to pass that on to other younger, or newer, poets than myself. Americans are very obsessed with being original, but in one sense there's no such thing as totally original literature, and if there is, since who knows what there is until it exists, then how would we recognize it? Don't we recognize what is good through the models of what's been beautiful in the past? We even recognize it as sometimes breaking a mold to make a different mold for beauty. I think one of the things that language poets are very involved with is getting away from conventional ideas of beauty, because those ideas contain a certain attitude toward women, certain attitudes toward sex, certain attitudes toward race, etc. And one of the great social movements of our times, the Black Power movement of the '60s and '70s, its slogan was "black is beautiful." Well, now it seems like you shouldn't have to say that. But, after all, black for centuries and centuries and centuries was the devil, it was evil, and if it was beautiful, it was tainted beauty. So, I think that what we're always doing is redefining the possibilities of beauty, but, don't get me wrong, I think that all of art is about beauty.

FOX: What makes a poem enduring?

WAKOSKI: I think that great poetry is the most interesting and complex use of the poet's language at that point in history, and so it's even more exciting when you read a poet like Yeats, almost one hundred years old now, and you think that perhaps no one can really top that. And it is exciting to see this consummate use of language that is complex and exists on many different levels of meaning as well as probably several different levels of intensity through the lyric and musical power that it has, but it's still just as beautiful, if not more beautiful in some cases. Sometimes the archaism of the language when it's spoken is why we are all in love with the Irish today. I think it's because they sound different and we like that different sound. Americans, of course, are always in love with accents [Fox laughs], since we "don't have any accent" [both laugh].

FOX: You mentioned Black Power. What do you think the role, if any, of the poet is in a political sense?

WAKOSKI: This is another area where I have earned many enemies over my lifetime. I am not political as a person. I do not read newspapers. I do not watch television. I am not interested in current events, although I will occasionally discuss them if other people want to discuss them. But I don't think that poetry is a good, to use a contemporary word, venue, for current events. I have finally been browbeaten to death by friends like David Ignatow who insist that all great poetry is political. And if that's true, then I'm political. But I am not political in the current events sense, and I have never wanted anyone to read my poetry that way. Case in point: I could be rich and famous now if I had just cooperated with the feminists of the '70s and said, "Yes, I'm a feminist. That is my agenda." Because, in fact, women, feminists, do read my poetry, and they read it often with the power of their political interpretation. I don't care; that's what poetry is supposed to do. It's supposed to be there for you to read and interpret, but what I've quarreled with all along, and I will continue to quarrel with even though I realize it's very counterproductive, is that I don't write from a political agenda or point of view or even the sense that I am a spokesman for a group of people. I write for Diane Wakoski. I am happy to be a woman. I happily use a female persona. My poems are almost all written as Diane. I don't have any problems with that, and if other women choose to identify with this, I think that's terrific.

I think that's what poetry does. It allows people to come together and identify with a common thing that is outside of themselves, but which they identify with from the interior. So, I've never been politically correct, even before that term was available to us [laughs], and I have really identified with other people who don't want to be read as just a Black poet, or just a woman poet, or just someone who represents a cause, an anti-Vietnam war poet. It seems to me to diminish what poetry can do, which is not to say that poems couldn't be terribly relevant to any of these political concerns, and some people, of course, do write with the political agenda or the ideology as a primary driving force for them. That's fine. I just don't want to be mistaken for one of those people.

FOX: Your poetry seems very personal.

WAKOSKI: Yes, and I can't in my own way see why men couldn't identify with the themes in my poetry just as much as women. So, again, I'm not trying to exclude anybody. I'm perfectly happy when I look out at an audience and it's all women. I always think it's kind of odd, but then, more women than men, I think, read and write poetry. Wouldn't you agree with me?

FOX: Yes. Yes, I would. Are you happy with your career as a poet?

WAKOSKI: I'm not unhappy. One, I have a wonderful publisher, Black Sparrow Press; as long as they exist, they will keep me in print. And they claim they sell very respectable numbers of my books, so I guess, and it's true, every place I go, my books are in libraries and on bookshelves. So it's not as if I'm invisible. But I still have never won that coveted Pulitzer Prize [laughs] that I've been joking about for twenty-five years, that I would so much love to win. And why don't they ever at least nominate me for an *L.A. Times* Prize. After all, I am a daughter of Orange County, born in Whittier.

FOX: I'm surprised. My tastes are different than most, I suppose, but for me your work is among that I like the best.

WAKOSKI: Well, let me interview you for a minute. [Fox laughs] In recent years, something that I didn't expect would happen has happened, and it's made me think twice, and obviously I'm going to circle around this as I circle around everything. I have always hated the term "confessional" and never considered myself a confessional poet, because historically, of course, I wasn't. I wasn't Plath, Sexton, Lowell or Berryman, and they are the seminal confessional poets. Although over the years, every once in a while people would refer to me as a confessional poet, and I understood why, being someone talking about not being beautiful, wanting sex, things that are not totally propitious. Well, in recent years, I've come across three different colleges or universities where they are teaching courses called "Confessional Poetry" and I am one of the twelve poets they've taught. Alan, what do you think, does that fit in with the way you think about my poetry?

FOX: Well, I would have to say yes. I think of you as a confessional poet but with me, that's not a bad term; I kind of like it. Because I'm interested in the human experience from someone else's perspective, things that I can identify with, that are said in ways that are new and interesting, and with as large as possible, a degree of personal insight. And I think, for me, the two things that I most like about your work is, first of all, it's written beautifully. When I read a book of part letters, part poetry, that format does not normally appeal to me—but you do it very, very well, and the letters are letters and the poetry is poetry, and they go together. And that's not often the case.

WAKOSKI: Thank you.

FOX: And the other thing I like is your transparency. I think we all have a need to be close to other people and we have impediments to that, and sometimes the impediment is that the other person doesn't know him or her self very well and can't help too much.

WAKOSKI: So is it the element of vulnerability that you see in my poems that makes you think of them in the confessional context? That's slightly different from what you were just saying.

FOX: Not vulnerable in a "here I am, look at me," sense. It's just "here I am."

WAKOSKI: Yes, it's very matter of fact. I don't see it as making me vulnerable. As I've said over and over again—believe me, I don't tell you anything I don't want you to know. And if I reveal a secret, at this point, it's a secret I'm ready to reveal, and I do think that one of the pleasures of reading poetry, that in fact, what the structure of a poem is all about, is that it builds up to some kind of revelation and discovery, so you always feel at the end of the poem that you have discovered something that you didn't know before, which is like a secret, even if it's the way the poet defines a word and turns it around to mean something else. And so in that sense, when you look at the word "confessional," this is the way I always looked at it: a confession to a priest is telling him your sins, a confession to a police officer is telling him your crimes, a confession to a psychologist is telling him or her something you're ashamed of. Well, I never felt I was talking about sins, crimes or things I was ashamed of, but I realize now that many people feel that what I have been talking about, which often is my failures, are things that I ought to be ashamed of. And that's where it's coming out of the closet of all these things we're supposed to be ashamed of, sex number one, of course, any kind of sex except married sex that made babies.

FOX: I find your work makes you accessible, and I probably wouldn't put you in the same category as those others. Sylvia Plath, to me, is angry, that's very clear; and I don't know if I know that much about her. I feel in your work that I know about you as a human being, and that's just thrilling, it's a relief.

WAKOSKI: All right, let me ask you one more question as long I'm interviewing you, Alan [laughs]. Do you think of me as a deep image poet? Or does that term mean anything to you at all? It's been around for a long time, really, since Jerry Rothenberg coined it in the late '50s, I guess, but it hasn't been used critically very much.

FOX: I don't too much like that term; maybe I don't understand it too well, and I think what it means is not what I would think it means if didn't know what it's supposed to mean. A deep image to me is an image which is very accurate, cuts to the heart of the issue. I'm not sure that's the way it's used. I think your poetry does tend to cut to the heart, which is what I'm interested in, the heart versus superficiality. I'm interested in the depth, so I think you certainly have depth.

WAKOSKI: I'm just curious about the ways we're sort of arranging the poetry that now we're a historical part of, and since I teach it also, I'm always thinking about how to explain these things to other people and make sense out of.

FOX: In terms of your voice do you notice an evolution in your work?

WAKOSKI: Other people have noticed more of an evolution than I have and so I'll try to tell you where I'm coming from and also relate it to what I think other people perceive. I have always wanted what I have now come to call the voice of personal narrative. That has always been the appealing voice in poetry. It started for me lyrically in Shakespeare's sonnets. Because it's talking in sentences, using imagery, and it's a very personal narrative voice in the sense of telling an emotional story. I don't think I had a lot of models for it when I was young. I found some in Robinson Jeffers, both in the lyric, short lyric, poems, and then in the long story poems, although I have basically not written story poems. Then I really found it in one poem by D. H. Lawrence called "Snake." It's an absolutely breathtakingly beautiful poem about going out in Sicily to the well and seeing two snakes, a golden one that is poisonous, and then feeling that he should have to kill this and not being able to do it. It's a gorgeous poem about coming to terms with what is the real power of the earth and one's own human limitations when it comes to confronting that, but it's spoken in this voice that has forever been a model for me, for the voice of poetry. When I was a young poet, though, I was in love with early Wallace Stevens' poetry, and then I fell in love with Garcia Lorca's poetry in translation, and I was also taking French classes and translating French surreal poetry. I don't think I knew how to transcend my Southern California plain speech through lyricism because, in spite of the fact that I tried to write sonnets, I really am not a lyric poet, but I wanted that lyric intensity. I discovered it through writing imagery, visual imagery, making descriptions, some of which uses figurative language, and other which is adjectives, but I quickly learned to get rid of the adjectives because they're more prose construction, adjective / noun, and tried "clocks in my elbows," and things like that. I became a very, very self-conscious user of surrealist imagery, and I think that attracted many people to my poetry. I still have access to that imagery, but I'm much more likely to use more mundane kinds of imagery, and I think a lot of people feel the surrealism has disappeared from my poetry. I don't feel it has. I think it's gone underground, and I use it more in a metaphorical sense than in a literal imagistic sense. I see you nodding. But a lot of people miss that, they would like the surface more studded with that surrealistic imagery, and I keep saying I agree with them "Blue Monday" is one of the best poems I ever wrote. It's pure surrealist imagery and it's all lyric, and if I could write another one tomorrow I would. I'd write ten of them. I have sat down once a year, every year, since I wrote that poem, to write another poem that does what that poem does, and it always goes off someplace else. So I can certainly see the evolution of my language where the extreme, almost baroque, use of surrealist imagery on the surface of my poems has been pushed under to much more complex metaphorical or troopaic structures, and the surface language is prosier. The only thing I've been able to do to discount that is to write more short poems interspersed with long poems, but my short poems rarely reach the level of what I would call lyric poetry. Maybe I have one in each book that can function that way. But I don't have that gift to condense my language into lyric. I can condense my language very tight in long structures so that there'll be a million different levels of something going on, but to turn it then into this little lyric stuff is not really what my gift is. Every once in a while, you know, the gods give you one [laughs].

FOX: How do you know that you're a poet as opposed to a novelist, or journalist, or something else?

WAKOSKI: Well, it is a little bit like religion. You really do know it. And I think you really do know it at a certain point. I am an avid reader of fiction and have been my entire life, and if I could be a fiction writer I would be a fiction writer. But I didn't write fiction in high school. I enrolled in a novel writing class when I was an undergraduate at Berkeley. I was already writing poetry very seriously and fairly successfully as an undergraduate. I had a wonderful professor, a novelist no one has ever heard of named George Stewart, who was wise and friendly, and every time I would bring one of my so-called chapters of the novel to class, they were very short, everyone would kind of be stunned and then they would say, "Well, that's very poetic, Diane." Now if there's one thing in the world I really hate it's poetic novels. I do not read James Joyce. I do not read books that are described as poetic in general with any pleasure. So at the end of the term I said, "Professor Stewart, well, what do you think?" And he was silent for a while, and I was a very embarrassed kind of person so I sat and I looked at him. I saw he was smiling and we both burst into laughter and together said, "Yes, Diane, it's very poetic." [Fox laughs] And I knew that I was not a novelist. I just knew that I wasn't. I don't sit around envying novelists. I love what they do. I like to read. I read more fiction at this point than poetry, partly 'cause it's work for me, and I cannot read a new book of poetry without being the poetry professor and saying, "How did they ever get that in the book?" [Fox laughs] or whatever. I start rewriting somebody famous's poetry. So it's a hard task for me to do that. Nevertheless,

I periodically every year, find a few new poets who really are exciting and wonderful to me. I love, as I say, passing the tradition on to new poets.

FOX: Do you find a vast gap between so-called academic poetry and poetry of the streets?

WAKOSKI: Well, not exactly. I think that we're in a funny period in contemporary poetry. The good side of it is: everything goes. The good side of that is for young poets they can really look around and find their voices. There is no "you have to sound like Robert Lowell or Richard Wilbur or you'll never get published" sense. There is no tyranny of voice for them right now. The other side of the coin, which is painful for many students, is they would like, they'd be happy to have more of a tyranny of voice because they don't know, there's so much, and actually I help them out by being a somewhat tyrannical teacher, and saying, "You have to learn this first," and give them something to fight against and so forth. But I think that my generation really made poetry, not into an oral art because it already was, but made people aware of the fact that it was. And it made people very poetry literate in the late '60s and all through the '70s because there were so many poetry readings in any area where there was either a university or an urban area, and so everyone could hear quite a lot of poetry. They didn't necessarily hear it 'cause it wasn't on TV, but they could, and if they were in school, they did, because most English classes emphasized that through high school and through university or college. And I was very excited when the phenomenon of performance poetry and poetry slams started trickling up and coming in, and thinking this is where Kenneth Rexroth's poetry with jazz has its logical next step. And I was always sorry that that didn't turn into something big. It was just a fringe part, not very many poets did it, the fringe part of the big poetry reading thing, and I think that is because the big forum for poetry reading was anti-Vietnam war protest. So I think it got diverted over into politics, with these big audiences wanting to hear about Vietnam, and then women's issues, and then Black issues, and so the whole lyrical aspect of poetry as performance rather than poetry as political speech was kind of shunted away. And I thought with performance poetry and, perhaps with the slams, that would come back. Unfortunately, we were already in the age of the comedy club—nothing wrong with comedy clubs—and MTV and stuff where the easy thing was bad poetry on stage and you performed it in the way that a stand-up comic does to get a whole lot of audience response that really isn't to the language. You let people judge it who are not judges of language at the slams. Performance poetry moved way, way over into video, dance, music, etc., and the language is the least interesting aspect for the most part. So now you have things like the Nuyorican Cafe in New York City, which again emphasizes being Puerto Rican or the politics, rather than language, and becomes the forum for oral poetry. It seems like a regression rather than a progression from where we were with the big poetry readings with Robert Bly reading his wonderful long poem, that I can't remember the title of now, but was written in pieces and was written as an anti-Vietnam poetry project, but in fact is something much bigger than that.

Example of the problems that that has created: In one of my poetry writing classes a few years ago a girl appeared whom I immediately felt was exceptionally talented. She didn't seem to have any idea of what poetry was, but she just wrote from the heart, what we were talking about, Alan, and she had stories to tell. She also learned very fast, and she learned language. Well, what I found out was that she had been, during her whole high school career, going to these poetry slams in Ann Arbor, and she had learned to be very passionate and win her poetry slam. Well, I had major quarrels and fights with her, but she was good, she stuck it out, and I stuck it out; she would give a little, and I would give a little. You know, "This is what you have to learn, Amy, if you're really going to be a poet," "but this is what I feel," "yes, I know, but—" She really by the end of that semester was writing very, very well-formed poems. She was continuing to go to these poetry slams and having very mixed results. If there was anybody there who knew anything about poetry she would win. She had a hard time handling that, 'cause she now heard how awful most of this poetry was that was being slammed out against her quite well written, and very passionate poems. By the time she graduated from college, which was last year she had more or less stopped going to them, she said, "There's no point; these people don't know, and it's not even gratifying emotionally to win." And I said, "But, Amy, I was counting on you and the others like you to turn these poetry events, the slams and so forth, into the new age of poetry where good poetry is also presented in this way that has a big audience and that has a dimension that is greater than just the page." The last time I saw her, she hadn't written any poetry for six months, 'cause clearly what was turning her on was to have an audience, whether it was in a classroom or in a slam, and not having any other avenue for that she just wasn't that interested in writing. Well, now, that's a terrible loss. And I think she'll come back. She's still in touch with me, and I have little informal sessions at my house for my former students.

FOX: That raises a question in my mind: How much do you write for yourself and how much do you write for your audience?

WAKOSKI: You know, that's a question that I think we all have to battle with over the years, and there probably are a number of places where your path diverges in the yellow woods or someplace else [laughs]. I tend to think that wherever you start, whether it's orally with people listening to you, or in the head, on the page, making shapes and forms and working intricately with language, as you perceive it through your mind, you eventually need to balance it with the other one. Someone who's a totally cerebral poet, Frank Bidart, maybe, I don't think he cares what anybody hears in his poetry although it's actually very good read-aloud poetry. And I think that what you take is from one to the other, so that you don't want something that sounds good to the audience unless it also fits in with the structure that you've been making. You want it come at the right place, you don't want them to laugh at the wrong place or to respond to the beauty of it as if it's finished when you still haven't finished making the structure of the poem. And by the same token, you don't want all the intricate and beautiful machinations of your language and your ideas to be so invisible that you read them aloud and absolutely, it's not just they go by too fast, it's just they're totally buried and someone needs a pitchfork to dig them out. So I think that we're constantly using the two different approaches to the poem to balance it.

I miss not giving as many poetry readings as I used to when I was younger, because I've learned, I mean I'm getting to the place where I will often write an invisible poem, and I won't know that it is until I read it, and since I don't give more than a dozen poetry readings a year anymore, and I tend to, giving so few readings, to read some of the same poems over and over again because I know what people want to hear, or I want to try out something new, and I feel this is one of my best new poems, that there are many, many poems that never get read aloud whereas that was hardly ever the case in my life before. When I lived in New York City, I went to open poetry readings almost every week in the cafes—that's what I want to write a book about—where you got to hear what had a shape and that had a dynamic, an oral dynamic, not just from the way the audience responded but from the way you could present it orally. And that gave you lots of clues for rewriting, reshaping the dramatic structure. But, I don't know, I think that kids get that out of their workshops. We make them usually read their poems aloud, but it's not quite the same as going into an audience and reading one poem every week and wanting to be the one that everybody likes. And if you have the luxury of doing it week after week you begin to have some taste and judgment. You know when you're being a circus performer and the difference between that and real drama and what is coming out of the integrity of the poem. And you also know the difference—when I was an undergraduate at Berkeley and studied with Thom Gunn who was fresh from studying with Yvor Winters at Stanford, plus his own very British sensibility, he would not allow us to read our poems aloud in class because he said, "You can dramatize them." Well, I and a few others quarreled with him and he said, "All right, you may read them in a monotone but not until halfway through the term, and I will read them aloud for you. If they have to be read aloud, I'll read them aloud, and I'll read them in a monotone, so you can't convince anybody with your forensic ability that you have written this great poem." And that was actually quite good discipline. It was a little frustrating for young, enthusiastic people, but it really made you understand that the voice of the poet is not necessarily to make it sound better; it's to give you a sense of where the language comes from. And, of course, Thom couldn't give us that with his British accent. We thought everything sounded better with his British accent [laughs] so at a certain point we sort of liked that.

FOX: You mentioned several poets or teachers who have been influential for you, and many poets have one or two people that they run their work by and discuss it with. Do you?

WAKOSKI: I never had that luxury in my life, and maybe I didn't seek it out because I'm a good critic and a fairly good self-critic. But, in recent years, my friend Judith Minty, a poet in Michigan, whom I like very much, both as a friend and as a writer, has become a very good reader of my poems. Several of the poems that I wrote last year, especially long ones, she gave me really valuable feedback for revisions. And I realized, my God, some people have this their whole life. It's a wonderful luxury to have that kind of friend or mentor. I still have former students who basically use me that way with their poetry.

FOX: Do you think your best work is behind you or ahead of you?

WAKOSKI: Let me give you a footnote to that before I answer it. My footnote is that I don't think that my poetry ever progressed. I think that my first poetry is as good as my last poetry. It's different, and I think that for better or worse, I mean some people will like certain periods of my writing better than other periods of my writing, just as I love early Wallace Stevens' poetry, and I virtually have no use for his later long poems that everyone thinks are his great work, so I just think that's a matter of taste. In that sense, I hope I have a lot of work ahead of me, and I don't think it's better. I do have to be realistic since I teach contemporary American poetry, and I think there are periods in poets' lives when they are part of the history of what's going on, especially if they're in a period that is perhaps making history. I do not think Alan Ginsberg's poem, "Howl," is a great poem but I think it's his most important poem because it made history. I think "Kaddish" is a great poem. I think that if we only have our choice in history of reading one Alan Ginsberg poem, it will always be "Howl" and that's because it made history. And I don't even resent that anymore. I think it's up to us who are seeking out models of poetry to discover the great things on our own. So, as a history maker, to whatever extent I was, it was the poetry that moved from *Inside the Blood Factory* to the *Motorcycle Betrayal Poems*, and where I was that poet that you might call confessional, the woman who was daring to go out there and stomp around and say that she was an Orpheus looking for her true love and willing to bring him back from Hell if she could find him. And also trying to do something that I think was a sort of step forward from the William Carlos Williams aesthetic which was to make poetry out of the everyday, to literally be able to write poetry that came out of my everyday life that became a kind of mythic biography of myself. And I think that's very common for people now, but I think I'm one of the people who invented that as a possibility. So, in that sense, what I'm writing now can't be better than what I wrote before, and people don't review my books the way they used to. I'm always moaning and groaning and lamenting, this is my most complex poetry, *The Archeology of Movies and Books*, those four books, and what I'm working on now, I think is doing something really exciting, but it's not any different from what I've been doing for all those years.

FOX: How do you rate yourself on passion in your work?

WAKOSKI: That's an interesting question. Well, I think most people would agree that the title *Dancing on the Grave of a Son of a Bitch* is a fairly passionate title, my most famous title. [Fox laughs] And, you know, we were talking earlier about poets of anger; I'm a poet of anger, but I'm a poet of somebody who goes past anger. It's been very important for me to use anger as, to blow up, and then find a resolution. And that's the secret or the surprise, that I like, or discovery, that I like to offer at the end of the poem: how I resolved the anger or the pain, so that I don't think you have to read me as a poet that is depressing. One of the most common things that people who are not very serious about poetry say is "Oh, I don't like to read poetry because it's so depressing." And what they mean is poets are frequently addressing problems, pain, difficulty, but I think of myself as someone who is looking for resolution for those things. I think I'm a fairly passionate poet, but I'm the same kind of poet that I am person. I have a very cool exterior most of the time, until I get embarrassed or angry, and then I'm a volcano, or just a mass of blushes. I sometimes am inappropriate in my emotions. Some people think I'm very cold and cruel because I just have this exterior of being, not really cool, it's not an emotional state, but I'm thinking about things rationally, I'm trying to analyze them. And then at other times, my emotions break through and they're totally out of control. So I'd say that I'm sort of a victim of inappropriate responses to things at times. But my poetry itself is about my passionate longing for beauty, my passionate desire for love and sex and romance and some kind of peaceful beauty. But the poems go through lots of turmoil to get there, frequently.

FOX: Are there areas you haven't written about because you don't want to hurt other people's feelings or reveal too much about yourself?

WAKOSKI: Yeah [clears throat, pauses], yeah. [Both laugh loudly]

FOX: Okay [still laughing].

WAKOSKI: But I don't discount ever writing about them. One of the things I loved about Anais Nin was something that I myself have never been able to do, because I suppose I have a need for a direct audience, but she passionately wrote those diaries and wrote everything into them, but was literary enough that she separated parts of them out and put them in the vault so they couldn't be used until either certain people were dead, or she was, or whatever. And I keep saying that there are at least a couple of stories or ongoing themes in my life that I should just be writing about now and putting in Anais Nin's vault, and yet I can't quite bring myself to write about things until I'm ready to shout them to the world. I keep saying I'm going to write this so-called memoir, 'cause I don't really want to write a memoir, of the '60s coffeehouse world of poetry where there was a real sense, better than poetry workshops and colleges, of honing your craft by these weekly open mike readings and, even though you didn't have specific criticism from other people, whatever people would say to you became a way that you would interpret as criticism of what didn't work and why it didn't work.

At any rate, I would like to write this book that is kind of a so-called memoir, talking about the people I knew, and what we did, and at the same time not really a memoir, but a book about poetics and esthetics, and what it was that allowed us to not be unworldly in the sense that we wanted money and fame, but be more concerned about what art was and the way we made it. Because I think that people would like to read that, and I don't quite know how to write it. And the reason your question suggested this is that I keep going through different ways I could possibly write this book; I don't have letters, journals, diaries, any of that stuff that gives you something to describe from in detail. I don't have that kind of detailed memory. And I know this always shocks people when I say this, but I wrote poetry because I needed love, sex and romance, and I didn't know any other way to go after it. So all my poetry has something to do with whatever man I was involved with, in love with, or living with, or having sex with [laughs] at that time in my life, and yet I'm not quite ready to write—I don't write overtly about sex in most of my poems, even though I'm always alluding to it or referring to it—and I don't really feel free to write about these men, most of whom are still alive, in a way that would be, what everybody would say, "Diane, write that book. . . ." [words lost in laughter]. "Maybe Diane can fill this in for us about your love life." I don't know how to write that. And I finally decided; I have a way of doing it that may turn into Anais Nin's write-it-and-stick-it-in-the-oven until everybody is so far gone that they want people to think that they had a sex life [both laugh loudly] . . . wives are not going to leave them as a result of knowing their involvement with Diane Wakoski. A friend, a critic, suggested to me when I started doing my so-called research for this in New York this spring, I was talking to him and telling him some of these same things I've been telling you, that it's so hard for me to figure out how to get started on this. He said, "Diane, it's so obvious. You love to write these letters describing your life, sometimes they're ten or twenty pages long, you've sent them to me; you obviously love the epistolary form, why don't you sit down and, I don't know, choose somebody to start writing letters to. You don't have to go chronologically, just remember." I said, "Leo, this is so obvious, this is what will get me to sit down and start creating this text; then I can figure out what to do with it." And I finally decided that probably what I'm going to do is start by writing one or some of these letters to the person I call the "motorcycle betrayer" whom I don't have any contact or correspondence with, and probably would be sort of afraid to open it up, because I have a perfectly happy life, and I don't want to mess up my life because of messing up my head.

FOX: Has it been difficult for you to juggle marriage, family, love, writing, teaching . . . ?

WAKOSKI: Well, I'm sort of a one-track-mind person. On the other hand, I like to juggle several things; I read several books at the same time. I have to say that because I came in the back door of the academy, I've never had the problems of juggling schoolwork with professional work and family that other people have, because I've always been a full professor, and I've always taught small classes with good students and a light teaching load. And so if I'm bitching and moaning, it's just, you know, Princess Diane who thinks that the world [Fox laughs] should give her anything, and she shouldn't have to do anything.

FOX: Of course, of course.

WAKOSKI: And I don't think I could have had an academic career if I'd had to do what most academics have to do to have it. I don't have children so I've never had to have that juggling. The men that I've been involved with have either left me or, as in Robert's case, stayed with me and been a nice husband because he's willing to live that life with me. There was a point around 1980, after Robert and I had been living together several years, just before we got married, when Robert said, "I'm not driving you around anymore to poetry readings." And so at that point I got MSU to fully fund my job so that I could stay there all year and not have to earn part of my living giving readings, and that's when I started doing a lot less reading, and we bought a house.

FOX: Well, you're kind of, I guess, becoming or have become an elder statesperson. How does that feel?

WAKOSKI: Yes, well, once you get used to it, it's actually, I keep saying, as soon as I get to my Georgia O'Keeffe period, I will be very happy. Everyone will notice, then they'll review me, then they'll give me prizes, then they'll be nice to me. Then they'll say, "Oh Diane, what do you need? [laughs] We'll come to you." And I'll say, "Oh, no, I'd rather go to you." But I haven't reached my Georgia O'Keeffe stage. Nobody cares who I am right now. And I believe that will happen if I can just keep the old age side of my genes going.

FOX: What would you like to be remembered for?

WAKOSKI: I'd like to be remembered for half a dozen poems, "Blue Monday," "Father of My Country," "I Have Had To Learn To Live With My Face," maybe a few poems from *The Archeology of Movies and Books,* like "Medea and the Sorceress." I'd really like to be remembered for those poems. Maybe for a title like *The Motorcycle Betrayal Poem, Dancing on the Grave of a Son of a Bitch,* or *Argonaut Rose.*

FOX: I think we've done terrifically well today. I've enjoyed our conversation.

WAKOSKI: I love talking to you.

FOX: It seems to me that your work will be important, describing what it was like to be a human being in this period of time and this milieu, someone who has a lot of insight and the verbal ability to describe it in interesting, understandable, and, hopefully, somewhat complex ways. If I had written what you've written, I'd be very proud of it.

WAKOSKI: Thank you. Actually, I am.